The Reading Teacher's Plan Book

A systematic, small-group reading program for your beginning readers

Written by Marjorie Conrad

Copyright © 2008 by The Reading Teacher's Plan Book. All rights reserved. No part of this publication may be reproduced or transmitted in any form or by any means, electronic, mechanical, photocopying, recording, or otherwise, without prior written permission of The Reading Teacher's Plan Book. Cover design by Stephanie Leonard. ISBN 978-0-557-17779-0

Welcome to *The Reading Teacher's Plan Book!*

Program Overview

The Reading Teacher's Plan Book has been designed to assist you in providing systematic, small-group reading instruction for your first grade students or other beginning readers. It also gives you the flexibility to differentiate instruction according to the varying reading level of your students. The plans are designed to complement any small-group, guided reading program.

The Reading Teacher's Plan Book

This resource book is divided into the following categories:

- The Plan Book – Instructions, Yearly Tracking and Pacing Planner, and Lesson Plans
- Teaching Week Resources
- Review Week Resources
- Advanced Week Resources
- Other Resources

The Lesson Plans

The Lesson Plans are divided into three categories: Teaching Weeks, Review Weeks, and Advanced Weeks. The weekly plans are divided into four 30-minute daily plans. Each daily plan is divided into four components: *Fluency Building, Word Work, Guided Reading, and Writing.*

Teaching Weeks

The Reading Teacher's Plan Book provides you with 20 Teaching Week Lesson Plans which systematically teach short vowels, long vowels, and other vowel patterns. All students, whether struggling, grade-level, or advanced, need a solid foundation in the fundamentals of reading which is provided with these plans.

Review Weeks

One key difference between advanced readers and struggling readers is the amount of time needed to master new concepts. Advanced readers often master new concepts right away and need minimal review throughout the year. Struggling readers, however, tend to need repeated exposure to new concepts. 15 Review Week Lesson Plans are included so you can provide extra practice and review of phonics concepts as needed.

Advanced Weeks

The 10 Advanced Week Lesson Plans are designed to support the needs of your advanced readers. These lesson plans teach students how to decode longer words, and they emphasize comprehension to a greater degree. While struggling readers will alternate between Teaching Weeks and Review Weeks, advanced readers will move more quickly through the Teaching Weeks, with minimal Review Weeks, and will have more time spent in Advanced Week lessons.

Considerations for Struggling Readers

Struggling readers are ready to begin these lessons when they have become proficient in beginning phonemic awareness skills, letter identification, the ability to track print in Guided Reading Level A books, and knowledge of basic sight words. Struggling first graders who receive two to three weeks of small-group instruction emphasizing these skills are usually ready to transition to *The Reading Teacher's Plan Book* lesson plans.

Planning Your Year

Consider the needs of your students as you plan your instruction. Students in a classroom are typically divided into four groups. Depending on the make-up of your classroom, Group 1 might be your below-level readers, Group 2 your slightly below-level readers, Group 3 your on-level readers, and Group 4 your above-level readers. These groups should be fluid, with students moving between groups throughout the year depending on their individual progress and needs.

The Reading Teacher's Plan Book is designed to be a spiral curriculum, moving forward then stepping back. If students are going to be successful at the next level of reading, they need instruction in the reading tasks required at that new level (moving forward). However, until a skill becomes automatic, students tend to forget what they have previously learned. They need periodic, regular review throughout the year to help them solidify and automatize these skills (stepping back).

A *Yearly Tracking and Pacing Planner* is provided to assist you in planning your different groups (see page 17).

Contents

The Plan Book . . . . **pages 6 - 119**
- Instructions
- Yearly Tracking and Pacing Planner
- Materials Needed
- Lesson Plans for Teaching Weeks, Review Weeks, and Advanced Weeks

Teaching Week Resources . . . . **pages 120 - 238**

Review Week Resources . . . . **pages 239 - 326**

Advanced Week Resources . . . . **pages 327 - 378**

Other Resources . . . . **pages 379 - 400**
- Sound/Spelling Boxes
- Writing Sorts
- Word Windows
- Graphic Organizers
- Vowel, Digraph, and Syllable Charts
- Comprehension Strategy Chart

PLAN BOOK INSTRUCTIONS

Check out our website at <u>www.readingteachersplanbook.com</u> to see helpful hints for assembling and storing your teaching resource materials.

Understanding the Lesson Plans

The Reading Teacher's Plan Book lesson plans are divided into the following components:

- Fluency Building
- Word Work
- Guided Reading
- Writing

The Reading Teacher's Plan Book lesson plans are fast paced, helping you use your instructional time more effectively. The entire plan is taught in 30-minute daily sessions with a suggested time frame given for each component. Times are listed in ranges (i.e. 5-7 minutes), since some activities take longer than others. As you begin your small-group instruction, it is beneficial to set a timer for each component of the plan to help you get a feel for the pacing.

Each Teaching Week and Review Week has a specific phonics focus, and each Advanced Week teaches a syllabication pattern. In the Teaching and Review Weeks, the majority of writing activities reinforce the phonics concepts being taught and reviewed. The writing activities in the Advanced Weeks reinforce the comprehension strategies being learned.

Preparing and Organizing Your Materials

You will be assembling materials to go with *The Reading Teacher's Plan Book* lesson plans. For convenience in storing and accessing these materials, it is recommended that you place all weekly materials in a gallon-size plastic storage bag. These bags can be kept in a large storage container giving you quick access to your instructional materials. Individual activities such as sets of "Making Words Letter Cards" or "Individual Sort Cards" can be stored in snack-size baggies within the larger gallon-size storage bag.

Read through the following instructions for directions on how to prepare the materials and teach *The Reading Teacher's Plan Book* activities.

Fluency Building

Purpose: There are two goals for "Fluency Building." The first goal is to help students develop fluency, which is the ability to read quickly, automatically, and with expression. The second goal is to develop independent reading skills and strategies.

Procedure: Place a variety of books on the group table. Include books which have recently been read during the "Guided Reading" component of the lesson plan, books which are on the students' independent reading level, and phonics books which reinforce concepts already taught.

Each student picks his own book to read, and independently reads his book aloud using a soft voice. When finished, he selects another book and continues reading until time is up. The teacher monitors the group, coaching individual students as needed.

Timed Fluency Passages: *Timed Fluency Passages are suggested on the Advanced Week Lesson Plans. Consider doing one-minute timings once a week with your students. This procedure consists of timing your students for one minute as they read a fluency passage. Each student should read out loud at the same time, but in a soft voice so they do not interfere with each other's reading. At the end of one minute, mark how far each student read. Repeat the process two more times, encouraging students to read a little quicker and smoother each time.*

Word Study – Blending Practice

Purpose: The purpose of daily blending practice is to review the vowel sounds being targeted and to develop the skill of blending sounds together.

Preparation: Copy "Group Word Sort Cards" or "Blending Cards" onto cardstock. Laminate and cut into individual cards.

Procedure: Refer to the vowel picture charts to teach the targeted vowel sound and patterns. Use the "Group Word Sort Cards" to practice reading words with those patterns. As a group, have students read the vowel pattern first, then blend the sounds together. At the beginning of the year, using a **_slinky_** is an excellent way to illustrate to students the concept of stretching out the sounds in words.

This part of the Word Study component should be very short, not more than 1-2 minutes.

Word Study – Picture Sort

Purpose: The purpose of the picture sort is to help students build their phonemic awareness, which is the ability to differentiate between sounds. If a student does not have an awareness of a sound, it is not likely he will produce that sound when reading.

Preparation: Copy "Picture Sort Cards" onto cardstock. Laminate and cut into individual cards. *(Free color copies of the "Picture Sort Cards" are available on our website.)*

Procedure: Picture sorts are an auditory exercise. Taking turns, students select a picture, say the name of the picture out loud, and listen to the sounds in the word. Next they look at the header cards and choose which sound matches their word. Lastly, they lay the picture card under the correct heading and proceed to the next word.

Example: When sorting between the *short o* and the *long o* sound (Teaching Week 9), lay the header cards at the top of two columns on the table. Show the first picture card (i.e. a picture of a *pot*). Help students stretch out the sounds in the word (*p-o-t*), emphasizing the *short o* sound in the middle. Students place the picture in the *short o* column.

Word Study – Word Sorts

Purpose: The purpose of a word sort is to help students notice patterns in words and to help students apply knowledge about vowel patterns when reading new words.

Group Sort Preparation: Copy "Group Word Sort Cards" onto cardstock. Laminate and cut into individual cards. (These word cards are also used for daily blending practice.)

Group Sort Procedure: In a Group Sort, the whole group sorts the cards together. Taking turns, students select a word and read the word **out loud**. Next they look at the header cards and choose which pattern matches their word. Lastly, they lay the word card under the correct heading and proceed to the next word. ***It is very important that students read their words out loud. Otherwise they will use visual cues to sort the words and not become proficient at actually reading the words.***

Example: When sorting between the *short a*, *short i*, and *short o* vowel sounds (Review Week 1), lay the header cards at the top of three columns on the table. Using the "Group Word Sort Cards," each student selects a card. The first student reads his word out loud to the group (i.e. *flag*), and places it in the *short a* column. Continue with the next student and repeat until all words have been sorted.

©The Reading Teacher's Plan Book

Individual Sort Preparation: Copy and cut a set of "Individual Sort Cards" *for each student*. To keep sets separate, consider using different colors of paper. Clip the individual sets together and store in a plastic baggie for future use.

Individual Sort Procedure: In an Individual Sort, each student independently sorts his own set of cards following the same procedure as for a Group Sort. Remind students to read each word **OUT LOUD** before laying it down. As students finish sorting their cards, they scramble their words and start again, sorting their words a little faster each time.

Word Study – Making Words (Letter Cards)

Purpose: Making Words is a hands-on activity where students manipulate letter cards to make new words. Students learn spelling patterns, and they learn that a little change can create a whole new word.

Preparation: Copy the "Making Words Letter Cards" onto cardstock. Cut one row of letter cards per student, and then cut each row into individual cards. Clip each set of cards together and store in a plastic baggie for future use.

Procedure: Each student is given a set of letter cards and makes the words listed on the lesson plan. For example, in Teaching Week 3 (Short O Families), students make the words *hot, rot, rob, cob, cop, hop, top, stop*. Instruct students to take three letters and make the word *hot*, then change one letter to make the word *rot*, and so on until all words have been made.

Word Study – Making Words (Syllable Match-Up)

Purpose: Syllable Match-Up is a hands-on activity where students manipulate syllable cards to make new words. Students learn to read multisyllabic words by reading words in chunks or syllables.

Preparation: Copy the "Syllable Match-Up Cards" onto cardstock. Laminate. Cut each strip into four cards and clip together. Keep sets separate. Store in a plastic baggie for future use. *(Free color copies of the "Syllable Match-Up Cards" are available on our website.)*

Procedure: Give each student a set of four syllable cards. Each student matches his cards together and makes two real words. Students read their words out loud, then scramble their cards and pass them to their neighbor. Continue until students have matched all sets.

Word Study – Onset and Rime

Purpose: Students learn how to successfully decode new words as they blend onsets and rimes together. The onset is the beginning sound/s in a word, and the rime is the part of the word from the vowel to the end, most commonly known as the word family.

Either cubes or cards/mats are used in this activity.

Cubes Preparation: Copy "Onset/Rime Cubes" onto cardstock; laminate. Cut along the edges. Fold along the lines and assemble with hot glue.

Onset/Rime Cube Procedure: Two cubes are used for this activity. Beginning sounds are written on the sides of the first cube, and rimes are written on the sides of the second cube. Students take turns rolling the cubes. As a group, blend the onset and rime together, and say the new word.

Cards and Mats Preparation: Copy one set of "Onset/Rime Cards and Mats" **for each student;** laminate. The cards are on the left, and the mat is on the right. Cut along the dotted lines to make individual cards. Clip one set of cards to each mat. Store the sets in a plastic baggie for future use. To keep sets separate, consider using different colors of paper.

Cards and Mats Procedure: Provide each student with a mat, cards, and paper/pencil. Show students how to place onset cards in front of the rimes to make new words. Give students three minutes to write as many "real" words as they can find.

Word Study – Other

Echo Game Preparation: Copy the "Echo Game Cards" onto cardstock. Laminate. Each page has two matching sets of cards. Clip each set of six cards together. Keep sets separate. Store cards in a plastic baggie for future use. *(Free color copies of the "Echo Game Cards" are available on our website.)*

Echo Game Procedures: Students play this game with partners. Each set of partners gets a matching set of cards. Both partners lay their cards on the table. Player A picks up one of his cards, reads it out loud, and places it in front of him. Player B quickly finds his matching card, and reads it out loud creating an echo. Player B then places his card next to Player A's card, and play continues until all the words have been used. The partners gather their cards and start again, this time beginning with Partner B. After both partners have had a turn, they pass their playing cards to the next set of partners, and start again.

Word Hunt (Cubes, Mats, and Bingo Chips) Preparation: Copy the **cube** onto cardstock. Laminate and cut along the outside edges. Fold along the lines and assemble with hot glue. Copy a **mat** for each student. (Three different mats are provided.) Provide an assortment of bingo chips, shiny stones, etc.

Word Hunt (Cubes, Mats, and Bingo Chips) Procedure: Each student gets a **Word Hunt Mat** and **bingo chips**. One student rolls the **cube**, and each student covers a word on his mat which matches the pattern on the cube. Students read their selected words out loud, and play continues until the first student to get three words in a row calls "Bingo." Students clear their boards and start again.

Word Hunt (Word Windows and Writing Mats) Preparation: Copy a **Writing Mat** and **Word Window** for each student. Copy Word Windows onto cardstock, and cut out windows with a razor.

Word Hunt (Word Windows and Writing Mats) Procedure: Give each student a **Word Window** and **Writing Mat.** You will also need to lay out an assortment of previously read guided reading books. Students use their Word Windows to hunt through the books and find words with the targeted patterns. They then write the words they find on their Writing Mats.

Guided Reading

Phonics books and leveled books (typically sold in sets of six) are used at this stage of the plan. (Phonics books and leveled books are not included with "The Reading Teacher's Plan Book.") Students begin the guided reading component by reading a phonics book that reinforces the weekly phonics focus. Students then read a leveled book using the guided reading procedures below. With lower levels, you will read a new book each day. With higher levels, you will read a section or a chapter of a book each day. After a leveled book or phonics book has been read during "Guided Reading," it is placed with the "Fluency Building" books.

Purpose: The purpose of Guided Reading is to help students develop and apply the strategies they need to become independent readers. Students practice these strategies as they read books at their instructional level.

Procedure: Prepare the students for a successful reading experience. The difficulty level of the book should be at the students' instructional level. This means the book is neither too easy nor too difficult, but just right. A "just right" book is one where students can read and comprehend 90-94% of the words correctly (approximately 9 out of every 10 words). A "just right" book is easy enough to ensure success, but at a difficulty level which matches the students' abilities to use phonics knowledge and other skills to decode unknown words.

Follow these steps during the Guided Reading component of the lesson plans:

1. Introduce the new book. Read the title together. Generate a **brief discussion** which connects the book to the students' experiences. (For example, if reading a book about a loose tooth, ask students if any of them have lost a tooth.)
2. Do a **brief "walk"** through the first few pages of the book. During this time, point out new sight words or teach how to decode a particularly difficult word. Draw attention to any patterns the book might have (i.e. the sentences on each page are repetitive or the book is written in a question/answer format). **Do not point out every unknown feature in the book. Students need to develop skills for decoding unknown words.**
3. Make predictions about what might happen in the story. Set a purpose for reading the story . . . "Let's read to see if our predictions are right. Let's read to see if . . ."
4. Give each student a copy of the book. All students read the book out loud using a soft voice. However, **this first reading is not a choral reading.** Each student should be reading independently at his own pace. Circulate around the table, listening to individual students as they read. Coach them with sounding out difficult words.
5. Discuss what happened in the story. Have students retell the important parts of the story or use the Question Die (p. 386) to discuss key story elements.
6. Reread the story (or a portion of the story) together as a group. This time do a choral reading with all students reading together.

Guided Reading for the Advanced Weeks
Comprehension and Writing

As students progress into the Advanced Week Lesson Plans, greater attention is given to comprehension. Half the lesson plan is devoted to reviewing comprehension strategies, reading new books, and responding to the reading, both verbally and in writing.

The following comprehension strategies are taught and practiced during this time:

- **Predict:** Good readers use their background knowledge and clues from the story to guess what will happen or what they will learn about.
- **Summarize:** Good readers retell the important parts or main ideas of a story.
- **Question:** Good readers ask and answer key questions (who, what, where, when, why, and how) about a story.

- **Clarify:** Good readers make sense of what they are reading. When they come to a word or an idea they do not understand, they use strategies to figure out the unknown word or idea.

Follow these steps during the "Guided Reading: Comprehension and Writing" component of the Advanced Week Lesson Plans:

1. Use the "What Good Readers Do" Strategy Chart (page 400) to review the comprehension strategies of **predicting, questioning, summarizing,** and **clarifying.**
2. Conduct a **brief preview** of today's portion of the book. Activate background knowledge by asking students to share what they already know about the story or topic. Encourage students to ask questions or make predictions about what might happen or what they might learn in today's reading.
3. Have students **independently read** today's portion of the story. Listen to individual students as they read. Coach them in sounding out difficult words.
4. Starting with checking predictions, discuss today's reading using the Strategy Chart. Check predictions, summarize the main events in the story, ask and answer questions, and clarify unknown words or ideas.
5. Have students respond in writing to the story using a Graphic Organizer (pages 385-390) or a written response to one of the questions listed in the "Writing – Response Sentences" section (page 16).

Writing – Sound Boxes
Refer to the vowel picture charts (pages 391-395) when doing writing activities.

Purpose: Students learn how to "sound out" words by isolating each individual sound.

Preparation: Copy a "Sound/Spelling Boxes" worksheet for each student (page 379).

Procedure: All students are given a "Sound/Spelling Boxes" worksheet and a pencil. Suggested words are listed on the lesson plans. Say the first word out loud. Students count the number of sounds in the word, and then underline that number of boxes in the first row of the "Sound/Spelling Boxes" worksheet. Help students spell the word, writing one sound in each box, *not necessarily one letter in each box*. Repeat these steps with each new word.

©The Reading Teacher's Plan Book

Example:

bat: b-a-t (3 sounds)

b	a	t

shop: sh-o-p (3 sounds)

sh	o	p

cheek: ch-ee-k (3 sounds)

ch	ee	k

jump: j-u-m-p (4 sounds)

j	u	m	p

Writing – White Boards
Refer to the vowel picture charts (pages 391-395) when doing writing activities.

White boards can be used with the following activities:

Sight Word Writing Fluency: Just as we want our students to read words automatically, we also want them to write words automatically. Choose five or more sight words from your guided reading books. Write the first word together. Give students 10 seconds to write the word as many times as they can. Start again and see if students can improve their score. Repeat this process with the other sight words.

Spelling Patterns: Teach students that learning to spell one word can help them spell other words. Suggested word families/vowel patterns are listed on your lesson plan. Help students write lists of words using the suggested families/patterns.

Slinky Words: Use the "Slinky Words Picture Cards" which accompany the lesson plan. Show the first picture, and instruct students to "stretch" the sounds in the word while pretending to stretch a slinky in their hands. Encourage students to think about the sounds they are saying and to spell the word correctly on their white boards. Repeat. *(Free color copies of the "Slinky Words Picture Cards" are available on our website.)*

Word Chains: Students write the first word on their white boards. Then they make one change (add one letter, take away one letter, or change one letter) to write the next word in the chain. Students see that changing one letter creates a whole new word. *Example: cat, can, man, men, ten, tin, pin, pan, pat, bat*

Writing – Writing Sort
Refer to the vowel picture charts (pages 391-395) when doing writing activities.

Purpose: The purpose of a Writing Sort is to help students notice patterns in words and to help them apply knowledge about vowel patterns when writing new words.

Preparation: Copy a "Writing Sort" worksheet for each student. Choose from 2-Column, 3-Column, or 4-Column Writing Sorts (pages 380-382).

Procedure: First, give each student a copy of the "Writing Sort" worksheet. Students write the targeted vowel patterns across the top of the columns. Next, read a word out loud using either the "Group Word Sort Cards" or "Individual Word Sort Cards" (see specific lesson plans). Students think about the pattern that is used to spell the word, and they write the word under the correct heading. Lastly, show the students the word card and let students check their work. Repeat with new words.

Example: When sorting between the *short a*, *short i*, and *short o* sounds (Review Week 1), use the "Group Word Sort Cards" and the "3-Column Writing Sort" worksheet. Students write *a*, *i*, and *o* across the top of the columns. Call out the first word (i.e. *pig*). Students sound out the word (*p-i-g*), think about the vowel sound they hear, and write the word in the *short i* column. Show students the word card, and let them check their work.

Writing – Dictation Sentences
Refer to the vowel picture charts (pages 391-395) when doing writing activities.

Purpose: The goal of writing dictation sentences is to allow students to apply what they know about word patterns and sight words as they write complete sentences.

Procedure: Suggested sentences are written on your lesson plan. Read the sentence out loud. Reread it slowly as students write the words in the sentence. Help any students who are having difficulty. **Step them through the process of sounding out an unknown word and referring to the vowel picture charts to help them target the spelling of that sound.**

Writing – Response Sentences
Refer to the vowel picture charts (pages 391-395) when doing writing activities.

Purpose: Story responses help students deepen their comprehension and make personal connections with the story. Students answer questions, write pattern sentences, or respond using graphic organizers.

Story Response Questions: Ask your students to respond to a question about the story you just read. Depending on the level of your group, you can either write the same sentence together or assist students in writing their own sentences. **Be sure to practice sounding out unknown words together, referring to the vowel picture charts.**

Suggested Story Response Questions:

- What was your favorite part of the story? Why?
- Who was your favorite character? Why?
- Did you like how the character solved the problem in the story? Why? What would you have done differently?
- Did this story make you think of something that has happened to you (or someone you know or something else you have read)? Write about it.

Pattern Writing: Beginning books often follow a repetitive pattern. Instruct students to write their own sentences following the pattern in their guided reading books. For example, in a book which lists favorite foods, students can follow the pattern and write their own sentences . . . *I like apples. I like bananas. I like pizza.*

Comprehension Graphic Organizers: Use the provided graphic organizers to help students predict, summarize, clarify, and ask questions about their guided reading books. (See pages 385-390.)

Yearly Tracking and Pacing Planner

Group: _____

Teaching Weeks:

Week 1 Short A Word Families at, an, ap	Week 2 Short I Word Families it, ig, in	Week 3 Short O Word Families ot, op, ob	Week 4 Short E Word Families et, ed, en	Week 5 Short U Word Families ut, un, ug	Week 6 ck families and ch, sh, th	Week 7 Long Vowel a_e	Week 8 Long Vowel i_e	Week 9 Long Vowel o_e, u_e	Week 10 Long Vowel Patterns ai, ay
Date: GRL:	Date: GRL:	Date: GRL:	Date: GRL:	Date: GRL:	Date: GRL:	Date: GRL:	Date: GRL:	Date: GRL:	Date: GRL:

Week 11 Long Vowel Patterns e, ee, ea	Week 12 Long Vowel Patterns o, oa, ow	Week 13 Long Vowel Patterns ie, igh, y	Week 14 Spooky Sound oo, ew, ue, u-e	Week 15 Hurt Sound ou, ow	Week 16 Bossy R Sound ar, are, er, ir, ur, or	Week 17 Whining Sound aw, au, all	Week 18 Bouncy Sound oi, oy Boxing Sound oo	Week 19 Endings ed, ing, er, ful, less, ly	Week 20 Compound Words
Date: GRL:	Date: GRL:	Date: GRL:	Date: GRL:	Date: GRL:	Date: GRL:	Date: GRL:	Date: GRL:	Date: GRL:	Date: GRL:

Review Weeks:

Review Week 1 Short A, I, O	Review Week 2 Short E, U	Review Week 3 Short Vowels	Review Week 4 Short Vowels	Review Week 5 Short Vowels	Review Week 6 Long Vowels/ Silent E	Review Week 7 Long Vowels/ Silent E	Review Week 8 Long Vowel Patterns	Review Week 9 Long Vowel Patterns	Review Week 10 Long Vowel Patterns
Date: GRL:	Date: GRL:	Date: GRL:	Date: GRL:	Date: GRL:	Date: GRL:	Date: GRL:	Date: GRL:	Date: GRL:	Date: GRL:

Review Week 11 "A Patterns"	Review Week 12 "E Patterns"	Review Week 13 "I Patterns"	Review Week 14 "O Patterns"	Review Week 15 "U Patterns"
Date: GRL:	Date: GRL:	Date: GRL:	Date: GRL:	Date: GRL:

Advanced Weeks:

Advanced Week 1 Syllabication Double Consonants	Advanced Week 2 Syllabication Consonant + le	Advanced Week 3 Syllabication Suffixes	Advanced Week 4 Syllabication Prefixes	Advanced Week 5 Syllabication Closed Syllables	Advanced Week 6 Syllabication Open Syllables	Advanced Week 7 Syllabication Silent E Pattern	Advanced Week 8 Syllabication Vowel Team Patterns	Advanced Week 9 Syllabication Bossy R Patterns	Advanced Week 10 Syllabication Dividing Words into Syllables
Date: GRL:	Date: GRL:	Date: GRL:	Date: GRL:	Date: GRL:	Date: GRL:	Date: GRL:	Date: GRL:	Date: GRL:	Date: GRL:

*GRL=Guided Reading Level

©The Reading Teacher's Plan Book

TEACHING WEEKS MATERIALS LIST

Teaching Week 1:   Short A Families — at, an, ap (Use the Short Vowels Picture Chart, p. 391.)
- Short A Families Lesson Plan
- Short A Families Group Sort Cards, pgs. 120-121
- Short A Families Onset/Rime Cubes, pgs. 122-123
- Short A Families Making Words Letter Cards, p. 124
- Short A Families Individual Sort Cards, p. 125
- Sound/Spelling Boxes, p. 379

Teaching Week 2: Short I Families — it, in, ig (Use the Short Vowels Picture Chart, p. 391.)
- Short I Families Lesson Plan
- Short I Families Group Sort Cards, pgs. 126-127
- Short I Families Onset/Rime Cubes, pgs. 128-129
- Short I Families Making Words Letter Cards, p. 130
- Short I Families Individual Sort Cards, p. 131
- Sound/Spelling Boxes, p. 379

Teaching Week 3: Short O Families — ot, op, ob (Use the Short Vowels Picture Chart, p. 391.)
- Short O Families Lesson Plan
- Short O Families Group Sort Cards, pgs. 132-133
- Short O Families Onset/Rime Cubes, pgs. 134-135
- Short O Families Making Words Letter Cards, p. 136
- Short O Families Individual Sort Cards, p. 137
- Sound/Spelling Boxes, p. 379

Teaching Week 4: Short E Families — et, ed, en (Use the Short Vowels Picture Chart, p. 391.)
- Short E Families Lesson Plan
- Short E Families Group Sort Cards, pgs. 138-139
- Short E Families Onset/Rime Cubes, pgs. 140-141
- Short E Families Making Words Letter Cards, p. 142
- Short E Families Individual Sort Cards, p. 143
- Sound/Spelling Boxes, p. 379

Teaching Week 5: Short U Families — ut, un, ug (Use the Short Vowels Picture Chart, p. 391.)
- Short U Families Lesson Plan
- Short U Families Group Sort Cards, pgs. 144-145
- Short U Families Onset/Rime Cubes, pgs. 146-147
- Short U Families Making Words Letter Cards, p. 148
- Short U Families Individual Sort Cards, p. 149
- Sound/Spelling Boxes, p. 379

©The Reading Teacher's Plan Book

Teaching Week 6: ck families and digraphs ch, sh, th (Use the [Digra]phs Picture Chart, pgs. 396-397.)
    ck, ch, sh, th Lesson Plan
    Ack, ick, ock, uck Group Sort Cards (6a), pgs. 150-151
    Ack, ick, ock, uck Onset/Rime Cubes, pgs. 152-153
    Ch, sh, th Group Sort Cards (6b), pgs. 154-155
    Ch, sh, th Picture Sort, p. 156
    Sound/Spelling Boxes, p. 379
    3-Column Writing Sort, p. 381

Teaching Week 7: Long A with Silent E (Use the Long Vowel Sound/Spelling Picture Chart, p. 392.)
    Long A with Silent E Lesson Plan
    Long A with Silent E Group Sort Cards, pgs. 157-158
    Long A with Silent E Onset/Rime Cubes, pgs. 159-160
    Short A/Long A Picture Sort, p. 161
    Long A with Silent E Individual Sort Cards, p. 162
    2-Column Writing Sort, p. 380

Teaching Week 8: Long I with Silent E (Use the Long Vowel Sound/Spelling Picture Chart, p. 392.)
    Long I with Silent E Lesson Plan
    Long I with Silent E Group Sort Cards, pgs. 163-164
    Long I with Silent E Onset/Rime Cubes, pgs. 165-166
    Short I/Long I Picture Sort, p. 167
    Long I with Silent E Making Words Letter Cards, p. 168
    Long I with Silent E Individual Sort Cards, p. 169
    2-Column Writing Sort, p. 380

Teaching Week 9: Long O, U with Silent E (Use the Long Vowel Sound/Spelling Picture Chart, p. 392.)
    Long O, U with Silent E Lesson Plan
    Long O, U with Silent E Group Sort Cards, pgs. 170-171
    Long O with Silent E Onset/Rime Cubes, pgs. 172-173
    Long U with Silent E Onset/Rime Cubes, pgs. 174-175
    Short O/Long O Picture Sort, p. 176
    Short U/Long U Picture Sort, p. 177
    Long O, U w/Silent E Making Words Letter Cards, p. 178
    Long O, U with Silent E Individual Sort Cards, p. 179
    2-Column Writing Sort, p. 380

Teaching Week 10: Long A Vowel Patterns ai, ay (Use the Long Vowel Sound/Spelling Picture Chart, p. 392.)
    Long A Vowel Patterns Lesson Plan
    Long A Vowel Patterns Group Sort Cards, pgs. 180-181

Long A Vowel Patterns Onset/Rime Cubes, pgs. 183-183
Long A Vowel Patterns Making Words Letter Cards, p. 184
Long A Vowel Patterns Individual Sort Cards, p. 185
Sound/Spelling Boxes, p. 379

Teaching Week 11: Long E Vowel Patterns e, ee, ea (Use the Long Vowel Sound/Spelling Picture Chart, p. 392.)

Long E Vowel Patterns Lesson Plan
Long E Vowel Patterns Group Sort Cards, pgs. 186-187
Long E Vowel Patterns Onset/Rime Cubes, pgs. 188-189
Long E Vowel Patterns Making Words Letter Cards, p. 190
Long E Vowel Patterns Individual Sort Cards, p. 191
Sound/Spelling Boxes, p. 379
2-Column Writing Sort, p. 380

Teaching Week 12: Long O Vowel Patterns o, oa, ow (Use the Long Vowel Sound/Spelling Picture Chart, p. 392.)

Long O Vowel Patterns Lesson Plan
Long O Vowel Patterns Group Sort Cards, pgs. 192-193
Long O Vowel Patterns Onset/Rime Cards and Mats, p. 194
Long O Vowel Patterns Making Words Cards, p. 195
Long O Vowel Patterns Individual Sort Cards, p. 196
Sound/Spelling Boxes, p. 379

Teaching Week 13: Long I Vowel Patterns ie, igh, y (Use the Long Vowel Sound/Spelling Picture Chart, p. 392.)

Long I Vowel Patterns Lesson Plan
Long I Vowel Patterns Group Sort Cards, pgs. 197-198
Long I Vowel Patterns Onset/Rime Cards and Mats, p. 199
Long I Vowel Patterns Making Words Cards, p. 200
Long I Vowel Patterns Individual Sort Cards, p. 201
Sound/Spelling Boxes, p. 379
3-Column Writing Sort, p. 381

Teaching Week 14: "Spooky Sound" oo, ew, ue, u-e (Use the Other Vowel Sounds Sound/Spelling Picture Chart, pgs. 393-395.)

Spooky Sound Patterns Lesson Plan
Spooky Sound Patterns Group Sort Cards, pgs. 202-203
Spooky Sound Patterns Onset/Rime Cards and Mats, p. 204
Spooky Sound Patterns Making Words Cards, p. 205
Spooky Sound Patterns Individual Sort Cards, p. 206
Sound/Spelling Boxes, p. 379

2-Column Writing Sort, p. 380

Teaching Week 15: "Hurt Sound" ou, ow (Use the Other Vowel Sounds Sound/Spelling Picture Chart, pgs. 393-395.)
Hurt Sound Patterns Lesson Plan
Hurt Sound Patterns Group Sort Cards, pgs. 207-208
Hurt Sound Patterns Onset/Rime Cards and Mats, p. 209
Hurt Sound Patterns Making Words Cards, p. 210
Hurt Sound Patterns Individual Sort Cards, p. 211
Sound/Spelling Boxes, p. 379

Teaching Week 16: "Bossy R Sounds" ar, are, er, ir, ur, or (Use the Other Vowel Sounds Sound/Spelling Picture Chart, pgs. 393-395.)
Bossy R Patterns Lesson Plan
Bossy R Patterns Group Sort Cards, pgs. 212-213
Bossy R Patterns Onset/Rime Cards and Mats, p. 214
Bossy R Patterns Making Words Cards, p. 215
Bossy R Patterns Individual Sort Cards, p. 216
Sound/Spelling Boxes, p. 379
3-Column Writing Sort, p. 381

Teaching Week 17: "Whining Sound" aw, au, all (Use the Other Vowel Sounds Sound/Spelling Picture Chart, pgs. 393-395.)
Whining Sound Patterns Lesson Plan
Whining Sound Patterns Group Sort Cards, pgs. 217-218
Whining Sound Patterns Onset/Rime Cards and Mats, p. 219
Whining Sound Patterns Making Words Cards, p. 220
Whining Sound Patterns Individual Sort Cards, p. 221
3-Column Writing Sort, p. 381

Teaching Week 18: "Bouncy Sound" oi, oy, "Boxing Sound" oo (Use the Other Vowel Sounds Sound/Spelling Picture Chart, pgs. 393-395.)
Oi, Oy, Oo Patterns Lesson Plan
Oi, Oy, Oo Patterns Group Sort Cards, pgs. 222-223
Oi, Oy, Oo Patterns Onset/Rime Cards and Mats, p. 224
Oi, Oy, Oo Patterns Making Words Cards, p. 225
Oi, Oy, Oo Patterns Individual Sort Cards, p. 226
Sound/Spelling Boxes, p. 379

Teaching Week 19: Endings ed, ing, er
Endings Lesson Plan
Endings Group Sort Cards 19a (Sounds of "-ed"), pgs. 227-228

Blending Cards 19b (ed, ing, er), pgs. 229-230
Word Windows, pgs. 383-384
Endings Word Hunt Writing Mats, p. 231
Endings Individual Sort Cards, p. 232
3-Column Writing Sort, p. 381
Comprehension Graphic Organizers, pgs. 385-390

Teaching Week 20: Compound Words
Compound Words Lesson Plan
Compound Words Blending Cards, pgs. 233-234
Compound Words Match-Up, pgs. 235-236
Compound Words Word Hunt Cube, Mats, and Bingo Chips, pgs. 237-238
4-Column Writing Sort, p. 382
Comprehension Graphic Organizers, pgs. 385-390

Teaching Week 1: Short A Word Families – at, an, ap
Use with activities on pages 120-125.

DAY 1:

Fluency Building (5-7 minutes)

Include:
*Previously read books
*Books from Level _____
*Phonics Books

Word Study (8-10 minutes)

- ✓ **Blending at, an, ap words** *(Use Group Word Sort Cards.)*
- • Picture/Sound Sort
- • Word Sorts –
  - Group   Individual
  - Making Words Activity
- ✓ **Onset/Rime Activity** *(Use the Onset/Rime Cubes.)*
- • Other:

Guided Reading (8-10 minutes)

- ✓ Phonics Book: _____ Book: _____
- ✓ Guided Reading Level: _____

Writing (5-7 minutes)

- ✓ **Sound Boxes** *(Use the Sound/Spelling Boxes.)*
- • White Boards
- • Writing Sort
- • Dictation Sentences
- • Response Sentences

<u>Words for Sound Boxes:</u>

c-a-t
h-a-t
r-a-n
c-a-n
m-a-p

Guided Reading Level _____

DAY 2:

Fluency Building (5-7 minutes)

Include:
*Previously read books
*Books from Level _____
*Phonics Books

Word Study (8-10 minutes)

- ✓ **Blending at, an, ap words** *(Use Group Word Sort Cards.)*
- • Picture/Sound Sort
- ✓ **Word Sorts – at, an, ap words** *(Use Group Word Sort Cards.)*
  - Group   Individual
  - Making Words Activity
- • Onset/Rime Activity
- • Other:

Guided Reading (8-10 minutes)

- ✓ Phonics Book: _____ Book: _____
- ✓ Guided Reading Level: _____

Writing (5-7 minutes)

- • Sound Boxes
- ✓ **White Boards**
- • Writing Sort
- • Dictation Sentences
- • Response Sentences

<u>Spelling Patterns:</u>
Write "at" words . . . then "an" words . . . then "ap" words

©The Reading Teacher's Plan Book

Teaching Week 1: Short A Word Families – at, an, ap (cont.)
Use with activities on pages 120-125.

DAY 3:

Fluency Building (5-7 minutes)

Include:
*Previously read books
*Books from Level _____
*Phonics Books

Word Study (8-10 minutes)

✓ <u>Blending at, an, ap words</u> *(Use Group Word Sort Cards.)*
- Picture/Sound Sort
- Word Sorts – Group   Individual
- **Making Words Activity**
- Onset/Rime Activity
- Other:

<u>Make these words:</u>
(Use the letter cards.)
can, pan, pat, cat, rat, ran, rap, trap

Guided Reading (8-10 minutes)

✓ Phonics Book: _____
✓ Guided Reading Level: _____ Book: _____

Writing (5-7 minutes)

- Sound Boxes
- White Boards
- Writing Sort
- Dictation Sentences
- ✓ **Response Sentences**

Pattern Sentences:
Use the pattern from today's guided reading book. Pick a group sentence. Write the sentence together.

Guided Reading Level _____

DAY 4:

Fluency Building (5-7 minutes)

Include:
*Previously read books
*Books from Level _____
*Phonics Books

Word Study (8-10 minutes)

✓ <u>Blending at, an, ap words</u> *(Use Group Word Sort Cards.)*
- Picture/Sound Sort
✓ <u>Word Sorts – at, an, ap words</u> *(Use Individual Sort Cards.)*
   Group   **Individual**
- Making Words Activity
- Onset/Rime Activity
- Other:

Guided Reading (8-10 minutes)

✓ Phonics Book: _____
✓ Guided Reading Level: _____ Book: _____

Writing (5-7 minutes)

- Sound Boxes
- White Boards
- Writing Sort
- ✓ **Dictation Sentences**
- Response Sentences

Dictation Sentences:
1. I see a fat cat.
2. The man ran fast.
3. I can clap my hands.

©The Reading Teacher's Plan Book

Teaching Week 2: Short I Word Families – *it, in, ig*
Use with activities on pages 126-131.

DAY 1:

Fluency Building (5-7 minutes)

Include:
Previously read books
Books from Level _____
Phonics Books

Word Study (8-10 minutes)

✓ <u>Blending it, in, ig words</u> *(Use Group Word Sort Cards.)*
- Picture/Sound Sort
- Word Sorts –
  - Group   Individual
- Making Words Activity
✓ <u>Onset/Rime Activity</u> *(Use the Onset/Rime Cubes.)*
- Other:

Guided Reading (8-10 minutes)

✓ Phonics Book: _____ Book: _____
✓ Guided Reading Level: _____

Writing (5-7 minutes)

✓ <u>Sound Boxes</u> *(Use the Sound/Spelling Boxes.)*
- White Boards
- Writing Sort
- Dictation Sentences
- Response Sentences

Guided Reading Level _____

DAY 2:

Fluency Building (5-7 minutes)

Include:
Previously read books
Books from Level _____
Phonics Books

Word Study (8-10 minutes)

✓ <u>Blending it, in, ig words</u> *(Use Group Word Sort Cards.)*
- Picture/Sound Sort
✓ <u>Word Sorts – it, in, ig words</u> *(Use Group Word Sort Cards.)*
  - Group   Individual
- Making Words Activity
- Onset/Rime Activity
- Other:

Guided Reading (8-10 minutes)

✓ Phonics Book: _____ Book: _____
✓ Guided Reading Level: _____

Writing (5-7 minutes)

- Sound Boxes
- **White Boards**
✓ Writing Sort
- Dictation Sentences
- Response Sentences

<u>*Words for Sound Boxes:*</u>

p-i-n
th-i-n
f-i-t
s-i-t
p-i-g

<u>*Spelling Patterns:*</u>
Write "it" words . . . then "in" words . . . then "ig" words

©The Reading Teacher's Plan Book

Teaching Week 2: Short I Word Families – it, in, ig (cont.)
Use with activities on pages 126-131.

DAY 3:

Fluency Building (5-7 minutes)

Include:
- *Previously read books
- *Books from Level _____
- *Phonics Books

Word Study (8-10 minutes)

- ✓ <u>Blending it, in, ig words</u> *(Use Group Word Sort Cards.)*
- • Picture/Sound Sort
- • Word Sorts – Group ____ Individual ____
- ✓ **Making Words Activity**
- • Onset/Rime Activity
- • Other: ____

Make these words:
(Use the letter cards.)
pig, big, bit, fit, fin, pin, win, twin, twig

Guided Reading (8-10 minutes)

- ✓ Phonics Book: _____ Book: _____
- ✓ Guided Reading Level: _____

Writing (5-7 minutes)

- • Sound Boxes
- • White Boards
- • Writing Sort
- • Dictation Sentences
- ✓ **Response Sentences**

Story Response Questions:
What is your favorite part of the story?
"I like _____."

Guided Reading Level _____

DAY 4:

Fluency Building (5-7 minutes)

Include:
- *Previously read books
- *Books from Level _____
- *Phonics Books

Word Study (8-10 minutes)

- ✓ <u>Blending it, in, ig words</u> *(Use Group Word Sort Cards.)*
- • Picture/Sound
- ✓ <u>Word Sorts – it, in, ig words</u> *(Use Individual Sort Cards.)*
  Group ____ **Individual**
- • Making Words Activity
- • Onset/Rime Activity
- • Other: ____

Guided Reading (8-10 minutes)

- ✓ Phonics Book: _____
- ✓ Guided Reading Level: _____ Book: _____

Writing (5-7 minutes)

- • Sound Boxes
- • White Boards
- • Writing Sort
- ✓ **Dictation Sentences**
- • Response Sentences

Dictation Sentences:
1. I like to dig.
2. I see the big pig.
3. I can hit with a bat.

©The Reading Teacher's Plan Book

Teaching Week 3: Short O Word Families – ot, op, ob

Use with activities on pages 132-137.

Guided Reading Level _____

DAY 1:

Fluency Building (5-7 minutes)

Include:
*Previously read books
*Books from Level _____
*Phonics Books

Word Study (8-10 minutes)

✓ **Blending ot, op, ob words** *(Use Group Word Sort Cards.)*
- Picture/Sound Sort
- Word Sorts –
  Group ____ Individual ____
- Making Words Activity
✓ **Onset/Rime Activity** *(Use the Onset/Rime Cubes.)*
- Other:

Guided Reading (8-10 minutes)

✓ Phonics Book: _____ Book: _____
✓ Guided Reading Level: _____

Writing (5-7 minutes)

✓ **Sound Boxes** *(Use the Sound/Spelling Boxes.)*
- White Boards
- Writing Sort
- Dictation Sentences
- Response Sentences

Words for Sound Boxes:

t-o-p
ch-o-p
r-o-b
c-o-b
s-p-o-t

DAY 2:

Fluency Building (5-7 minutes)

Include:
*Previously read books
*Books from Level _____
*Phonics Books

Word Study (8-10 minutes)

✓ **Blending ot, op, ob words** *(Use Group Word Sort Cards.)*
- Picture/Sound Sort
✓ **Word Sorts – ot, op, ob words** *(Use Group Word Sort Cards.)*
  Group ____ Individual ____
- Making Words Activity
- Onset/Rime Activity
- Other:

Guided Reading (8-10 minutes)

✓ Phonics Book: _____ Book: _____
✓ Guided Reading Level: _____

Writing (5-7 minutes)

- Sound Boxes
✓ **White Boards**
- Writing Sort
- Dictation Sentences
- Response Sentences

<u>*Spelling Patterns:*</u>
Write "ot" words . . . then "op" words . . . then "ob" words

©The Reading Teacher's Plan Book

Teaching Week 3: Short O Word Families – ot, op, ob (cont.)
Use with activities on pages 132-137.

Guided Reading Level _____

DAY 3:

**Fluency Building
(5-7 minutes)**

Include:
*Previously read books
*Books from Level _____
*Phonics Books

**Word Study
(8-10 minutes)**

✓ Blending ot, op, ob words *(Use Group Word Sort Cards.)*
• Picture/Sound Sort
• Word Sorts –
  Group   Individual
✓ **Making Words Activity**
• Onset/Rime Activity
• Other:

*Make these words:
(Use the letter cards.)
hot, rot, rob, cob, cop,
hop, top, stop*

**Guided Reading
(8-10 minutes)**

✓ Phonics Book: _____ Book: _____
✓ Guided Reading Level: _____

**Writing
(5-7 minutes)**

• Sound Boxes
• White Boards
• Writing Sort
• Dictation Sentences
✓ **Response Sentences**

Pattern Sentences:
Use the pattern from today's guided reading book. Pick a group sentence. Write the sentence together.

DAY 4:

**Fluency Building
(5-7 minutes)**

Include:
*Previously read books
*Books from Level _____
*Phonics Books

**Word Study
(8-10 minutes)**

✓ Blending ot, op, ob words *(Use Group Word Sort Cards.)*
• Picture/Sound
✓ Word Sorts – ot, op, ob words *(Use Individual Sort Cards.)*
  Group   **Individual**
• Making Words Activity
• Onset/Rime Activity
• Other:

**Guided Reading
(8-10 minutes)**

✓ Phonics Book: _____ Book: _____
✓ Guided Reading Level: _____

**Writing
(5-7 minutes)**

• Sound Boxes
• White Boards
• Writing Sort
✓ **Dictation Sentences**
• Response Sentences

Dictation Sentences:
1. The pot is hot.
2. We like to hop.
3. My mom has a job.

©The Reading Teacher's Plan Book

Teaching Week 4: Short E Word Families – et, ed, en

Use with activities on pages 138-143.

DAY 1:

Fluency Building (5-7 minutes)

Include:
*Previously read books
*Books from Level _____
*Phonics Books

Word Study (8-10 minutes)

✓ Blending et, ed, en words *(Use Group Word Sort Cards.)*
• Picture/Sound Sort
• Word Sorts –
   Group   Individual
   Making Words Activity
✓ Onset/Rime Activity *(Use the Onset/Rime Cubes.)*
• Other:

Guided Reading (8-10 minutes)

✓ Phonics Book: _____ Book: _____
✓ Guided Reading Level: _____

Writing (5-7 minutes)

✓ **Sound Boxes** *(Use the Sound/Spelling Boxes.)*
• White Boards
• Writing Sort
• Dictation Sentences
• Response Sentences

Guided Reading Level _____

DAY 2:

Fluency Building (5-7 minutes)

Include:
*Previously read books
*Books from Level _____
*Phonics Books

Word Study (8-10 minutes)

✓ **Blending et, ed, en words** *(Use Group Word Sort Cards.)*
• Picture/Sound Sort
✓ **Word Sorts – et, ed, en words** *(Use Group Word Sort Cards.)*
   Group   Individual
   Making Words Activity
• Onset/Rime Activity
• Other:

Guided Reading (8-10 minutes)

✓ Phonics Book: _____
✓ Guided Reading Level: _____ Book: _____

Writing (5-7 minutes)

• Sound Boxes
✓ **White Boards**
• Writing Sort
• Dictation Sentences
• Response Sentences

Words for Sound Boxes:

th-e-n
m-e-n
s-l-e-d
w-e-t
y-e-t

<u>*Spelling Patterns:*</u>
Write "et" words . . . then "ed" words . . . then "en" words

©The Reading Teacher's Plan Book

Teaching Week 4: Short E Word Families – et, ed, en (cont.)
Use with activities on pages 138-143.

DAY 3:

Fluency Building (5-7 minutes)

Include:
*Previously read books
*Books from Level _____
*Phonics Books

Word Study (8-10 minutes)

✓ **Blending et, ed, en words** *(Use Group Word Sort Cards.)*
• Picture/Sound Sort
✓ Word Sorts –   Group   Individual
• **Making Words Activity**   *Make these words:*
  (Use the letter cards.)
  ten, pen, men, met, pet, let, led, sled
• Onset/Rime Activity
• Other:

Guided Reading (8-10 minutes)

✓ Phonics Book: _____ Book: _____
✓ Guided Reading Level: _____

Writing (5-7 minutes)

• Sound Boxes
• White Boards
• Writing Sort
• Dictation Sentences
✓ **Response Sentences**

Story Response Questions:
What is your favorite part of the story?
"I like _____."

DAY 4:

Fluency Building (5-7 minutes)

Include:
*Previously read books
*Books from Level _____
*Phonics Books

Word Study (8-10 minutes)

✓ **Blending et, ed, en words** *(Use Group Word Sort Cards.)*
• Picture/Sound Sort
✓ **Word Sorts – et, ed, en words** *(Use Individual Sort Cards.)*
       Group   **Individual**
• Making Words Activity
• Onset/Rime Activity
• Other:

Guided Reading (8-10 minutes)

✓ Phonics Book: _____ Book: _____
✓ Guided Reading Level: _____

Writing (5-7 minutes)

• Sound Boxes
• White Boards
• Writing Sort
✓ **Dictation Sentences**
• Response Sentences

Dictation Sentences:
1. We will get a new pet.
2. Do you like my red sled?
3. Ten men got wet in the pond.

Guided Reading Level _____

©The Reading Teacher's Plan Book

Teaching Week 5: Short U Word Families – ut, un, ug
Use with activities on pages 144-149.

DAY 1:

Fluency Building
(5-7 minutes)

Include:
*Previously read books
*Books from Level ____
*Phonics Books

Word Study
(8-10 minutes)

✓ **Blending ut, un, ug words** *(Use Group Word Sort Cards.)*
- Picture/Sound Sort
- Word Sorts –
   Group   Individual
- Making Words Activity
✓ **Onset/Rime Activity** *(Use the Onset/Rime Cubes.)*
- Other: ____

Guided Reading
(8-10 minutes)

✓ Phonics Book: _____ Book: _____
✓ Guided Reading Level: _____ Book: _____

Writing
(5-7 minutes)

✓ **Sound Boxes** *(Use the Sound/Spelling Boxes.)*
- White Boards
- Writing Sort
- Dictation Sentences
- Response Sentences

Words for Sound Boxes:

j-u-g
s-l-u-g
h-u-t
sh-u-t
f-u-n

Guided Reading Level ____

DAY 2:

Fluency Building
(5-7 minutes)

Include:
*Previously read books
*Books from Level ____
*Phonics Books

Word Study
(8-10 minutes)

✓ **Blending ut, un, ug words** *(Use Group Word Sort Cards.)*
- Picture/Sound Sort
✓ **Word Sorts – ut, un, ug words** *(Use Group Word Sort Cards.)*
   Group   Individual
- Making Words Activity
- Onset/Rime Activity
- Other: ____

Guided Reading
(8-10 minutes)

✓ Phonics Book: _____ Book: _____
✓ Guided Reading Level: _____ Book: _____

Writing
(5-7 minutes)

- Sound Boxes
✓ **White Boards**
- Writing Sort
- Dictation Sentences
- Response Sentences

Spelling Patterns:
Write "ut" words . . . then "un" words . . . then "ug" words

©The Reading Teacher's Plan Book

Teaching Week 5: Short U Word Families – ut, un, ug (cont.)

Use with activities on pages 144-149.

Guided Reading Level _____

DAY 3:

Fluency Building
(5-7 minutes)

Include:
*Previously read books
*Books from Level _____
*Phonics Books

Word Study
(8-10 minutes)

- ✓ **Blending ut, un, ug words** *(Use Group Word Sort Cards.)*
- Picture/Sound Sort
- ✓ Word Sorts –
  - Group   Individual
- **Making Words Activity**   *Make these words:*
  (Use the letter cards.)
  bug, rug, run, sun, bun,
  but, nut, hut, shut
- Onset/Rime Activity
- Other:

Guided Reading
(8-10 minutes)

- ✓ Phonics Book: _____ Book: _____
- ✓ Guided Reading Level: _____

Writing
(5-7 minutes)

- Sound Boxes
- White Boards
- Writing Sort
- **Dictation Sentences**
- Response Sentences

Dictation Sentences:
1. A bug is on the rug.
2. A nut fell on the hut.
3. When can we run in the sun?

DAY 4:

Fluency Building
(5-7 minutes)

Include:
*Previously read books
*Books from Level _____
*Phonics Books

Word Study
(8-10 minutes)

- ✓ **Blending ut, un, ug words** *(Use Group Word Sort Cards.)*
- Picture/Sound Sort
- ✓ **Word Sorts – ut, un, ug words** *(Use Individual Sort Cards.)*
  - Group   **Individual**
- Making Words Activity
- Onset/Rime Activity
- Other:

Guided Reading
(8-10 minutes)

- ✓ Phonics Book: _____ Book: _____
- ✓ Guided Reading Level: _____

Writing
(5-7 minutes)

- Sound Boxes
- White Boards
- Writing Sort
- Dictation Sentences
- ✓ **Response Sentences**

Story Response Questions:
Students respond to a question about today's Guided Reading book.

©The Reading Teacher's Plan Book

Teaching Week 6: ack, ick, ock, uck and digraphs ch, sh, th
Use with activities on pages 150-156.

Guided Reading Level _____

DAY 1:

Fluency Building (5-7 minutes)

Include:
*Previously read books
*Books from Level _____
*Phonics Books

Word Study (8-10 minutes)

✓ Blending <u>ack, ick, ock, uck words</u> *(Use Group Word Sort Cards 6a.)*
- P_cture/Sound Sort
- Word Sorts –
  Group   Individual
  Making Words Activity
✓ **Onset/Rime Activity** *(Use the Onset/Rime Cubes.)*
- Other:

Guided Reading (8-10 minutes)

✓ Phonics Book: _____ Book: _____
✓ Guided Reading Level: _____

Writing (5-7 minutes)

✓ **Sound Boxes** *(Use the Sound/Spelling Boxes.)*
- White Boards
- Writing Sort
- Dictation Sentences
- Response Sentences

Words for Sound Boxes:

s-a-ck
s-o-ck
sh-o-ck
t-r-u-ck
t-r-i-ck

DAY 2:

Fluency Building (5-7 minutes)

Include:
*Previously read books
*Books from Level _____
*Phonics Books

Word Study (8-10 minutes)

✓ Blending ack, ick, ock, uck words *(Use Group Word Sort Cards 6a.)*
- Picture/Sound Sort
✓ Word Sorts – <u>ack, ick, ock, uck words</u> *(Use Group Word Sort Cards 6a.)*
  Group   Individual
  Making Words Activity
- Onset/Rime Activity
- Other:

Guided Reading (8-10 minutes)

✓ Phonics Book: _____ Book: _____
✓ Guided Reading Level: _____

Writing (5-7 minutes)

- Sound Boxes
✓ **White Boards**
- Writing Sort
- Dictation Sentences
- Response Sentences

<u>*Spelling Patterns:*</u>
Write "ack" words . . . then "ick" words . . . then "ock" words . . . then "uck" words

©The Reading Teacher's Plan Book

Teaching Week 6: ack, ick, ock, uck and digraphs ch, sh, th (cont.)
Use with activities on pages 150-156.

Guided Reading Level _____

DAY 3:

Fluency Building
(5-7 minutes)

Include:
*Previously read books
*Books from Level _____
*Phonics Books

Word Study
(8-10 minutes)

✓ **Blending ch, sh, th words** (*Use Group Word Sort Cards 6b.*)
✓ Picture/Sound Sort (*Use ch, sh, th Picture Sort Cards.*)
• Word Sorts —
   Group   Individual
• Making Words Activity
• Onset/Rime Activity
• Other:

Guided Reading
(8-10 minutes)

✓ Phonics Book: _____ Book: _____
✓ Guided Reading Level: _____

Writing
(5-7 minutes)

• Sound Boxes
• White Boards
✓ **Writing Sort**   (*Use the words in Group Sort 6b
                               and the 3-Column Writing Sort.*)
• Dictation Sentences   ch   sh   th
• Response Sentences

DAY 4:

Fluency Building
(5-7 minutes)

Include:
*Previously read books
*Books from Level _____
*Phonics Books

Word Study
(8-10 minutes)

✓ **Blending ch, sh, th words** (*Use Group Word Sort Cards 6b.*)
• Picture/Sound Sort
✓ **Word Sorts – ch, sh, th words** (*Use Group Word Sort Cards 6b.*)
   Group   Individual
• Making Words Activity
• Onset/Rime Activity
• Other:

Guided Reading
(8-10 minutes)

✓ Phonics Book: _____ Book: _____
✓ Guided Reading Level: _____

Writing
(5-7 minutes)

• Sound Boxes
• White Boards
• Writing Sort
✓ **Dictation Sentences**
• Response Sentences

Dictation Sentences:
1. *Put the chicks in the shed.*
2. *Can we step on the thick grass?*
3. *I like chips in my lunch!*

©The Reading Teacher's Plan Book

Teaching Week 7: Long A Vowel Pattern with Silent E

Use with activities on pages 157-162.

DAY 1:

Fluency Building (5-7 minutes)

Include:
*Previously read books
*Books from Level ____
*Phonics Books

Word Study (8-10 minutes)

- ✓ Blending Short A, Long A Silent E words (Use Group Word Sort Cards.)
- ✓ Picture/Sound Sort (Use Short A/Long A Picture Sort Cards.)
- Word Sorts –
  - Group   Individual
- Making Words Activity
- Onset/Rime Activity
- Other:

Guided Reading (8-10 minutes)

- ✓ Phonics Book: _____ Book: _____
- ✓ Guided Reading Level: _____

Writing (5-7 minutes)

- Sound Boxes
- ✓ White Boards
- Writing Sort
- Dictation Sentences
- Response Sentences

Spelling Patterns:
Write "ake" words . . . then "ame" words . . . then "ape" words

---

Guided Reading Level _____

DAY 2:

Fluency Building (5-7 minutes)

Include:
*Previously read books
*Books from Level ____
*Phonics Books

Word Study (8-10 minutes)

- ✓ Blending Short A, Long A Silent E words (Use Group Word Sort Cards.)
- Picture/Sound Sort
- Word Sorts –
  - Group   Individual
- Making Words Activity
- ✓ Onset/Rime Activity (Use the Onset/Rime Cubes.)
- Other:

Guided Reading (8-10 minutes)

- ✓ Phonics Book: _____ Book: _____
- ✓ Guided Reading Level: _____

Writing (5-7 minutes)

- Sound Boxes
- White Boards
- ✓ Writing Sort
- Dictation Sentences
- Response Sentences

(Use words from the Group Sort Cards and the 2-Column Writing Sort.)
Short A   Long A with Silent E

©The Reading Teacher's Plan Book

Teaching Week 7: Long A Vowel Pattern with Silent E (cont.)
Use with activities on pages 157-162.

DAY 3:

Fluency Building (5-7 minutes)

Include:
*Previously read books
*Books from Level _____
*Phonics Books

Word Study (8-10 minutes)

- ✓ **Blending** Short A, Long A Silent E words *(Use Group Word Sort Cards.)*
- Picture/Sound Sort
- ✓ **Word Sorts – Short A, Long A words** *(Use Group Word Sort Cards.)*
  Group Individual
- Making Words Activity
- Onset/Rime Activity
- Other:

Guided Reading (8-10 minutes)

- ✓ Phonics Book: _____ Book: _____
- ✓ Guided Reading Level: _____

Writing (5-7 minutes)

- Sound Boxes
- White Boards
- Writing Sort
- ✓ **Dictation Sentences**
- Response Sentences

Dictation Sentences:
1. This is a fun game.
2. I like my name.
3. Can we bake a cake?

Guided Reading Level _____

DAY 4:

Fluency Building (5-7 minutes)

Include:
*Previously read books
*Books from Level _____
*Phonics Books

Word Study (8-10 minutes)

- ✓ **Blending** Short A, Long A Silent E words *(Use Group Word Sort Cards.)*
- Picture/Sound Sort
- ✓ **Word Sorts – Short A, Long A words** *(Use Individual Sort Cards.)*
  Group **Individual**
- Making Words Activity
- Onset/Rime Activity
- Other:

Guided Reading (8-10 minutes)

- ✓ Phonics Book: _____ Book: _____
- ✓ Guided Reading Level: _____

Writing (5-7 minutes)

- Sound Boxes
- White Boards
- Writing Sort
- Dictation Sentences
- ✓ **Response Sentences**

Story Response Questions:
Students respond to a question about today's Guided Reading book.

©The Reading Teacher's Plan Book

Teaching Week 8: Long I Vowel Pattern with Silent E
Use with activities on pages 163-169.

DAY 1:

Fluency Building (5-7 minutes)

Include:
*Previously read books
*Books from Level ____
*Phonics Books

Word Study (8-10 minutes)

- ✓ Blending **Short I, Long I with Silent E words** *(Use Group Sort Cards.)*
- ✓ **Picture/Sound Sort** *(Use Short I/Long I Picture Sort Cards.)*
- • Word Sorts –
    Group ____ Individual ____
    Making Words Activity
- ✓ **Onset/Rime Activity** *(Use the Onset/Rime Cubes.)*
- • Other: ____

Guided Reading (8-10 minutes)

- ✓ Phonics Book: ____ Book: ____
- ✓ Guided Reading Level: ____ Book: ____

Writing (5-7 minutes)

- • Sound Boxes
- ✓ **White Boards**
- • Writing Sort
- • Dictation Sentences
- • Response Sentences

Spelling Patterns:
Write "ike" words... then "ide" words... then "ice" words

Guided Reading Level ____

DAY 2:

Fluency Building (5-7 minutes)

Include:
*Previously read books
*Books from Level ____
*Phonics Books

Word Study (8-10 minutes)

- ✓ Blending **Short I, Long I with Silent E words** *(Use Group Sort Cards.)*
- • Picture/Sound Sort
- ✓ **Word Sorts – Short I, Long I words** *(Use Group Sort Cards.)*
    Group ____ Individual ____
- • Making Words Activity
- • Onset/Rime Activity
- • Other: ____

Guided Reading (8-10 minutes)

- ✓ Phonics Book: ____ Book: ____
- ✓ Guided Reading Level: ____ Book: ____

Writing (5-7 minutes)

- • Sound Boxes
- • White Boards
- ✓ **Writing Sort**
- • Dictation Sentences
- • Response Sentences

(Use words from the Group Sort Cards and the 2-Column Writing Sort.)
Short I ____ Long I with Silent E ____

©The Reading Teacher's Plan Book

Teaching Week 8: Long I Vowel Pattern with Silent E (cont.)
Use with activities on pages 163-169.

DAY 3:

Fluency Building
(5-7 minutes)

Include:
*Previously read books
*Books from Level ____
*Phonics Books

Word Study
(8-10 minutes)

Blending Short I, Long I with Silent E words (Use Group Sort Cards.)
- Picture/Sound Sort
- Word Sorts –
  Group   Individual
- **Making Words Activity**
- Onset/Rime Activity
- Other:

Make these words:
(Use the letter cards.)

man, mane, cane, can, pan, pane, pine, pin, fin, fine, mine

Guided Reading
(8-10 minutes)

✓ Phonics Book: _____
✓ Guided Reading Level: ____ Book: _____

Writing
(5-7 minutes)

- Sound Boxes
✓ **White Boards**
- Writing Sort
- Dictation Sentences
- Response Sentences

Sight Word Writing Fluency:
Use words from today's Guided Reading book. Give students 10 seconds to write each word as many times as they can.

Guided Reading Level ____

DAY 4:

Fluency Building
(5-7 minutes)

Include:
*Previously read books
*Books from Level ____
*Phonics Books

Word Study
(8-10 minutes)

Blending Short I, Long I with Silent E words (Use Group Sort Cards.)
- Picture/Sound Sort
✓ **Word Sorts – Long A, Long I words** (Use Individual Sort Cards.)
  Group   **Individual**
- Making Words Activity
- Onset/Rime Activity
- Other:

Guided Reading
(8-10 minutes)

✓ Phonics Book: _____
✓ Guided Reading Level: ____ Book: _____

Writing
(5-7 minutes)

- Sound Boxes
- White Boards
- Writing Sort
✓ **Dictation Sentences**
- Response Sentences

Dictation Sentences:
1. Can you ride bikes with me?
2. Be nice to the little white mice.
3. Let's go on a hike.

©The Reading Teacher's Plan Book

Teaching Week 9: Long O, U with Silent E
Use with activities on pages 170-179.

DAY 1:

Fluency Building (5-7 minutes)

Include:
- *Previously read books*
- *Books from Level* _____
- *Phonics Books*

Word Study (8-10 minutes)

- ✓ **Blending** Long O, Long U Silent E words (*Use Group Word Sort Cards.*)
- ✓ Picture/Sound Sort (*Use Short O/Long O Picture Sort Cards.*)
- Word Sorts –
  - Group   Individual
  - Making Words Activity
- ✓ **Onset/Rime Activity** (*Use the "o_e" Onset/Rime Cubes.*)
- Other: _____

Guided Reading (8-10 minutes)

- ✓ Phonics Book: _____
- ✓ Guided Reading Level: _____ Book: _____

Writing (5-7 minutes)

- Sound Boxes
- ✓ **White Boards**
- Writing Sort
- Dictation Sentences
- Response Sentences

Spelling Patterns:
Write "ose" words . . . then "oke" words . . . then "u_e" words

---

Guided Reading Level _____

DAY 2:

Fluency Building (5-7 minutes)

Include:
- *Previously read books*
- *Books from Level* _____
- *Phonics Books*

Word Study (8-10 minutes)

- ✓ **Blending** Long O, Long U Silent E words (*Use Group Word Sort Cards.*)
- ✓ Picture/Sound Sort (*Use Short U/Long U Picture Sort Cards.*)
- Word Sorts –
  - Group   Individual
  - Making Words Activity
- ✓ **Onset/Rime Activity** (*Use the "u-e" Onset/Rime Cubes.*)
- Other: _____

Guided Reading (8-10 minutes)

- ✓ Phonics Book: _____
- ✓ Guided Reading Level: _____ Book: _____

Writing (5-7 minutes)

- Sound Boxes
- White Boards
- ✓ **Writing Sort**
- Dictation Sentences
- Response Sentences

(*Use words from the Group Sort Cards and the 2-Column Writing Sort.*)

<u>o-e</u>   <u>u-e</u>

©The Reading Teacher's Plan Book

Guided Reading Level _____

Teaching Week 9: Long O, U with Silent E (cont.)
Use with activities on pages 170-179.

DAY 3:

Fluency Building (5-7 minutes)

Include:
*Previously read books
*Books from Level _____
*Phonics Books

Word Study (8-10 minutes)

✓ Blending Long O, Long U Silent E words *(Use Group Word Sort Cards.)*
• Picture/Sound Sort
• Word Sorts –   Group   Individual
✓ **Making Words Activity**

Make these words:
(Use the letter cards.)
hop, hope, cope, cop, cup,
cub, cube, cute, cut

• Onset/Rime Activity
• Other:

Guided Reading (8-10 minutes)

✓ Phonics Book: _____
✓ Guided Reading Level: _____ Book: _____

Writing (5-7 minutes)

• Sound Boxes
• White Boards
• Writing Sort
✓ **Dictation Sentences**

Dictation Sentences:
1. Did you smell the rose with your nose?
2. The strong mule broke the rope.
3. I hope we can play at my home.

• Response Sentences

DAY 4:

Fluency Building (5-7 minutes)

Include:
*Previously read books
*Books from Level _____
*Phonics Books

Word Study (8-10 minutes)

✓ Blending Long O, Long U Silent E words *(Use Group Word Sort Cards.)*
• Picture/Sound Sort
✓ Word Sorts – Long O, Long U words *(Use Individual Sort Cards.)*
    Group   **Individual**
• Making Words Activity
• Onset/Rime Activity
• Other:

Guided Reading (8-10 minutes)

✓ Phonics Book: _____
✓ Guided Reading Level: _____ Book: _____

Writing (5-7 minutes)

• Sound Boxes
• White Boards
• Writing Sort
• Dictation Sentences
✓ **Response Sentences**

Story Response Questions:
Students respond to a question about today's Guided Reading book.

©The Reading Teacher's Plan Book

Teaching Week 10: Long A Vowel Patterns ai, ay
Use with activities on pages 180-185.

DAY 1:

Fluency Building (5-7 minutes)

Include:
*Previously read books
*Books from Level ___
*Phonics Books

Word Study (8-10 minutes)

✓ **Blending ai and ay words** *(Use Group Word Sort Cards.)*
- Picture/Sound Sort
- Word Sorts –
    Group   Individual
- Making Words Activity
✓ **Onset/Rime Activity** *(Use the Onset/Rime Cubes.)*
- Other:

Guided Reading (8-10 minutes)

✓ Phonics Book: _____ Book: _____
✓ Guided Reading Level: _____ Book: _____

Writing (5-7 minutes)

✓ **Sound Boxes** *(Use the Sound/Spelling Boxes.)*
- White Boards
- Writing Sort
- Dictation Sentences
- Response Sentences

Words for Sound Boxes:
r-ai-n
ch-ai-n
t-r-ai-l
s-ay
p-l-ay

Guided Reading Level _____

DAY 2:

Fluency Building (5-7 minutes)

Include:
*Previously read books
*Books from Level ___
*Phonics Books

Word Study (8-10 minutes)

✓ **Blending ai and ay words** *(Use Group Word Sort Cards.)*
- Picture/Sound Sort
✓ **Word Sorts – Short A, ai, and ay words** *(Use Group Word Sort Cards.)*
    Group   Individual
- Making Words Activity
- Onset/Rime Activity
- Other:

Guided Reading (8-10 minutes)

✓ Phonics Book: _____ Book: _____
✓ Guided Reading Level: _____ Book: _____

Writing (5-7 minutes)

- Sound Boxes
✓ **White Boards**
- Writing Sort
- Dictation Sentences
- Response Sentences

Spelling Patterns:
Write "ain" words . . . then "ail" words . . . then "ay" words

©The Reading Teacher's Plan Book

Guided Reading Level _____

Teaching Week 10: Long A Vowel Patterns ai, ay (cont.)
Use with activities on pages 180-185.

DAY 3:

Fluency Building (5-7 minutes)

Include:
*Previously read books
*Books from Level _____
*Phonics Books

Word Study (8-10 minutes)

✓ **Blending ai and ay words** *(Use Group Word Sort Cards.)*
• Picture/Sound Sort
✓ Word Sorts –   Group   Individual
✓ **Making Words Activity**
• Onset/Rime Activity
• Other:

Make these words:
(Use the letter cards.)
ran, rain, pain, pail, rail, mail, main, man, may, ray, pay, play

Guided Reading (8-10 minutes)

✓ Phonics Book: _____   Book: _____
✓ Guided Reading Level: _____

Writing (5-7 minutes)

• Sound Boxes
• White Boards
• Writing Sort
• Dictation Sentences
✓ **Response Sentences**

Story Response Questions:
Students respond to a question about today's Guided Reading book.

DAY 4:

Fluency Building (5-7 minutes)

Include:
*Previously read books
*Books from Level _____
*Phonics Books

Word Study (8-10 minutes)

✓ **Blending ai and ay words** *(Use Group Word Sort Cards.)*
• Picture/Sound Sort
✓ Word Sorts – **Short A, ai, and ay words** *(Use Individual Sort Cards.)*
   Group   **Individual**
• Making Words Activity
• Onset/Rime Activity
• Other:

Guided Reading (8-10 minutes)

✓ Phonics Book: _____   Book: _____
✓ Guided Reading Level: _____

Writing (5-7 minutes)

• Sound Boxes
• White Boards
• Writing Sort
✓ **Dictation Sentences**
• Response Sentences

Dictation Sentences:
1. The snail likes to play in the rain.
2. Put your tray away.
3. We waited all day for the mail.

©The Reading Teacher's Plan Book

Teaching Week 11: Long E Vowel Patterns e, ee, ea

Use with activities on pages 186-191.

DAY 1:

Fluency Building (5-7 minutes)

Include:
*Previously read books
*Books from Level _____
*Phonics Books

Word Study (8-10 minutes)

✓ **Blending e, ee, and ea words** (*Use Group Word Sort Cards.*)
• Picture/Sound Sort
• Word Sorts –
  Group ___ Individual ___
  Making Words Activity
✓ **Onset/Rime Activity** (*Use the Onset/Rime Cubes.*)
• Other: _____

Guided Reading (8-10 minutes)

✓ Phonics Book: _____ Book: _____
✓ Guided Reading Level: _____

Writing (5-7 minutes)

✓ **Sound Boxes** (*Use the Sound/Spelling Boxes.*)
• White Boards
• Writing Sort
• Dictation Sentences
• Response Sentences

Words for Sound Boxes:

sh-ee-t
j-ee-p
t-r-ea-t
ch-ea-t
c-l-ea-n

DAY 2:

Fluency Building (5-7 minutes)

Include:
*Previously read books
*Books from Level _____
*Phonics Books

Word Study (8-10 minutes)

✓ **Blending e, ee, and ea words** (*Use Group Word Sort Cards.*)
• Picture/Sound Sort
✓ **Word Sorts – e, ee, and ea words** (*Use Group Word Sort Cards.*)
  Group ___ Individual ___
• Making Words Activity
• Onset/Rime Activity
• Other: _____

Guided Reading (8-10 minutes)

✓ Phonics Book: _____ Book: _____
✓ Guided Reading Level: _____

Writing (5-7 minutes)

• Sound Boxes
✓ **White Boards**
• Writing Sort
• Dictation Sentences
• Response Sentences

Spelling Patterns:
Write "ea" words . . . then "ee" words . . . then "e" words

Guided Reading Level _____

©The Reading Teacher's Plan Book

Teaching Week 11: Long E Vowel Patterns e, ee, ea (cont.)

Use with activities on pages 186-191.

Guided Reading Level ____

DAY 3:

Fluency Building (5-7 minutes)

Include:
*Previously read books
*Books from Level ____
*Phonics Books

Word Study (8-10 minutes)

✓ **Blending e, ee, and ea words** *(Use Group Word Sort Cards.)*
- Picture/Sound Sort
- Word Sorts – Group ____ Individual ____
- ✓ **Making Words Activity** *(Make these words: (Use the letter cards.) be, beg, bet, beat, heat, seat, sea, see, bee, beet, sheet, she)*
- Onset/Rime Activity
- Other: ____

Guided Reading (8-10 minutes)

✓ Phonics Book: ____ Book: ____
✓ Guided Reading Level: ____

Writing (5-7 minutes)

- Sound Boxes
- ✓ **White Boards**
- Writing Sort
- Dictation Sentences
- Response Sentences

Sight Word Writing Fluency: Use words from today's Guided Reading book. Give students 10 seconds to write each word as many times as they can.

DAY 4:

Fluency Building (5-7 minutes)

Include:
*Previously read books
*Books from Level ____
*Phonics Books

Word Study (8-10 minutes)

✓ **Blending e, ee, and ea words** *(Use Group Word Sort Cards.)*
- Picture/Sound Sort
- ✓ **Word Sorts – e, ee, and ea words** *(Use Individual Sort Cards.)* Group ____ **Individual** ____
- Making Words Activity
- Onset/Rime Activity
- Other: ____

Guided Reading (8-10 minutes)

✓ Phonics Book: ____ Book: ____
✓ Guided Reading Level: ____

Writing (5-7 minutes)

- Sound Boxes
- White Boards
- ✓ **Writing Sort** *(Use words from the Individual Sort Cards and the 2-Column Writing Sort.)*
  short e   ee
- Dictation Sentences
- Response Sentences

©The Reading Teacher's Plan Book

Teaching Week 12: Long O Vowel Patterns *o, oa, ow*

Use with activities on pages 192-196.

DAY 1:

Fluency Building
(5-7 minutes)

Include:
*Previously read books
*Books from Level _____
*Phonics Books

Word Study
(8-10 minutes)

✓ **Blending o, oa, and ow words** *(Use Group Word Sort Cards.)*
  • Picture/Sound Sort
✓ **Word Sorts – o, oa, and ow words** *(Use Group Word Sort Cards.)*
  Group   Individual
  • Making Words Activity
  • Onset/Rime Activity
  • Other: _____

Guided Reading
(8-10 minutes)

✓ Phonics Book: _____ Book: _____
✓ Guided Reading Level: _____

Writing
(5-7 minutes)

✓ **Sound Boxes** *(Use the Sound/Spelling Boxes.)*
  • White Boards
  • Writing Sort
  • Dictation Sentences
  • Response Sentences

Words for Sound Boxes:

g-oa-t
g-r-ow
s-l-ow
c-oa-ch
s-n-ow

Guided Reading Level _____

DAY 2:

Fluency Building
(5-7 minutes)

Include:
*Previously read books
*Books from Level _____
*Phonics Books

Word Study
(8-10 minutes)

✓ **Blending o, oa, and ow words** *(Use Group Word Sort Cards.)*
  • Picture/Sound Sort
  • Word Sorts –
    Group   Individual
  • **Making Words Activity**   *Make these words:*
  • Onset/Rime Activity   *(Use the letter cards.)*
  • Other: *so, go, got, goat, boat, bow,*
                                        blow, low, tow

Guided Reading
(8-10 minutes)

✓ Phonics Book: _____
✓ Guided Reading Level: _____ Book: _____

Writing
(5-7 minutes)

  • Sound Boxes
  • White Boards
  • Writing Sort
  • Dictation Sentences
✓ **Response Sentences**

Story Response Questions:
Students respond to a question about today's Guided Reading book.

©The Reading Teacher's Plan Book

Teaching Week 12: Long O Vowel Patterns o, oa, ow (cont.)
Use with activities on pages 192-196.

DAY 3:

Fluency Building (5-7 minutes)

Include:
*Previously read books
*Books from Level _____
*Phonics Books

Word Study (8-10 minutes)

✓ **Blending o, oa, and ow words** *(Use Group Word Sort Cards.)*
• Picture/Sound Sort
• Word Sorts –
   Group   Individual
• Making Words Activity
✓ **Onset/Rime Activity** *(Use the Onset/Rime Cards and Mats.)*
• Other:

Guided Reading (8-10 minutes)

✓ Phonics Book: _____ Book: _____
✓ Guided Reading Level: _____ Book: _____

Writing (5-7 minutes)

• Sound Boxes
• **White Boards**
• Writing Sort
• Dictation Sentences
• Response Sentences

Spelling Patterns:
Write "o" words . . . then "oa" words . . . then "ow" words

Guided Reading Level _____

DAY 4:

Fluency Building (5-7 minutes)

Include:
*Previously read books
*Books from Level _____
*Phonics Books

Word Study (8-10 minutes)

✓ **Blending o, oa, and ow words** *(Use Group Word Sort Cards.)*
• Picture/Sound Sort
✓ **Word Sorts – o, oa, and ow words** *(Use Individual Sort Cards.)*
   Group   **Individual**
• Making Words Activity
• Onset/Rime Activity
• Other:

Guided Reading (8-10 minutes)

✓ Phonics Book: _____
✓ Guided Reading Level: _____ Book: _____

Writing (5-7 minutes)

• Sound Boxes
• White Boards
• Writing Sort
✓ **Dictation Sentences**
• Response Sentences

Dictation Sentences:
1. The boat will float across the pond.
2. We drove home on a bumpy road.
3. Do not throw a snowball at school!

©The Reading Teacher's Plan Book

Teaching Week 13: Long I Vowel Patterns ie, igh, y
Use with activities on pages 197-201.

DAY 1:

Fluency Building
(5-7 minutes)

Include:
*Previously read books
*Books from Level _____
*Phonics Books

Word Study
(8-10 minutes)

✓ **Blending ie, igh, y words** *(Use Group Word Sort Cards.)*
- Picture/Sound Sort
✓ **Word Sorts – ie, igh, y words** *(Use Group Word Sort Cards.)*
  Group   Individual
- Making Words Activity
- Onset/Rime Activity
- Other:

Guided Reading
(8-10 minutes)

✓ **Phonics Book:** _____ **Book:** _____
✓ **Guided Reading Level:** _____

Writing
(5-7 minutes)

✓ **Sound Boxes** *(Use the Sound/Spelling Boxes.)*
- White Boards
- Writing Sort
- Dictation Sentences
- Response Sentences

Words for Sound Boxes:

s-p-y
t-ie
p-ie
f-igh-t
l-igh-t

Guided Reading Level _____

DAY 2:

Fluency Building
(5-7 minutes)

Include:
*Previously read books
*Books from Level _____
*Phonics Books

Word Study
(8-10 minutes)

✓ **Blending ie, igh, y words** *(Use Group Word Sort Cards.)*
- Picture/Sound Sort
- Word Sorts –
  Group   Individual
- Making Words Activity
✓ **Onset/Rime Activity** *(Use the Onset/Rime Cards and Mats.)*
- Other:

Guided Reading
(8-10 minutes)

✓ **Phonics Book:** _____ **Book:** _____
✓ **Guided Reading Level:** _____

Writing
(5-7 minutes)

- Sound Boxes
✓ **White Boards**
- Writing Sort
- Dictation Sentences
- Response Sentences

Spelling Patterns:
Write "y" words . . . then "ie" words . . . then "igh" words

©The Reading Teacher's Plan Book

Teaching Week 13: Long I Vowel Patterns ie, igh, y (cont.)
Use with activities on pages 197-201.

Guided Reading Level _____

DAY 3:

Fluency Building (5-7 minutes)

Include:
*Previously read books
*Books from Level _____
*Phonics Books

Word Study (8-10 minutes)

- ✓ Blending ie, igh, y words *(Use Group Word Sort Cards.)*
- • Picture/Sound Sort
- • Word Sorts – Group ____ Individual ____
- ✓ Making Words Activity   *Make these words: (Use the letter cards.) tie, pie, pies, ties, lies, lie, light, sight, might, my, spy, sly*
- • Onset/Rime Activity
- • Other: _____

Guided Reading (8-10 minutes)

- ✓ Phonics Book: _____ Book: _____
- ✓ Guided Reading Level: _____

Writing (5-7 minutes)

- • Sound Boxes
- • White Boards
- • Writing Sort
- • Dictation Sentences
- ✓ Response Sentences   *Story Response Questions: Students respond to a question about today's Guided Reading book.*

DAY 4:

Fluency Building (5-7 minutes)

Include:
*Previously read books
*Books from Level _____
*Phonics Books

Word Study (8-10 minutes)

- ✓ Blending ie, igh, y words *(Use Group Word Sort Cards.)*
- • Picture/Sound Sort
- ✓ Word Sorts – ie, igh, y words *(Use Individual Sort Cards.)* Group ____ Individual ____
- • Making Words Activity
- • Onset/Rime Activity
- • Other: _____

Guided Reading (8-10 minutes)

- ✓ Phonics Book: _____ Book: _____
- ✓ Guided Reading Level: _____

Writing (5-7 minutes)

- • Sound Boxes
- • White Boards
- ✓ Writing Sort   *(Use words from the Individual Sort Cards and the 3-Column Writing Sort.)* short i ____ igh ____ y
- • Dictation Sentences
- • Response Sentences

©The Reading Teacher's Plan Book

Teaching Week 14: "Spooky Sound" Vowel Patterns oo, ew, ue, u_e
Use with activities on pages 202-206.

DAY 1:

Fluency Building (5-7 minutes)

Include:
*Previously read books
*Books from Level ____
*Phonics Books

Word Study (8-10 minutes)

- ✓ **Blending oo, ew, ue, u-e words** *(Use Group Word Sort Cards.)*
- ✓ **Word Sorts – oo, ew, ue, u-e words** *(Use Group Word Sort Cards.)*
  Group   Individual
- Picture/Sound Sort
- Making Words Activity
- Onset/Rime Activity
- Other:

Guided Reading (8-10 minutes)

- ✓ Phonics Book: _____ Book: _____
- ✓ Guided Reading Level: _____

Writing (5-7 minutes)

- ✓ **Sound Boxes** *(Use the Sound/Spelling Boxes.)*
- White Boards
- Writing Sort
- Dictation Sentences
- Response Sentences

Words for Sound Boxes:

s-p-oo-k
t-oo-th
g-r-ew
ch-ew
b-l-ue

Guided Reading Level ____

DAY 2:

Fluency Building (5-7 minutes)

Include:
*Previously read books
*Books from Level ____
*Phonics Books

Word Study (8-10 minutes)

- ✓ **Blending oo, ew, ue, u-e words** *(Use Group Word Sort Cards.)*
- Picture/Sound Sort
- Word Sorts –
  Group   Individual
- Making Words Activity
- ✓ **Onset/Rime Activity** *(Use the Onset/Rime Cards and Mats.)*
- Other:

Guided Reading (8-10 minutes)

- ✓ Phonics Book: _____ Book: _____
- ✓ Guided Reading Level: _____

Writing (5-7 minutes)

- Sound Boxes
- ✓ **White Boards**
- Writing Sort
- Dictation Sentences
- Response Sentences

Spelling Patterns:
Write "oo" words . . . then "ew" words . . . then "ue" words

©The Reading Teacher's Plan Book

Teaching Week 14: "Spooky Sound" Vowel Patterns oo, ew, ue, u_e (cont.)   *Guided Reading Level* _____
Use with activities on pages 202-206.

DAY 3:

Fluency Building (5-7 minutes)

Include:
*Previously read books
*Books from Level _____
*Phonics Books

Word Study (8-10 minutes)

✓ <mark>Blending oo, ew, ue, u-e words</mark> *(Use Group Word Sort Cards.)*
• Picture/Sound Sort
• Word Sorts – Group   Individual
• <mark>Making Words Activity</mark>

Make these words:
(Use the letter cards.)
rule, tool, stool, boot, boost, stew, brew, blew, blue

• Onset/Rime Activity
• Other: _____

Guided Reading (8-10 minutes)

✓ Phonics Book: _____ Book: _____
✓ Guided Reading Level: _____ Book: _____

Writing (5-7 minutes)

• Sound Boxes
• White Boards
✓ <mark>Writing Sort</mark>
• Dictation Sentences
• Response Sentences

(Use words from the Group Sort Cards and the 2-Column Writing Sort.)

<u>oo</u>   <u>ew</u>

DAY 4:

Fluency Building (5-7 minutes)

Include:
*Previously read books
*Books from Level _____
*Phonics Books

Word Study (8-10 minutes)

✓ <mark>Blending oo, ew, ue, u-e words</mark> *(Use Group Word Sort Cards.)*
• Picture/Sound Sort
✓ <mark>Word Sorts – oo, ew, ue words</mark> *(Use Individual Sort Cards.)*
   Group   **Individual**
• Making Words Activity
• Onset/Rime Activity
• Other: _____

Guided Reading (8-10 minutes)

✓ Phonics Book: _____ Book: _____
✓ Guided Reading Level: _____ Book: _____

Writing (5-7 minutes)

• Sound Boxes
• White Boards
• Writing Sort
✓ **Dictation Sentences**
• Response Sentences

<mark>*Dictation Sentences:*</mark>
1. Let's make a big splash in the pool.
2. Don't forget to chew your food.
3. We blew on our hot stew.

©The Reading Teacher's Plan Book

Teaching Week 15: "Hurt Sound" Vowel Patterns ou, ow
Use with activities on pages 207-211.

Guided Reading Level ____

DAY 1:

Fluency Building (5-7 minutes)

Include:
- *Previously read books*
- *Books from Level ____*
- *Phonics Books*

Word Study (8-10 minutes)

- ✓ **Blending ou, ow words** (*Use Group Word Sort Cards.*)
  - Picture/Sound Sort
- ✓ **Word Sorts – ou, ow words** (*Use Group Word Sort Cards.*)
  - Group   Individual
  - Making Words Activity
  - Onset/Rime Activity
  - Other:

Guided Reading (8-10 minutes)

- ✓ Phonics Book: _____ Book: _____
- ✓ Guided Reading Level: _____

Writing (5-7 minutes)

- ✓ **Sound Boxes** (*Use the Sound/Spelling Boxes.*)
  - White Boards
  - Writing Sort
  - Dictation Sentences
  - Response Sentences

Words for Sound Boxes:

sh-ou-t
c-l-ou-d
d-ow-n
b-r-ow-n
c-ou-ch

DAY 2:

Fluency Building (5-7 minutes)

Include:
- *Previously read books*
- *Books from Level ____*
- *Phonics Books*

Word Study (8-10 minutes)

- ✓ **Blending ou, ow words** (*Use Group Word Sort Cards.*)
  - Picture/Sound Sort
- Word Sorts –
  - Group   Individual
  - **Making Words Activity**
  - Onset/Rime Activity
  - Other:

Make these words:
(Use the letter cards.)
out, shout, show, how, tow, town, down, now

Guided Reading (8-10 minutes)

- ✓ Phonics Book: _____
- ✓ Guided Reading Level: _____ Book: _____

Writing (5-7 minutes)

- Sound Boxes
- **White Boards**
- ✓ Writing Sort
- Dictation Sentences
- Response Sentences

<u>*Spelling Patterns:*</u>
Write "ou" words . . . then "ow" words

©The Reading Teacher's Plan Book

Teaching Week 15: "Hurt Sound" Vowel Patterns ou, ow (cont.)
Use with activities on pages 207-211.

Guided Reading Level ____

DAY 3:

Fluency Building (5-7 minutes)

Include:
*Previously read books
*Books from Level ____
*Phonics Books

Word Study (8-10 minutes)

✓ **Blending ou, ow words** *(Use Group Word Sort Cards.)*
- Picture/Sound Sort
- Word Sorts –
  - Group   Individual
- Making Words Activity
✓ **Onset/Rime Activity** *(Use the Onset/Rime Cards and Mats.)*
- Other:

Guided Reading (8-10 minutes)

✓ Phonics Book: ____
✓ Guided Reading Level: ____ Book: ____

Writing (5-7 minutes)

- Sound Boxes
- White Boards
- Writing Sort
- Dictation Sentences
✓ Response Sentences

Story Response Questions:
Students respond to a question about today's Guided Reading book.

DAY 4:

Fluency Building (5-7 minutes)

Include:
*Previously read books
*Books from Level ____
*Phonics Books

Word Study (8-10 minutes)

✓ **Blending ou, ow words** *(Use Group Word Sort Cards.)*
- Picture/Sound Sort
✓ **Word Sorts – ou, ow words** *(Use Individual Sort Cards.)*
  - Group   **Individual**
- Making Words Activity
- Onset/Rime Activity
- Other:

Guided Reading (8-10 minutes)

✓ Phonics Book: ____
✓ Guided Reading Level: ____ Book: ____

Writing (5-7 minutes)

- Sound Boxes
- White Boards
- Writing Sort
✓ **Dictation Sentences**
- Response Sentences

Dictation Sentences:
1. The owl flew to the top of the tower.
2. How high can you count?
3. Plow the ground south of town.

©The Reading Teacher's Plan Book

Teaching Week 16: "Bossy R Sound" Vowel Patterns ar, are, er, ir, ur, or _Guided Reading Level _____
Use with activities on pages 212-216.

DAY 1:

Fluency Building
(5-7 minutes)

Include:
*Previously read books
*Books from Level _____
*Phonics Books

Word Study
(8-10 minutes)

✓ <u>Blending Bossy R words</u> *(Use Group Word Sort Cards.)*
- Picture/Sound Sort
✓ <u>Word Sorts – Bossy R words</u> *(Use Group Word Sort Cards.)*
  Group   Individual
- Making Words Activity
- Onset/Rime Activity
- Other:

Guided Reading
(8-10 minutes)

✓ Phonics Book: _____ Book: _____
✓ Guided Reading Level: _____

Writing
(5-7 minutes)

✓ <u>Sound Boxes</u> *(Use the Sound/Spelling Boxes.)*
- White Boards
- Writing Sort
- Dictation Sentences
- Response Sentences

<u>Words for Sound Boxes:</u>
c-ar-d
p-ar-k
s-c-are
s-t-are
f-or-t

DAY 2:

Fluency Building
(5-7 minutes)

Include:
*Previously read books
*Books from Level _____
*Phonics Books

Word Study
(8-10 minutes)

✓ <u>Blending Bossy R words</u> *(Use Group Word Sort Cards.)*
- Picture/Sound Sort
- Word Sorts –
  Group   Individual
✓ **Making Words Activity**
- Onset/Rime Activity
- Other:

<u>Make these words:</u>
(Use the letter cards.)
tar, car, cart, care, mare, more, tore, torn, turn

Guided Reading
(8-10 minutes)

✓ Phonics Book: _____ Book: _____
✓ Guided Reading Level: _____

Writing
(5-7 minutes)

- Sound Boxes
✓ **White Boards**
- Writing Sort
- Dictation Sentences
- Response Sentences

<u>Spelling Patterns:</u>
Write "ar" words . . . then "are" words . . . then "ir" words . . . then "or" words

©The Reading Teacher's Plan Book

Teaching Week 16: "Bossy R Sound" Vowel Patterns ar, are, er, ir, ur, or (cont.) __Guided Reading Level_____
Use with activities on pages 212-216.

DAY 3:

Fluency Building (5-7 minutes)

Include:
*Previously read books
*Books from Level _____
*Phonics Books

Word Study (8-10 minutes)

✓ **Blending Bossy R words** *(Use Group Word Sort Cards.)*
• Picture/Sound Sort
• Word Sorts –   Group   Individual
• Making Words Activity
✓ **Onset/Rime Activity** *(Use the Onset/Rime Cards and Mats.)*
• Other:

Guided Reading (8-10 minutes)

✓ Phonics Book: _____ Book: _____
✓ Guided Reading Level: _____

Writing (5-7 minutes)

• Sound Boxes
• White Boards
✓ **Writing Sort**   *(Use words from the Group Sort Cards and the 3-Column Writing Sort.)*
   __ar__   __are__   __or__
• Dictation Sentences
• Response Sentences

DAY 4:

Fluency Building (5-7 minutes)

Include:
*Previously read books
*Books from Level _____
*Phonics Books

Word Study (8-10 minutes)

✓ **Blending Bossy R words** *(Use Group Word Sort Cards.)*
• Picture/Sound Sort
✓ **Word Sorts – Bossy R words** *(Use Individual Sort Cards.)*
       Group   **Individual**
• Making Words Activity
• Onset/Rime Activity
• Other:

Guided Reading (8-10 minutes)

✓ Phonics Book: _____ Book: _____
✓ Guided Reading Level: _____

Writing (5-7 minutes)

• Sound Boxes
• White Boards
• Writing Sort
• Dictation Sentences
✓ **Response Sentences**

Story Response Questions:
Students respond to a question about today's Guided Reading book.

©The Reading Teacher's Plan Book

Teaching Week 17: "Whining Sound" Vowel Patterns aw, au, all
Use with activities on pages 217-221.

Guided Reading Level _____

DAY 1:

Fluency Building (5-7 minutes)

Include:
*Previously read books
*Books from Level _____
*Phonics Books

Word Study (8-10 minutes)

- ✓ <u>**Blending aw, au, all words**</u> *(Use Group Word Sort Cards.)*
  - Picture/Sound Sort
- ✓ <u>**Word Sorts** – aw, au, all words</u> *(Use Group Word Sort Cards.)*
  - **Group**   Individual
  - Making Words Activity
  - Onset/Rime Activity
  - Other:

Guided Reading (8-10 minutes)

- ✓ Phonics Book: _____ Book: _____
- ✓ Guided Reading Level: _____

Writing (5-7 minutes)

- Sound Boxes
- ✓ **White Boards**
- Writing Sort
- Dictation Sentences
- Response Sentences

DAY 2:

Fluency Building (5-7 minutes)

Include:
*Previously read books
*Books from Level _____
*Phonics Books

Word Study (8-10 minutes)

- ✓ <u>**Blending aw, au, all words**</u> *(Use Group Word Sort Cards.)*
  - Picture/Sound Sort
  - Word Sorts –
    - Group   Individual
- ✓ **Making Words Activity**
  - Onset/Rime Activity
  - Other:

Make these words:
(Use the letter cards.)
tan, can, car, cart, call,
tall, law, claw, raw, lawn

Guided Reading (8-10 minutes)

- ✓ Phonics Book: _____ Book: _____
- ✓ Guided Reading Level: _____

Writing (5-7 minutes)

- Sound Boxes
- White Boards
- Writing Sort
- Dictation Sentences
- ✓ **Response Sentences**

Spelling Patterns:
Write "aw" words . . . then "au" words . . . then "all" words

Story Response Questions:
Students respond to a question about today's Guided Reading book.

©The Reading Teacher's Plan Book

Teaching Week 17: "Whining Sound" Vowel Patterns aw, au, all (cont.)   *Guided Reading Level* _____
Use with activities on pages 217-221.

DAY 3:

**Fluency Building
(5-7 minutes)**

Include:
*Previously read books
*Books from Level _____
*Phonics Books

**Word Study
(8-10 minutes)**

✓ **Blending aw, au, all words** *(Use Group Word Sort Cards.)*
• Picture/Sound Sort
• Word Sorts –
   Group   Individual
• Making Words Activity
✓ **Onset/Rime Activity** *(Use the Onset/Rime Cards and Mats.)*
• Other:

**Guided Reading
(8-10 minutes)**

✓ Phonics Book: _____
✓ Guided Reading Level: _____ Book: _____

**Writing
(5-7 minutes)**

• Sound Boxes
• White Boards
✓ **Writing Sort**   *(Use words from the Group Sort Cards and the 3-Column Writing Sort.)*
   <u>aw</u>   <u>all</u>   <u>ar</u>
• Dictation Sentences
• Response Sentences

DAY 4:

**Fluency Building
(5-7 minutes)**

Include:
*Previously read books
*Books from Level _____
*Phonics Books

**Word Study
(8-10 minutes)**

✓ **Blending aw, au, all words** *(Use Group Word Sort Cards.)*
• Picture/Sound Sort
✓ **Word Sorts – aw, all, ar words** *(Use Individual Sort Cards.)*
   Group   **Individual**
• Making Words Activity
• Onset/Rime Activity
• Other:

**Guided Reading
(8-10 minutes)**

✓ Phonics Book: _____
✓ Guided Reading Level: _____ Book: _____

**Writing
(5-7 minutes)**

• Sound Boxes
• White Boards
• Writing Sort
✓ **Dictation Sentences**
• Response Sentences

<u>*Dictation Sentences:*</u>
1. Do not draw on the wall.
2. Can I drink my milk with a straw?
3. The barn is too small for the cows.

©The Reading Teacher's Plan Book

Teaching Week 18: "Bouncy Sound" oi, oy; "Boxing Sound" oo

Use with activities on pages 222-226.

Guided Reading Level _____

DAY 1:

Fluency Building (5-7 minutes)

Include:
*Previously read books
*Books from Level _____
*Phonics Books

Word Study (8-10 minutes)

✓ Blending oi, oy, oo words *(Use Group Word Sort Cards.)*
• Picture/Sound Sort
✓ Word Sorts – oi, oy, oo words *(Use Group Word Sort Cards.)*
   Group   Individual
• Making Words Activity
• Onset/Rime Activity
• Other:

Guided Reading (8-10 minutes)

✓ Phonics Book: _____
✓ Guided Reading Level: _____ Book: _____

Writing (5-7 minutes)

✓ Sound Boxes *(Use the Sound/Spelling Boxes.)*
• White Boards
• Writing Sort
• Dictation Sentences
• Response Sentences

Words for Sound Boxes:

b-oy
j-oy
c-oi-n
ch-oi-ce
b-oo-k

DAY 2:

Fluency Building (5-7 minutes)

Include:
*Previously read books
*Books from Level _____
*Phonics Books

Word Study (8-10 minutes)

✓ Blending oi, oy, oo words *(Use Group Word Sort Cards.)*
• Picture/Sound Sort
• Word Sorts –
   Group   Individual
✓ Making Words Activity
• Onset/Rime Activity
• Other:

Make these words:
(Use the letter cards.)
boy, boil, toil, toy, joy, join, coin, coil, coy

Guided Reading (8-10 minutes)

✓ Phonics Book: _____
✓ Guided Reading Level: _____ Book: _____

Writing (5-7 minutes)

• Sound Boxes
✓ White Boards
• Writing Sort
• Dictation Sentences
• Response Sentences

Sight Word Writing Fluency:
Use words from today's Guided Reading book. Give students 10 seconds to write each word as many times as they can.

©The Reading Teacher's Plan Book

Teaching Week 18: "Bouncy Sound" oi, oy; "Boxing Sound" oo (cont.)
Use with activities on pages 222-226.

Guided Reading Level _____

DAY 3:

Fluency Building (5-7 minutes)

Include:
*Previously read books
*Books from Level _____
*Phonics Books

Word Study (8-10 minutes)

✓ **Blending oi, oy, oo words** *(Use Group Word Sort Cards.)*
• Picture/Sound Sort
✓ Word Sorts –
   Group ____ Individual ____
• Making Words Activity
✓ **Onset/Rime Activity** *(Use the Onset/Rime Cards and Mats.)*
• Other:

Guided Reading (8-10 minutes)

✓ Phonics Book: _____ Book: _____
✓ Guided Reading Level: _____

Writing (5-7 minutes)

• Sound Boxes
✓ **White Boards**
• Writing Sort
• Dictation Sentences
• Response Sentences

Spelling Patterns:
Write "oy" words . . . then "oil" words . . . then "oo" words

DAY 4:

Fluency Building (5-7 minutes)

Include:
*Previously read books
*Books from Level _____
*Phonics Books

Word Study (8-10 minutes)

✓ **Blending oi, oy, oo words** *(Use Group Word Sort Cards.)*
• Picture/Sound Sort
✓ **Word Sorts – oi, oy, oo words** *(Use Individual Sort Cards.)*
   Group ____ **Individual** ____
• Making Words Activity
• Onset/Rime Activity
• Other:

Guided Reading (8-10 minutes)

✓ Phonics Book: _____ Book: _____
✓ Guided Reading Level: _____

Writing (5-7 minutes)

• Sound Boxes
• White Boards
• Writing Sort
• Dictation Sentences
✓ **Response Sentences**

Story Response Questions:
Students respond to a question about today's Guided Reading book.

©The Reading Teacher's Plan Book

Teaching Week 19: "Endings" –ed, -ing, -er

Use with activities on pages 227-232.

DAY 1:

Fluency Building (5-7 minutes)

Include:
*Previously read books
*Books from Level ____
*Phonics Books

Word Study (8-10 minutes)

✓ **Blending Sounds of "–ed"** *(Use Group Word Sort Cards.)*
- Picture/Sound Sort
✓ **Word Sorts – Sounds of "–ed"** *(Use Group Word Sort Cards 19a.)*
  Group   Individual
- Making Words Activity
- Onset/Rime Activity
- Other: _____

Guided Reading (8-10 minutes)

✓ Phonics Book: _____ Book: _____
✓ Guided Reading Level: _____

Writing (5-7 minutes)

- Sound Boxes
- White Boards
- Writing Sort
- Dictation Sentences
✓ **Response Sentences** *Use a Comprehension Graphic Organizer.*

Guided Reading Level _____

DAY 2:

Fluency Building (5-7 minutes)

Include:
*Previously read books
*Books from Level ____
*Phonics Books

Word Study (8-10 minutes)

✓ **Blending Sounds of "–ed"** *(Use Group Word Sort Cards 19a.)*
- Picture/Sound Sort
- Word Sorts –
  Group   Individual   *(Use words from the Group Sort Cards and the 3-Column Writing Sort.)*
- Making Words Activity   *Sounds of "-ed" –*
- Onset/Rime Activity   /t/   /d/   /ed/
✓ **Other: Writing Sort**

Guided Reading (8-10 minutes)

✓ Phonics Book: _____ Book: _____
✓ Guided Reading Level: _____

Writing (5-7 minutes)

- Sound Boxes
- White Boards
- Writing Sort
- Dictation Sentences
✓ **Response Sentences** *Use a Comprehension Graphic Organizer.*

©The Reading Teacher's Plan Book

Guided Reading Level _____

DAY 4:

Fluency Building (5-7 minutes)

Include:
*Previously read books
*Books from Level _____
*Phonics Books

Word Study (8-10 minutes)

✓ **Blending Endings –ed, -ing, -er** *(Use Blending Cards 19b.)*
• Picture/Sound Sort
✓ **Word Sorts – Endings –ed, -ing, -er** *(Use Individual Sort Cards.)*
    Group   **Individual**
• Making Words Activity
• Onset/Rime Activity
• Other: _____

Guided Reading (8-10 minutes)

✓ Phonics Book: _____ Book: _____
✓ Guided Reading Level: _____ Book: _____

Writing (5-7 minutes)

• Sound Boxes
• White Boards
• Writing Sort
• Dictation Sentences
✓ **Response Sentences** *Use a Comprehension Graphic Organizer.*

Teaching Week 19: "Endings"–-ed, -ing, -er (cont.)
Use with activities on pages 227-232.

DAY 3:

Fluency Building (5-7 minutes)

Include:
*Previously read books
*Books from Level _____
*Phonics Books

Word Study (8-10 minutes)

✓ **Blending Endings –ed, -ing, -er** *(Use Blending Cards 19b.)*
• Picture/Sound Sort
• Word Sorts – Group   Individual
• Making Words Activity
• Onset/Rime Activity
✓ Other: **Word Hunt** *(Use the Word Windows and Writing Mats.)*

Guided Reading (8-10 minutes)

✓ Phonics Book: _____ Book: _____
✓ Guided Reading Level: _____ Book: _____

Writing (5-7 minutes)

• Sound Boxes
• White Boards
• Writing Sort
• Dictation Sentences
✓ **Response Sentences** *Use a Comprehension Graphic Organizer.*

©The Reading Teacher's Plan Book

Teaching Week 20: Compound Words
Use with activities on pages 233-238.

DAY 1:

Fluency Building (5-7 minutes)

Include:
- *Previously read books*
- *Books from Level* _____
- *Phonics Books*

Word Study (8-10 minutes)

✓ **Blending Compound Words** *(Use Blending Cards.)*
- Picture/Sound Sort
- Word Sorts –
  - Group ____ Individual ____
✓ **Making Words Activity – Compound Word Match-Up** *(Use the Compound Word Match-Up Cards. Follow same directions as for Syllable Match-Up.)*
- Onset/Rime Activity
- Other: _____

Guided Reading (8-10 minutes)

Guided Reading Level: _____
Book: _____

Writing (5-7 minutes)

- Sound Boxes
- White Boards
- Writing Sort
- Dictation Sentences
✓ **Response Sentences** *Use a Comprehension Graphic Organizer.*

Guided Reading Level _____

DAY 2:

Fluency Building (5-7 minutes)

Include:
- *Previously read books*
- *Books from Level* _____
- *Phonics Books*

Word Study (8-10 minutes)

✓ **Blending Compound Words** *(Use Blending Cards.)*
- Picture/Sound Sort
- Word Sorts –
  - Group ____ Individual ____
- Making Words Activity
- Onset/Rime Activity
✓ **Other: Writing Sort** *(Use words from the Blending Cards and the 4-Column Writing Sort.)* *"down" "up" "over" "where"*

Guided Reading (8-10 minutes)

Guided Reading Level: _____
Book: _____

Writing (5-7 minutes)

- Sound Boxes
- White Boards
- Writing Sort
- Dictation Sentences
✓ **Response Sentences** *Use a Comprehension Graphic Organizer.*

©The Reading Teacher's Plan Book

Teaching Week 20: Compound Words (cont.)
Use with activities on pages 233-238.

DAY 3:

Fluency Building (5-7 minutes)

Include:
* *Previously read books*
* *Books from Level* _____
* *Phonics Books*

Word Study (8-10 minutes)

✓ **Blending Compound Words** *(Use Blending Cards.)*
* Picture/Sound Sort
* Word Sorts –
  Group   Individual
* Making Words Activity
* Onset/Rime Activity
✓ **Other: Word Hunt** *(Use Word Hunt Cube, Mats, and bingo chips.)*

Guided Reading (8-10 minutes)

Guided Reading Level: _____
Book: _____

Writing (5-7 minutes)

* Sound Boxes
* White Boards
* Writing Sort
* Dictation Sentences
✓ **Response Sentences** *Use a Comprehension Graphic Organizer.*

Guided Reading Level _____

DAY 4:

Fluency Building (5-7 minutes)

Include:
* *Previously read books*
* *Books from Level* _____
* *Phonics Books*

Word Study (8-10 minutes)

✓ **Blending Compound Words** *(Use Blending Cards.)*
* Picture/Sound Sort
* Word Sorts –
  Group   Individual
* Making Words Activity
* Onset/Rime Activity
✓ **Other: Dictation Sentences**

<u>*Dictation Sentences:*</u>
1. *The lighthouse shines brightly at sunset.*
2. *Can I eat a hotdog at the football game?*
3. *We will do our homework in the clubhouse.*

Guided Reading (8-10 minutes)

Guided Reading Level: _____
Book: _____

Writing (5-7 minutes)

* Sound Boxes
* White Boards
* Writing Sort
* Dictation Sentences
✓ **Response Sentences** *Use a Comprehension Graphic Organizer.*

©The Reading Teacher's Plan Book

REVIEW WEEKS MATERIALS LIST

Review Week 1: Short A, I, O (Use the Short Vowels Picture Chart, p. 391.)
    Short A, I, O Lesson Plan
    Short A, I, O Group Sort Cards, pgs. 239-240
    Short A, I, O Making Words Cards, p. 241
    Short A, I, O Onset/Rime Cards and Mats, p. 242
    Short A, I, O Individual Sort Cards, p. 243
    Sound/Spelling Boxes, p. 379
    3-Column Writing Sort, p. 381

Review Week 2: Short E, U (Use the Short Vowels Picture Chart, p. 391.)
    Short E, U Lesson Plan
    Short E, U Group Sort Cards, pgs. 244-245
    Short E, U Making Words Cards, p. 246
    Short E, U Onset/Rime Cards and Mats, p. 247
    Short E, U Individual Sort Cards, p. 248
    Sound/Spelling Boxes, p. 379
    2-Column Writing Sort, p. 380

Review Week 3: Short Vowels (Use the Short Vowels Picture Chart, p. 391.)
    Short Vowels Review Lesson Plan (Week 3)
    Short Vowels Blending Cards, p. 249
    Short Vowels Review Onset/Rime Cards and Mats, p. 250
    Short Vowels Review Making Words Cards, p. 251
    Short Vowels Review Individual Sort Cards, p. 252
    Short Vowels Review Echo Game Cards, pgs. 253-255
    Short Vowels Review Slinky Words Picture Cards, p. 256
    3-Column Writing Sort, p. 381

Review Week 4: Short Vowels (Use the Short Vowels Picture Chart, p. 391.)
    Short Vowels Review Lesson Plan (Week 4)
    Short Vowels Review Blending Cards, p. 257
    Short Vowels Review Onset/Rime Cards and Mats, p. 258
    Short Vowels Review Making Words Cards, p. 259
    Short Vowels Review Individual Sort Cards, p. 260
    Short Vowels Review Echo Game Cards, pgs. 261-263
    Short Vowels Review Slinky Words Picture Cards, p. 264
    3-Column Writing Sort, p. 381

©The Reading Teacher's Plan Book

Review Week 5: Short Vowels (Use the Short Vowels Picture Chart, p. 391.)
    Short Vowels Review Lesson Plan (Week 5)
    Short Vowels Review Blending Cards, p. 265
    Short Vowels Review Onset/Rime Cards and Mats, p. 266
    Short Vowels Review Making Words Cards, p. 267
    Short Vowels Review Individual Sort Cards, p. 268
    Short Vowels Review Echo Game Cards, pgs. 269-271
    Short Vowels Review Slinky Words Picture Cards, p. 272
    3-Column Writing Sort, p. 381

Review Week 6: Long Vowels/Silent E (Use the Long Vowels Picture Chart, p. 392.)
    Long Vowels/Silent E Review Lesson Plan (Week 6)
    Long Vowels/Silent E Review Blending Cards, p. 273
    Long Vowels/Silent E Review Onset/Rime Cards, p. 274
    Long Vowels/Silent E Review Making Words Cards, p. 275
    Long Vowels/Silent E Review Individual Sort Cards, p. 276
    Long Vowels/Silent E Review Echo Game Cards, pgs. 277-279
    3-Column Writing Sort, p. 381

Review Week 7: Long Vowels/Silent E (Use the Long Vowels Picture Chart, p. 392.)
    Long Vowels/Silent E Review Lesson Plan (Week 7)
    Long Vowels/Silent E Review Blending Cards, p. 280
    Long Vowels/Silent E Review Onset/Rime Cards, p. 281
    Long Vowels/Silent E Review Making Words Cards, p. 282
    Long Vowels/Silent E Review Individual Sort Cards, p. 283
    Long Vowels/Silent E Review Echo Game Cards, pgs. 284-286
    3-Column Writing Sort, p. 381

Review Week 8: Long Vowel Patterns (Use the Long Vowels Picture Chart, p. 392.)
    Long Vowel Patterns Review Lesson Plan (Week 8)
    Long Vowel Patterns Review Blending Cards, p. 287
    Long Vowel Patterns Review Onset/Rime Cards and Mats, p. 288
    Long Vowel Patterns Review Individual Sort Cards, p. 289
    Long Vowel Patterns Review Echo Game Cards, pgs. 290-292
    Long Vowel Patterns Review Slinky Words Picture Cards, p. 293
    Word Windows, pgs. 383-384
    Long Vowel Patterns Review Word Hunt Writing Mats, p. 294
    4-Column Writing Sort, p. 382

Review Week 9: Long Vowel Patterns (Use the Long Vowels Picture Chart, p. 392.)
    Long Vowel Patterns Review Lesson Plan (Week 9)
    Long Vowel Patterns Review Blending Cards, p. 295
    Long Vowel Patterns Review Onset/Rime Cards and Mats, p. 296
    Long Vowel Patterns Review Individual Sort Cards, p. 297
    Long Vowel Patterns Review Echo Game Cards, pgs. 298-300
    Long Vowel Patterns Review Slinky Words Picture Cards, p. 301
    Word Windows, pgs. 383-384
    Long Vowel Patterns Review Word Hunt Writing Mats, p. 302
    4-Column Writing Sort, p. 382

Review Week 10: Long Vowel Patterns (Use the Long Vowels Picture Chart, p. 392.)
    Long Vowel Patterns Review Lesson Plan (Week 10)
    Long Vowel Patterns Review Blending Cards, p. 303
    Long Vowel Patterns Review Onset/Rime Cards and Mats, p. 304
    Long Vowel Patterns Review Individual Sort Cards, p. 305
    Long Vowel Patterns Review Echo Game Cards, pgs. 306-308
    Long Vowel Patterns Review Slinky Words Picture Cards, p. 309
    Word Windows, pgs. 383-384
    Long Vowel Patterns Review Word Hunt Writing Mats, p. 310
    4-Column Writing Sort, p. 382

Review Week 11: A Patterns
    "A Patterns" Review Lesson Plan
    "A Patterns" Review Blending Cards, p. 311
    "A Patterns" Review Making Words Cards, p. 312
    Word Windows, pgs. 383-384
    "A Patterns" Review Word Hunt Writing Mats, p. 313
    3-Column Writing Sort, p. 381
    Comprehension Graphic Organizers, pgs. 385-390

Review Week 12: E Patterns
    "E Patterns" Review Lesson Plan
    "E Patterns" Review Blending Cards, p. 314
    "E Patterns" Review Making Words Cards, p. 315
    Word Windows, pgs. 383-384
    "E Patterns" Review Word Hunt Writing Mats, p. 316
    3-Column Writing Sort, p. 381
    Comprehension Graphic Organizers, pgs. 385-390

Review Week 13: I Patterns
    "I Patterns" Review Lesson Plan
    "I Patterns" Review Blending Cards, p. 317
    "I Patterns" Review Making Words Cards, p. 318
    Word Windows, pgs. 383-384
    "I Patterns" Review Word Hunt Writing Mats, p. 319
    3-Column Writing Sort, p. 381
    Comprehension Graphic Organizers, pgs. 385-390

Review Week 14: O Patterns
    "O Patterns" Review Lesson Plan
    "O Patterns" Review Blending Cards, p. 320
    "O Patterns" Review Making Words Cards, p. 321
    Word Windows, pgs. 383-384
    "O Patterns" Review Word Hunt Writing Mats, p. 322
    3-Column Writing Sort, p. 381
    Comprehension Graphic Organizers, pgs. 385-390

Review Week 15: U Patterns
    "U Patterns" Review Lesson Plans
    "U Patterns" Review Blending Cards, p. 323
    "U Patterns" Review Making Words Cards, p. 324
    "U Patterns" Review Word Hunt Cube, Mats, & Bingo Chips, pgs. 325-326
    3-Column Writing Sort, p. 381
    Comprehension Graphic Organizers, pgs. 385-390

Review Week 1: Short Vowels A, I, O
Use with activities on pages 239-243.

DAY 1:

Fluency Building (5-7 minutes)

Include:
*Previously read books
*Books from Level ___
*Phonics Books

Word Study (8-10 minutes)

✓ **Blending short a, i, o words** *(Use Group Word Sort Cards.)*
  - Picture/Sound Sort
✓ **Word Sorts – short a, i, o words** *(Use Group Word Sort Cards.)*
  - Group   Individual
  - Making Words Activity
  - Onset/Rime Activity
  - Other:

Guided Reading (8-10 minutes)

✓ Phonics Book: _____ Book: _____
✓ Guided Reading Level: _____

Writing (5-7 minutes)

✓ **Sound Boxes** *(Use the Sound/Spelling Boxes.)*
  - White Boards
  - Writing Sort
  - Dictation Sentences
  - Response Sentences

Words for Sound Boxes:
s-t-o-p
sh-o-t
t-r-a-p
p-i-n-ch
th-i-n

Guided Reading Level ___

DAY 2:

Fluency Building (5-7 minutes)

Include:
*Previously read books
*Books from Level ___
*Phonics Books

Word Study (8-10 minutes)

✓ **Blending short a, i, o words** *(Use Group Word Sort Cards.)*
  - Picture/Sound Sort
  - Word Sorts –
    Group   Individual
  - Making Words Activity
✓ **Onset/Rime Activity** *(Use the Onset/Rime Cards and Mats.)*
  - Other:

Guided Reading (8-10 minutes)

✓ Phonics Book: _____ Book: _____
✓ Guided Reading Level: _____

Writing (5-7 minutes)

  - Sound Boxes
  - White Boards
✓ **Writing Sort**
  - Dictation Sentences
  - Response Sentences

(Use words from the Individual Sort Cards and the 3-Column Writing Sort.)

a___   i___   o___

©The Reading Teacher's Plan Book

Guided Reading Level _____

Review Week 1: Short Vowels A, I, O (cont.)
Use with activities on pages 239-243.

DAY 3:

Fluency Building (5-7 minutes)

Include:
*Previously read books
*Books from Level _____
*Phonics Books

Word Study (8-10 minutes)

- ✓ **Blending short a, i, o words** *(Use Group Word Sort Cards.)*
  - Picture/Sound Sort
- • Word Sorts –
  - Group   Individual
- ✓ **Making Words Activity**   **Make these words:** *(Use the letter cards.)* pat, sat, sit, spit, spot, pot, lot, lit, lip, slip, slap, tap, tap, top
- • Onset/Rime Activity
- • Other:

Guided Reading (8-10 minutes)

- ✓ Phonics Book: _____
- ✓ Guided Reading Level: ___ Book: _____

Writing (5-7 minutes)

- • Sound Boxes
- ✓ **White Boards**
- • Writing Sort
- • Dictation Sentences
- • Response Sentences

Sight Word Writing Fluency: Use words from today's Guided Reading book. Give students 10 seconds to write each word as many times as they can.

DAY 4:

Fluency Building (5-7 minutes)

Include:
*Previously read books
*Books from Level _____
*Phonics Books

Word Study (8-10 minutes)

- ✓ **Blending short a, i, o words** *(Use Group Word Sort Cards.)*
- • Picture/Sound
- ✓ **Word Sorts – short a, i, o words** *(Use Individual Sort Cards.)*
  - Group   **Individual**
- • Making Words Activity
- • Onset/Rime Activity
- • Other:

Guided Reading (8-10 minutes)

- ✓ Phonics Book: _____
- ✓ Guided Reading Level: ___ Book: _____

Writing (5-7 minutes)

- • Sound Boxes
- • White Boards
- • Writing Sort
- • Dictation Sentences
- ✓ **Response Sentences**

Story Response Questions: Students respond to a question about today's Guided Reading book.

©The Reading Teacher's Plan Book

Review Week 2: Short Vowels E, U
Use with activities on pages 244-248.

DAY 1:

Fluency Building (5-7 minutes)

Include:
* *Previously read books*
* *Books from Level* ____
* *Phonics Books*

Word Study (8-10 minutes)

✓ <u>Blending short e, u words</u> *(Use Group Word Sort Cards.)*
* Picture/Sound Sort
✓ <u>Word Sorts – short e, u words</u> *(Use Group Word Sort Cards.)*
  Group   Individual
* Making Words Activity
* Onset/Rime Activity
* Other:

Guided Reading (8-10 minutes)

✓ Phonics Book: _____ Book: _____
✓ Guided Reading Level: _____

Writing (5-7 minutes)

✓ <u>Sound Boxes</u> *(Use the Sound/Spelling Boxes.)*
* White Boards
* Writing Sort
* Dictation Sentences
* Response Sentences

<u>Words for Sound Boxes:</u>

ch-e-ck
n-e-s-t
s-p-e-ll
j-u-m-p
s-t-u-m-p

Guided Reading Level ____

DAY 2:

Fluency Building (5-7 minutes)

Include:
* *Previously read books*
* *Books from Level* ____
* *Phonics Books*

Word Study (8-10 minutes)

✓ <u>Blending short e, u words</u> *(Use Group Word Sort Cards.)*
* Picture/Sound Sort
* Word Sorts –
  Group   Individual
✓ **Making Words Activity**
* Onset/Rime Activity
* Other:

<u>Make these words:</u>
(Use the letter cards.)
pet, bet, best, pest, past,
mast, must, stump, bump

Guided Reading (8-10 minutes)

✓ Phonics Book: _____ Book: _____
✓ Guided Reading Level: _____

Writing (5-7 minutes)

* Sound Boxes
✓ **White Boards**
■ Writing Sort
* Dictation Sentences
* Response Sentences

<u>Spelling Patterns:</u>
Write "ed" words . . . then "ell"
words . . . then "un" words . . . then
"ump" words

©The Reading Teacher's Plan Book

Guided Reading Level _____

DAY 4:

Fluency Building
(5-7 minutes)

Include:
*Previously read books
*Books from Level _____
*Phonics Books

Word Study
(8-10 minutes)

✓ **Blending short e, u words** *(Use Group Word Sort Cards.)*
• Picture/Sound Sort
✓ **Word Sorts – short e, u words** *(Individual Sort Cards.)*
    Group   **Individual**
• Making Words Activity
• Onset/Rime Activity
• Other:

Guided Reading
(8-10 minutes)

✓ Phonics Book: _____
✓ Guided Reading Level: _____ Book: _____

Writing
(5-7 minutes)

• Sound Boxes
• White Boards
• Writing Sort
• Dictation Sentences
✓ **Response Sentences**

Story Response Questions:
Students respond to a question about today's Guided Reading book.

Review Week 2: Short Vowels E, U (cont.)
Use with activities on pages 244-248.

DAY 3:

Fluency Building
(5-7 minutes)

Include:
*Previously read books
*Books from Level _____
*Phonics Books

Word Study
(8-10 minutes)

✓ **Blending short e, u words** *(Use Group Word Sort Cards.)*
• Picture/Sound Sort
• Word Sorts –
    Group   Individual
• Making Words Activity
✓ **Onset/Rime Activity** *(Use the Onset/Rime Cards and Mats.)*
• Other:

Guided Reading
(8-10 minutes)

✓ Phonics Book: _____
✓ Guided Reading Level: _____ Book: _____

Writing
(5-7 minutes)

• Sound Boxes
• White Boards
✓ **Writing Sort**
• Dictation Sentences
• Response Sentences

(Use words from the Group Sort Cards and the 2-Column Writing Sort.)

e   u

©The Reading Teacher's Plan Book

Review Week 3: Short Vowel Review

Use with activities on pages 249-256.

DAY 1:

Fluency Building (5-7 minutes)

Include:
* *Previously read books*
* *Books from Level* ___
* *Phonics Books*

Word Study (8-10 minutes)

- ✓ <u>Blending Short Vowel Words</u> *(Use Blending Cards.)*
- • P_cture/Sound Sort
- • Word Sorts –
   Group   Individual
   Making Words Activity
- ✓ <u>Onset/Rime Activity</u>   *(Use the Onset/Rime Cards and Mats.)*
   Emphasize speed and automaticity.
- • Other:

Guided Reading (8-10 minutes)

- ✓ Phonics Book: _____ Book: _____
- ✓ Guided Reading Level: _____

Writing (5-7 minutes)

- • Sound Boxes
- ✓ **White Boards**
- • Writing Sort
- • Dictation Sentences
- • Response Sentences

<u>Slinky Words:</u>
(Use the Slinky Words Picture Cards.)
jump, chick, lock, crash, flag, sun, sled, bells

Guided Reading Level ___

DAY 2:

Fluency Building (5-7 minutes)

Include:
* *Previously read books*
* *Books from Level* ___
* *Phonics Books*

Word Study (8-10 minutes)

- ✓ <u>Blending Short Vowel Words</u> *(Use Blending Cards.)*
- • Picture/Sound Sort
- • Word Sorts –
   Group   Individual
- ✓ **Making Words Activity**
- • Onset/Rime Activity
- • Other:

<u>Make these words:</u>
(Use the letter cards.)
met, mat, hat, hot, shot, shut, hut, hum

Guided Reading (8-10 minutes)

- ✓ Phonics Book: _____ Book: _____
- ✓ Guided Reading Level: _____

Writing (5-7 minutes)

- • Sound Boxes
- • White Boards
- ✓ **Writing Sort**
- • Dictation Sentences
- • Response Sentences

(Use words from the Blending Cards and the 3-Column Writing Sort.)

<u>e</u>   <u>i</u>   <u>o</u>

©The Reading Teacher's Plan Book

Guided Reading Level _____

DAY 4:

Fluency Building (5-7 minutes)

Include:
*Previously read books
*Books from Level _____
*Phonics Books

Word Study (8-10 minutes)

✓ **Blending Short Vowel Words** *(Use Blending Cards.)*
- Picture/Sound
- Word Sorts –
  - Group   Individual
- Making Words Activity
- Onset/Rime Activity
- **Other: Echo Game** *(Use Echo Game Cards.)*

Guided Reading (8-10 minutes)

✓ Phonics Book: _____ Book: _____
✓ Guided Reading Level: _____

Writing (5-7 minutes)

- Sound Boxes
- White Boards
- Writing Sort
- Dictation Sentences
- **Response Sentences**

Story Response Questions: Students respond to a question about today's Guided Reading book.

Review Week 3: Short Vowel Review (cont.)
Use with activities on pages 249-256.

DAY 3:

Fluency Building (5-7 minutes)

Include:
*Previously read books
*Books from Level _____
*Phonics Books

Word Study (8-10 minutes)

✓ **Blending Short Vowel Words** *(Use Blending Cards.)*
- Picture/Sound Sort
✓ **Word Sorts – Short Vowel Words** *(Use Individual Sort Cards.)*
  - Group   **Individual**   Emphasize speed and automaticity.
- Making Words Activity
- Onset/Rime Activity
- Other:

Guided Reading (8-10 minutes)

✓ Phonics Book: _____ Book: _____
✓ Guided Reading Level: _____

Writing (5-7 minutes)

- Sound Boxes
✓ **White Boards**
- Writing Sort
- Dictation Sentences
- Response Sentences

Word Chains:
1. *hen, pen, pet, pit, fit, fix, fox*
2. *cat, cut, cub, rub, rug, dug, dog*

©The Reading Teacher's Plan Book

Review Week 4: Short Vowel Review
Use with activities on pages 257-264.

DAY 1:

**Fluency Building
(5-7 minutes)**

Include:
*Previously read books
*Books from Level _____
*Phonics Books

**Word Study
(8-10 minutes)**

✓ **Blending Short Vowel Words** *(Use Blending Cards.)*
• Picture/Sound Sort
• Word Sorts –
  Group_____ Individual_____
• Making Words Activity
✓ **Onset/Rime Activity** *(Use the Onset/Rime Cards and Mats.)*
• Other: *Emphasize speed and automaticity.*

**Guided Reading
(8-10 minutes)**

✓ Phonics Book: _____ Book: _____
✓ Guided Reading Level: _____

**Writing
(5-7 minutes)**

• Sound Boxes
✓ White Boards
• Writing Sort
• Dictation Sentences
• Response Sentences

Slinky Words:
(Use the Slinky Words Picture Cards.)
sand, mop, fish, clock, cut, shell, nest, brush

Guided Reading Level _____

DAY 2:

**Fluency Building
(5-7 minutes)**

Include:
*Previously read books
*Books from Level _____
*Phonics Books

**Word Study
(8-10 minutes)**

✓ **Blending Short Vowel Words** *(Use Blending Cards.)*
• Picture/Sound Sort
• Word Sorts –
  Group_____ Individual_____
✓ **Making Words Activity**
• Onset/Rime Activity
• Other:

Make these words:
(Use the letter cards.)
led, sled, slid, slip, slap, clap, clip, tip

**Guided Reading
(8-10 minutes)**

✓ Phonics Book: _____ Book: _____
✓ Guided Reading Level: _____

**Writing
(5-7 minutes)**

• Sound Boxes
• White Boards
✓ **Writing Sort**
• Dictation Sentences
• Response Sentences

(Use words from the Blending Cards and the 3-Column Writing Sort.)

<u>a</u>   <u>o</u>   <u>u</u>

©The Reading Teacher's Plan Book

Review Week 4: Short Vowel Review (cont.)
Use with activities on pages 257-264.

DAY 3:

Fluency Building (5-7 minutes)

Include:
*Previously read books
*Books from Level _____
*Phonics Books

Word Study (8-10 minutes)

✓ **Blending Short Vowel Words** *(Use Blending Cards.)*
✓ **Word Sorts – Short Vowel Words** *(Use Individual Sort Cards.)* *Emphasize speed and automaticity.*
  - Picture/Sound Sort
  - **Individual**
  - Making Words Activity
  - Onset/Rime Activity
  - Other:

Guided Reading (8-10 minutes)

✓ Phonics Book: _____ Book: _____
✓ Guided Reading Level: _____

Writing (5-7 minutes)

- Sound Boxes
- White Boards
- Writing Sort
- Dictation Sentences
- ✓ **Response Sentences**

Story Response Questions: Students respond to a question about today's Guided Reading book.

Guided Reading Level _____

DAY 4:

Fluency Building (5-7 minutes)

Include:
*Previously read books
*Books from Level _____
*Phonics Books

Word Study (8-10 minutes)

✓ **Blending Short Vowel Words** *(Use Blending Cards.)*
  - Picture/Sound
  - Word Sorts –
    - Group   Individual
  - Making Words Activity
  - Onset/Rime Activity
✓ **Other: Echo Game** *(Use Echo Game Cards.)*

Guided Reading (8-10 minutes)

✓ Phonics Book: _____ Book: _____
✓ Guided Reading Level: _____

Writing (5-7 minutes)

- Sound Boxes
- White Boards
- Writing Sort
- ✓ **Dictation Sentences**
- Response Sentences

Dictation Sentences:
1. There was a spot on his chin.
2. The pigs want to play in the mud.
3. Do not step on that tack.

©The Reading Teacher's Plan Book

Review Week 5: Short Vowel Review
Use with activities on pages 265-272.

DAY 1:

Fluency Building
(5-7 minutes)

Include:
*Previously read books
*Books from Level ____
*Phonics Books

Word Study
(8-10 minutes)

✓ **Blending Short Vowel Words** *(Use the Blending Cards.)*
 • Picture/Sound Sort
 • Word Sorts –
   Group   Individual
   Making Words Activity
✓ **Onset/Rime Activity** *(Use the Onset/Rime Cards and Mats.)*
 • Other: *Emphasize speed and automaticity.*

Guided Reading
(8-10 minutes)

✓ Phonics Book: _____ Book: _____
✓ Guided Reading Level: _____ Book: _____

Writing
(5-7 minutes)

 • Sound Boxes
 ✓ **White Boards**
 • Writing Sort
 • Dictation Sentences
 • Response Sentences

Slinky Words:
(Use the Slinky Words Picture Cards.)
swim, map, twins, pen, lunch, pond, truck, check

Guided Reading Level ____

DAY 2:

Fluency Building
(5-7 minutes)

Include:
*Previously read books
*Books from Level ____
*Phonics Books

Word Study
(8-10 minutes)

✓ **Blending Short Vowel Words** *(Use the Blending Cards.)*
 • Picture/Sound Sort
 • Word Sorts –
   Group   Individual
   Making Words Activity
 ✓ Onset/Rime Activity
 • Other:

Guided Reading
(8-10 minutes)

✓ Phonics Book: _____
✓ Guided Reading Level: _____ Book: _____

Writing
(5-7 minutes)

 • Sound Boxes
 • White Boards
 ✓ **Writing Sort**
 • Dictation Sentences
 • Response Sentences

Make these words:
(Use the letter cards.)
shop, hop, hot, shot, shut, hut, hug, tug, tag, tap, lap, slap

(Use words from the Blending Cards and the 3-Column Writing Sort.)
<u>a</u>   <u>e</u>   <u>u</u>

©The Reading Teacher's Plan Book

Review Week 5: Short Vowel Review (cont.)
Use with activities on pages 265-272.

DAY 3:

Fluency Building (5-7 minutes)

Include:
*Previously read books
*Books from Level _____
*Phonics Books

Word Study (8-10 minutes)

- ✓ **Blending Short Vowel Words** *(Use the Blending Cards.)*
- ✓ **Word Sorts – Short Vowel Words** *(Use Individual Sort Cards.)*
  - Picture/Sound Sort
  - Group **Individual** *Emphasize speed and automaticity.*
  - Making Words Activity
  - Onset/Rime Activity
  - Other: _____

Guided Reading (8-10 minutes)

- ✓ Phonics Book: _____ Book: _____
- ✓ Guided Reading Level: _____

Writing (5-7 minutes)

- Sound Boxes
- ✓ **White Boards**
- Writing Sort
- Dictation Sentences
- Response Sentences

Word Chains:
1. *fish, dish, dash, bash, bath, bat, bag, bog, fog, frog*
2. *cat, rat, rag, rug, dug, dog*

DAY 4:

Fluency Building (5-7 minutes)

Include:
*Previously read books
*Books from Level _____
*Phonics Books

Word Study (8-10 minutes)

- ✓ **Blending Short Vowel Words** *(Use the Blending Cards.)*
  - Picture/Sound
  - Word Sorts –
    - Group   Individual
  - Making Words Activity
  - Onset/Rime Activity
- ✓ Other: **Echo Game** *(Use Echo Game Cards.)*

Guided Reading (8-10 minutes)

- ✓ Phonics Book: _____ Book: _____
- ✓ Guided Reading Level: _____

Writing (5-7 minutes)

- Sound Boxes
- White Boards
- Writing Sort
- Dictation Sentences
- ✓ **Response Sentences**

Story Response Questions: Students respond to a question about today's Guided Reading book.

©The Reading Teacher's Plan Book

Review Week 6: Long Vowel Patterns with Silent E Review

Use with activities on pages 273-279.

DAY 1:

Fluency Building (5-7 minutes)

Include:
*Previously read books
*Books from Level _____
*Phonics Books

Word Study (8-10 minutes)

✓ **Blending Long Vowel/Silent E Words** *(Use the Blending Cards.)*
- Picture/Sound Sort
- Word Sorts –
  Group   Individual
- Making Words Activity
✓ **Onset/Rime Activity** *(Use the Onset/Rime Cards and Mats.)*
- Other: *Emphasize speed and automaticity.*

Guided Reading (8-10 minutes)

✓ Phonics Book: _____ Book: _____
✓ Guided Reading Level: _____

Writing (5-7 minutes)

- Sound Boxes
✓ White Boards
- Writing Sort
- Dictation Sentences
- Response Sentences

Spelling Patterns:
Write "ake" words... then "ide" words... then "ose" words... then "u_e" words

---

Guided Reading Level _____

DAY 2:

Fluency Building (5-7 minutes)

Include:
*Previously read books
*Books from Level _____
*Phonics Books

Word Study (8-10 minutes)

✓ **Long Vowel/Silent E Words** *(Use the Blending Cards.)*
- Picture/Sound Sort
- Word Sorts –
  Group   Individual
✓ **Making Words Activity**
- Onset/Rime Activity
- Other:

Make these words:
(Use the letter cards.)
Pete, pet, pen, pin, pine, fine, mine, mane, man, pan, pane

Guided Reading (8-10 minutes)

✓ Phonics Book: _____ Book: _____
✓ Guided Reading Level: _____

Writing (5-7 minutes)

- Sound Boxes
- White Boards
✓ Writing Sort
- Dictation Sentences
- Response Sentences

(Use words from the Blending Cards and the 3-Column Writing Sort.)

a-e   i-e   o-e

©The Reading Teacher's Plan Book

Review Week 6: Long Vowel Patterns with Silent E Review (cont.)
Use with activities on pages 273-279.

Guided Reading Level _____

DAY 3:

Fluency Building (5-7 minutes)

Include:
- *Previously read books*
- *Books from Level _____*
- *Phonics Books*

Word Study (8-10 minutes)

- ✓ **Long Vowel/Silent E Words** *(Use the Blending Cards.)*
- • Picture/Sound Sort
- ✓ **Word Sorts – Short Vowel Words** *(Use Individual Sort Cards.)*
  - Group   **Individual**   Emphasize speed and automaticity.
- • Making Words Activity
- • Onset/Rime Activity
- • Other: _____

Guided Reading (8-10 minutes)

- ✓ Phonics Book: _____ Book: _____
- ✓ Guided Reading Level: _____ Book: _____

Writing (5-7 minutes)

- • Sound Boxes
- • White Boards
- • Writing Sort
- ✓ **Dictation Sentences**
- • Response Sentences

Dictation Sentences:
1. Can I ride your new bike?
2. We will help mom bake a cake.
3. Smell the rose with your nose.

DAY 4:

Fluency Building (5-7 minutes)

Include:
- *Previously read books*
- *Books from Level _____*
- *Phonics Books*

Word Study (8-10 minutes)

- ✓ **Long Vowel/Silent E Words** *(Use the Blending Cards.)*
- • Picture/Sound Sort
- • Word Sorts –
  - Group   Individual
- • Making Words Activity
- • Onset/Rime Activity
- ✓ **Other: Echo Game** *(Use Echo Game Cards.)*

Guided Reading (8-10 minutes)

- ✓ Phonics Book: _____
- ✓ Guided Reading Level: _____ Book: _____

Writing (5-7 minutes)

- • Sound Boxes
- • White Boards
- • Writing Sort
- • Dictation Sentences
- ✓ **Response Sentences**

Story Response Questions:
Students respond to a question about today's Guided Reading book.

©The Reading Teacher's Plan Book

Review Week 7: Long Vowel Patterns with Silent E Review

Use with activities on pages 280-286.

Guided Reading Level ___

DAY 1:

Fluency Building (5-7 minutes)

Include:
*Previously read books
*Books from Level ___
*Phonics Books

Word Study (8-10 minutes)

✓ <u>Blending Long Vowel/Silent E Words</u> *(Use the Blending Cards.)*
• Picture/Sound Sort
• Word Sorts –
  Group   Individual
• Making Words Activity
✓ Onset/Rime Activity *(Use the Onset/Rime Cards and Mats.)*
• Other: ___ Emphasize speed and automaticity.

Guided Reading (8-10 minutes)

✓ Phonics Book: ___
✓ Guided Reading Level: ___ Book: ___

Writing (5-7 minutes)

• Sound Boxes
• **White Boards**
• Writing Sort
• Dictation Sentences
• Response Sentences

<u>Spelling Patterns:</u>
Write "ace" words . . . then "age" words . . . then "ice" words . . . then "ike" words

DAY 2:

Fluency Building (5-7 minutes)

Include:
*Previously read books
*Books from Level ___
*Phonics Books

Word Study (8-10 minutes)

✓ <u>Long Vowel/Silent E Words</u> *(Use the Blending Cards.)*
• Picture/Sound Sort
• Word Sorts –
  Group   Individual
• **Making Words Activity**
• Onset/Rime Activity
• Other: ___

<u>Make these words:</u>
(Use the letter cards.)
mice, mike, make, lake, lace, place, pace, page, cage, cake

Guided Reading (8-10 minutes)

✓ Phonics Book: ___
✓ Guided Reading Level: ___ Book: ___

Writing (5-7 minutes)

• Sound Boxes
• White Boards
✓ **Writing Sort**
• Dictation Sentences
• Response Sentences

(Use words from the Blending Cards and the 3-Column Writing Sort.)

<u>ace</u>   <u>ice</u>   <u>age</u>

©The Reading Teacher's Plan Book

Review Week 7: Long Vowel Patterns with Silent E Review (cont.)

Use with activities on pages 280-286.

Guided Reading Level _____

DAY 3:

Fluency Building (5-7 minutes)

Include:
*Previously read books
*Books from Level _____
*Phonics Books

Word Study (8-10 minutes)

- ✓ <u>**Long Vowel/Silent E Words**</u> *(Use the Blending Cards.)*
- ✓ <u>**Word Sorts – Short Vowel Words**</u> *(Use Individual Sort Cards.)*
  - Picture/Sound Sort
  - Group   **Individual**   *Emphasize speed and automaticity.*
- • Making Words Activity
- • Onset/Rime Activity
- • Other: _____

Guided Reading (8-10 minutes)

- ✓ Phonics Book: _____ Book: _____
- ✓ Guided Reading Level: _____

Writing (5-7 minutes)

- • Sound Boxes
- ✓ **White Boards**
- • Writing Sort
- • Dictation Sentences
- • Response Sentences

<u>**Sight Word Writing Fluency:**</u>
Use words from today's Guided Reading book. Give students 10 seconds to write each word as many times as they can.

DAY 4:

Fluency Building (5-7 minutes)

Include:
*Previously read books
*Books from Level _____
*Phonics Books

Word Study (8-10 minutes)

- ✓ <u>**Long Vowel/Silent E Words**</u> *(Use the Blending Cards.)*
  - Picture/Sound Sort
  - Word Sorts –
    - Group   Individual
- • Making Words Activity
- • Onset/Rime Activity
- ✓ Other: <u>**Echo Game**</u> *(Use Echo Game Cards.)*

Guided Reading (8-10 minutes)

- ✓ Phonics Book: _____ Book: _____
- ✓ Guided Reading Level: _____

Writing (5-7 minutes)

- • Sound Boxes
- • White Boards
- • Writing Sort
- ✓ **Dictation Sentences**
- • Response Sentences

<u>**Dictation Sentences:**</u>
1. Do you see the white mice in the cage?
2. Put a smile on your face!
3. Our family will hike to the lake.

©The Reading Teacher's Plan Book

Review Week 8: Long Vowel Patterns

Use with activities on pages 287-294.

DAY 1:

Fluency Building (5-7 minutes)

Include:
*Previously read books
*Books from Level _____
*Phonics Books

Word Study (8-10 minutes)

✓ **Blending Long Vowel Words** *(Use the Blending Cards.)*
- Picture/Sound Sort
- Word Sorts –
  Group   Individual
- Making Words Activity
✓ **Onset/Rime Activity** *(Use the Onset/Rime Cards and Mats.)*
- Other: Emphasize speed and automaticity.

Guided Reading (8-10 minutes)

✓ Phonics Book: _____ Book: _____
✓ Guided Reading Level: _____ Book: _____

Writing (5-7 minutes)

- Sound Boxes
✓ **White Boards**
- Writing Sort
- Dictation Sentences
- Response Sentences

Slinky Words:
(Use the Slinky Words Picture Cards.)
tray, clay, cheese, wheel, pie, fries, snow, crow

Guided Reading Level _____

DAY 2:

Fluency Building (5-7 minutes)

Include:
*Previously read books
*Books from Level _____
*Phonics Books

Word Study (8-10 minutes)

✓ **Long Vowel Words** *(Use the Blending Cards.)*
- Picture/Sound Sort
- Word Sorts –
  Group   Individual
- Making Words Activity
- Onset/Rime Activity
✓ **Other: Word Hunt** *(Use the Word Windows and Writing Mats.)*

Guided Reading (8-10 minutes)

✓ Phonics Book: _____ Book: _____
✓ Guided Reading Level: _____ Book: _____

Writing (5-7 minutes)

- Sound Boxes
- White Boards
✓ **Writing Sort**
- Dictation Sentences
- Response Sentences

(Use words from the Blending Cards and the 4-Column Writing Sort.)

<u>ay</u>   <u>ee</u>   <u>ie</u>   <u>ow</u>

©The Reading Teacher's Plan Book

Review Week 8: Long Vowel Patterns (cont.)

Use with activities on pages 287-294.

DAY 3:

Fluency Building (5-7 minutes)

Include:
*Previously read books
*Books from Level _____
*Phonics Books

Word Study (8-10 minutes)

✓ **Long Vowel Words** *(Use the Blending Cards.)*
• Picture/Sound Sort
✓ **Word Sorts – Long Vowel Words** *(Use Individual Sort Cards.)* *Emphasize speed and automaticity.*
   Group   **Individual**
• Making Words Activity
• Onset/Rime Activity
• Other:

Guided Reading (8-10 minutes)

✓ Phonics Book: _____ Book: _____
✓ Guided Reading Level: _____

Writing (5-7 minutes)

• Sound Boxes
• White Boards
• Writing Sort
✓ **Dictation Sentences**
• Response Sentences

Dictation Sentences:
1. Keep the sheep away from the road.
2. Will you tie a pretty bow on the gift?
3. I want to play with clay all day!

Guided Reading Level _____

DAY 4:

Fluency Building (5-7 minutes)

Include:
*Previously read books
*Books from Level _____
*Phonics Books

Word Study (8-10 minutes)

✓ **Long Vowel Words** *(Use the Blending Cards.)*
• Picture/Sound
  Word Sorts –
   Group   Individual
• Making Words Activity
• Onset/Rime Activity
✓ **Other: Echo Game** *(Use Echo Game Cards.)* *Emphasize speed and automaticity.*

Guided Reading (8-10 minutes)

✓ Phonics Book: _____
✓ Guided Reading Level: _____ Book: _____

Writing (5-7 minutes)

• Sound Boxes
• White Boards
• Writing Sort
• Dictation Sentences
✓ **Response Sentences**

Story Response Questions:
Students respond to a question about today's Guided Reading book.

©The Reading Teacher's Plan Book

Review Week 9: Long Vowel Patterns
Use with activities on pages 295-302.

DAY 1:

Fluency Building (5-7 minutes)

Include:
*Previously read books
*Books from Level _____
*Phonics Books

Word Study (8-10 minutes)

✓ **Blending Long Vowel Words** *(Use the Blending Cards.)*
- Picture/Sound Sort
- Word Sorts –
  Group   Individual
- Making Words Activity
✓ **Onset/Rime Activity** *(Use the Onset/Rime Cards and Mats.)*
- Other: Emphasize speed and automaticity.

Guided Reading (8-10 minutes)

✓ Phonics Book: _____ Book: _____
✓ Guided Reading Level: _____

Writing (5-7 minutes)

- Sound Boxes
✓ White Boards
- Writing Sort
- Dictation Sentences
- Response Sentences

Slinky Words:
(Use the Slinky Words Picture Cards.)
paint, snail, peach, dream, knight, light, float, toast

Guided Reading Level _____

DAY 2:

Fluency Building (5-7 minutes)

Include:
*Previously read books
*Books from Level _____
*Phonics Books

Word Study (8-10 minutes)

✓ **Long Vowel Words** *(Use the Blending Cards.)*
- Picture/Sound Sort
- Word Sorts –
  Group   Individual
- Making Words Activity
- Onset/Rime Activity
✓ Other: **Word Hunt** *(Use the Word Windows and Writing Mats.)*

Guided Reading (8-10 minutes)

✓ Phonics Book: _____ Book: _____
✓ Guided Reading Level: _____

Writing (5-7 minutes)

- Sound Boxes
- White Boards
✓ **Writing Sort**
- Dictation Sentences
- Response Sentences

(Use words from the Blending Cards and the 4-Column Writing Sort.)
<u>ai</u>   <u>ea</u>   <u>igh</u>   <u>oa</u>

©The Reading Teacher's Plan Book

Review Week 9: Long Vowel Patterns (cont.)
Use with activities on pages 295-302.

DAY 3:

Fluency Building (5-7 minutes)

Include:
*Previously read books
*Books from Level _____
*Phonics Books

Word Study (8-10 minutes)

- ✓ **Long Vowel Words** *(Use the Blending Cards.)*
- Picture/Sound Sort
- ✓ **Word Sorts – Long Vowel Words** *(Use Individual Sort Cards.)*
  - Group   **Individual**   *Emphasize speed and automaticity.*
- Making Words Activity
- Onset/Rime Activity
- Other:

Guided Reading (8-10 minutes)

- ✓ Phonics Book: _____ Book: _____
- ✓ Guided Reading Level: _____

Writing (5-7 minutes)

- Sound Boxes
- White Boards
- Writing Sort
- ✓ **Dictation Sentences**
- Response Sentences

Dictation Sentences:
1. Let's pick peaches from the tree.
2. We will go sailing in our new boat.
3. Please let me read with a nightlight!

Guided Reading Level _____

DAY 4:

Fluency Building (5-7 minutes)

Include:
*Previously read books
*Books from Level _____
*Phonics Books

Word Study (8-10 minutes)

- ✓ **Long Vowel Words** *(Use the Blending Cards.)*
- Picture/Sound Sort
- **Word Sorts –**
  - Group   Individual
- Making Words Activity
- Onset/Rime Activity
- ✓ Other: **Echo Game** *(Use Echo Game Cards.)* *Emphasize speed and automaticity.*

Guided Reading (8-10 minutes)

- ✓ Phonics Book: _____ Book: _____
- ✓ Guided Reading Level: _____

Writing (5-7 minutes)

- Sound Boxes
- White Boards
- Writing Sort
- Dictation Sentences
- ✓ **Response Sentences**

Story Response Questions:
Students respond to a question about today's Guided Reading book.

©The Reading Teacher's Plan Book

Review Week 10: Long Vowel Patterns
Use with activities on pages 303-310.

DAY 1:

Fluency Building
(5-7 minutes)

Include:
*Previously read books
*Books from Level _____
*Phonics Books

Word Study
(8-10 minutes)

✓ **Blending Long Vowel Words** *(Use the Blending Cards.)*
- Picture/Sound Sort
- Word Sorts –
  - Group   Individual
- Making Words Activity
✓ **Onset/Rime Activity** *(Use the Onset/Rime Cards and Mats.)*
- Other: Emphasize speed and automaticity.

Guided Reading
(8-10 minutes)

✓ Phonics Book: _____   Book: _____
✓ Guided Reading Level: _____

Writing
(5-7 minutes)

- Sound Boxes
✓ **White Boards**
- Writing Sort
- Dictation Sentences
- Response Sentences

Slinky Words:
(Use the Slinky Words Picture Cards.)
hay, spray, beach, treat, blow, row, fly, spy

Guided Reading Level _____

DAY 2:

Fluency Building
(5-7 minutes)

Include:
*Previously read books
*Books from Level _____
*Phonics Books

Word Study
(8-10 minutes)

✓ **Long Vowel Words** *(Use the Blending Cards.)*
- Picture/Sound Sort
- Word Sorts –
  - Group   Individual
- Making Words Activity
- Onset/Rime Activity
✓ Other: **Word Hunt** *(Use the Word Windows and Writing Mats.)*

Guided Reading
(8-10 minutes)

✓ Phonics Book: _____   Book: _____
✓ Guided Reading Level: _____

Writing
(5-7 minutes)

- Sound Boxes
- White Boards
✓ **Writing Sort**
- Dictation Sentences
- Response Sentences

(Use words from the Blending Cards and the 4-Column Writing Sort.)

<u>ay</u>   <u>ea</u>   <u>y</u>   <u>ow</u>

©The Reading Teacher's Plan Book

Review Week 10: Long Vowel Patterns (cont.)
Use with activities on pages 303-310.

DAY 3:

Fluency Building (5-7 minutes)

Include:
*Previously read books
*Books from Level ____
*Phonics Books

Word Study (8-10 minutes)

- ✓ <u>Long Vowel Words</u> *(Use the Blending Cards.)*
- Picture/Sound Sort
- ✓ <u>Word Sorts – **Long Vowel Words**</u> *(Use Individual Sort Cards.)* **Individual** *Emphasize speed and automaticity.*
  - Group
  - Making Words Activity
  - Onset/Rime Activity
  - Other:

Guided Reading (8-10 minutes)

- ✓ Phonics Book: _____ Book: _____
- ✓ Guided Reading Level: ____

Writing (5-7 minutes)

- Sound Boxes
- White Boards
- Writing Sort
- ✓ **Dictation Sentences**
- Response Sentences

Dictation Sentences:
1. I love to fly my kite in the sky.
2. Please may I eat a yummy treat?
3. The wind is blowing leaves off the trees.

Guided Reading Level ____

DAY 4:

Fluency Building (5-7 minutes)

Include:
*Previously read books
*Books from Level ____
*Phonics Books

Word Study (8-10 minutes)

- ✓ <u>Long Vowel Words</u> *(Use the Blending Cards.)*
- Picture/Sound Sort
- Word Sorts –
  - Group   Individual
  - Making Words Activity
  - Onset/Rime Activity
- ✓ Other: **Echo Game** *(Use Echo Game Cards.)*

Guided Reading (8-10 minutes)

- ✓ Phonics Book: _____ Book: _____
- ✓ Guided Reading Level: ____

Writing (5-7 minutes)

- Sound Boxes
- White Boards
- Writing Sort
- Dictation Sentences
- ✓ **Response Sentences**

Story Response Questions:
Students respond to a question about today's Guided Reading book.

©The Reading Teacher's Plan Book

Review Week 11: "A Patterns"
Use with activities on pages 311-313.

DAY 1:

Fluency Building (5-7 minutes)

Include:
*Previously read books
*Books from Level _____
*Phonics Books

Word Study (8-10 minutes)

✓ Blending "A Patterns" Review *(Use the Blending Cards.)*
- Picture/Sound Sort
- Word Sorts –
  Group ____ Individual ____
✓ **Making Words Activity**
- Onset/Rime Activity
- Other: _____

Make these words:
(Use the letter cards.)
bat, bar, ball, bail, fail, fall, far, star, stall, tall, tail, rail, rat

Guided Reading (8-10 minutes)

✓ Phonics Book: _____ Book: _____
✓ Guided Reading Level: _____ Book: _____

Writing (5-7 minutes)

- Sound Boxes
- White Boards
- Writing Sort
- Dictation Sentences
✓ **Response Sentences** *Use a Comprehension Graphic Organizer.*

Guided Reading Level _____

DAY 2:

Fluency Building (5-7 minutes)

Include:
*Previously read books
*Books from Level _____
*Phonics Books

Word Study (8-10 minutes)

✓ Blending "A Patterns" Review *(Use the Blending Cards.)*
- Picture/Sound Sort
- Word Sorts –
  Group ____ Individual ____
- Making Words Activity
- Onset/Rime Activity
✓ **Other: Writing Sort**

(Use words from the Blending Cards and the 3-Column Writing Sort.)

<u>ai</u>   <u>all</u>   <u>ar</u>

Guided Reading (8-10 minutes)

✓ Phonics Book: _____ Book: _____
✓ Guided Reading Level: _____ Book: _____

Writing (5-7 minutes)

- Sound Boxes
- White Boards
- Writing Sort
- Dictation Sentences
✓ **Response Sentences** *Use a Comprehension Graphic Organizer*

©The Reading Teacher's Plan Book

Guided Reading Level _____

DAY 4:

Fluency Building
(5-7 minutes)

Include:
*Previously read books
*Books from Level _____
*Phonics Books

Word Study
(8-10 minutes)

✓ **Blending "A Patterns" Review** *(Use the Blending Cards.)*
- Picture/Sound Sort
- Word Sorts –
  Group   Individual
- Making Words Activity
- Onset/Rime Activity
✓ **Other: Dictation Sentences**

Dictation Sentences:
1. Did you see that falling star?
2. The snail was crawling along the trail.
3. We are waiting for the race to start.

Guided Reading
(8-10 minutes)

✓ Phonics Book: _____ Book: _____
✓ Guided Reading Level: _____ Book: _____

Writing
(5-7 minutes)

- Sound Boxes
- White Boards
- Writing Sort
- Dictation Sentences
✓ **Response Sentences** *Use a Comprehension Graphic Organizer.*

©The Reading Teacher's Plan Book

Review Week 11: "A Patterns" (cont.)
Use with activities on pages 311-313.

DAY 3:

Fluency Building
(5-7 minutes)

Include:
*Previously read books
*Books from Level _____
*Phonics Books

Word Study
(8-10 minutes)

✓ **Blending "A Patterns" Review** *(Use the Blending Cards.)*
- Picture/Sound Sort
- Word Sorts –
  Group   Individual
- Making Words Activity
- Onset/Rime Activity
✓ **Other: Word Hunt** *(Use the Word Windows and Writing Mats.)*

Guided Reading
(8-10 minutes)

✓ Phonics Book: _____ Book: _____
✓ Guided Reading Level: _____ Book: _____

Writing
(5-7 minutes)

- Sound Boxes
- White Boards
- Writing Sort
- Dictation Sentences
✓ **Response Sentences** *Use a Comprehension Graphic Organizer.*

Guided Reading Level _____

Review Week 12: "E Patterns"
Use with activities on pages 314-316.

DAY 1:

Fluency Building (5-7 minutes)

Include:
- *Previously read books*
- *Books from Level _____*
- *Phonics Books*

Word Study (8-10 minutes)

✓ Blending "E Patterns" Review *(Use the Blending Cards.)*
- Picture/Sound Sort
- Word Sorts –
   Group   Individual
✓ Making Words Activity
- Onset/Rime Activity
- Other: _____

Make these words:
(Use the letter cards.)
perk, peak, peck, neck, new, net, neat, heat, cheat, chew

Guided Reading (8-10 minutes)

✓ Phonics Book: _____ Book: _____
✓ Guided Reading Level: _____

Writing (5-7 minutes)

- Sound Boxes
- White Boards
- Writing Sort
- Dictation Sentences
✓ Response Sentences *Use a Comprehension Graphic Organizer.*

DAY 2:

Fluency Building (5-7 minutes)

Include:
- *Previously read books*
- *Books from Level _____*
- *Phonics Books*

Word Study (8-10 minutes)

✓ Blending "E Patterns" Review *(Use the Blending Cards.)*
- Picture/Sound Sort
- Word Sorts –
   Group   Individual
- Making Words Activity
- Onset/Rime Activity
✓ Other: **Writing Sort**

(Use words from the Blending Cards and the 3-Column Writing Sort.)

<u>er</u>   <u>ea</u>   <u>ew</u>

Guided Reading (8-10 minutes)

✓ Phonics Book: _____ Book: _____
✓ Guided Reading Level: _____

Writing (5-7 minutes)

- Sound Boxes
- White Boards
- Writing Sort
- Dictation Sentences
✓ Response Sentences *Use a Comprehension Graphic Organizer*

©The Reading Teacher's Plan Book

Review Week 12: "E Patterns" (cont.)
Use with activities on pages 314-316.

DAY 3:

Fluency Building (5-7 minutes)

Include:
* *Previously read books*
* *Books from Level* _____
* *Phonics Books*

Word Study (8-10 minutes)

- ✓ Blending "E Patterns" Review *(Use the Blending Cards.)*
- • Picture/Sound Sort
- • Word Sorts –
  Group   Individual
- • Making Words Activity
- • Onset/Rime Activity
- ✓ Other: Word Hunt *(Use the Word Windows and Writing Mats.)*

Guided Reading (8-10 minutes)

- ✓ Phonics Book: _____ Book: _____
- ✓ Guided Reading Level: _____ Book: _____

Writing (5-7 minutes)

- • Sound Boxes
- • White Boards
- • Writing Sort
- • Dictation Sentences
- ✓ Response Sentences *Use a Comprehension Graphic Organizer.*

Guided Reading Level _____

DAY 4:

Fluency Building (5-7 minutes)

Include:
* *Previously read books*
* *Books from Level* _____
* *Phonics Books*

Word Study (8-10 minutes)

- ✓ Blending "E Patterns" Review *(Use the Blending Cards.)*
- • Picture/Sound Sort
- • Word Sorts –
  Group   Individual
- • Making Words Activity
- • Onset/Rime Activity
- ✓ Other: Dictation Sentences

<u>Dictation Sentences:</u>
1. *The beans in my garden grew two feet tall.*
2. *We will pack a treat to eat at the beach.*
3. *Mom puts meat and herbs in her stew.*

Guided Reading (8-10 minutes)

- ✓ Phonics Book: _____ Book: _____
- ✓ Guided Reading Level: _____ Book: _____

Writing (5-7 minutes)

- • Sound Boxes
- • White Boards
- • Writing Sort
- • Dictation Sentences
- ✓ Response Sentences *Use a Comprehension Graphic Organizer.*

©The Reading Teacher's Plan Book

Review Week 13: "I Patterns"
Use with activities on pages 317-319.

DAY 1:

Fluency Building (5-7 minutes)

Include:
*Previously read books
*Books from Level ____
*Phonics Books

Word Study (8-10 minutes)

✓ **Blending "I Patterns" Review** *(Use the Blending Cards.)*
- Picture/Sound Sort
- Word Sorts –
  Group   Individual
- **Making Words Activity**   *Make these words: (Use the letter cards.) stir, sir, sigh, sight, sit, pit, pie, tie, tin, pin, pine, pink, sink, sing, ring*
- Onset/Rime Activity
- Other: ____

Guided Reading (8-10 minutes)

✓ Phonics Book: ____ Book: ____
✓ Guided Reading Level: ____ Book: ____

Writing (5-7 minutes)

- Sound Boxes
- White Boards
- Writing Sort
- Dictation Sentences
✓ **Response Sentences** *Use a Comprehension Graphic Organizer.*

Guided Reading Level ____

DAY 2:

Fluency Building (5-7 minutes)

Include:
*Previously read books
*Books from Level ____
*Phonics Books

Word Study (8-10 minutes)

✓ **Blending "I Patterns" Review** *(Use the Blending Cards.)*
- Picture/Sound Sort
- Word Sorts –
  Group   Individual
- Making Words Activity
- Onset/Rime Activity
- **Other: Writing Sort**   *(Use words from the Blending Cards and the 3-Column Writing Sort.)*
  ir   ing   igh

Guided Reading (8-10 minutes)

✓ Phonics Book: ____ Book: ____
✓ Guided Reading Level: ____ Book: ____

Writing (5-7 minutes)

- Sound Boxes
- White Boards
- Writing Sort
- Dictation Sentences
✓ **Response Sentences** *Use a Comprehension Graphic Organizer*

©The Reading Teacher's Plan Book

Review Week 13: "I Patterns" (cont.)
Use with activities on pages 317-319.

DAY 3:

Fluency Building (5-7 minutes)

Include:
- *Previously read books*
- *Books from Level ____*
- *Phonics Books*

Word Study (8-10 minutes)

✓ **Blending "I Patterns" Review** *(Use the Blending Cards.)*
- Picture/Sound Sort
- Word Sorts –
  - Group   Individual
- Making Words Activity
- Onset/Rime Activity
✓ **Other: Word Hunt** *(Use the Word Windows and Writing Mats.)*

Guided Reading (8-10 minutes)

✓ Phonics Book: _____ Book: _____
✓ Guided Reading Level: _____ Book: _____

Writing (5-7 minutes)

- Sound Boxes
- White Boards
- Writing Sort
- Dictation Sentences
✓ **Response Sentences** *Use a Comprehension Graphic Organizer.*

Guided Reading Level ____

DAY 4:

Fluency Building (5-7 minutes)

Include:
- *Previously read books*
- *Books from Level ____*
- *Phonics Books*

Word Study (8-10 minutes)

✓ **Blending "I Patterns" Review** *(Use the Blending Cards.)*
- Picture/Sound Sort
- Word Sorts –
  - Group   Individual
- Making Words Activity
- Onset/Rime Activity
✓ **Other: Dictation Sentences**

<u>*Dictation Sentences:*</u>
1. The crickets were chirping all night.
2. Can I have pie for my birthday?
3. The birds like to sing in the morning.

Guided Reading (8-10 minutes)

✓ Phonics Book: _____ Book: _____
✓ Guided Reading Level: _____ Book: _____

Writing (5-7 minutes)

- Sound Boxes
- White Boards
- Writing Sort
- Dictation Sentences
✓ **Response Sentences** *Use a Comprehension Graphic Organizer.*

©The Reading Teacher's Plan Book

Review Week 14: "O Patterns"

Use with activities on pages 320-322.

DAY 1:

Fluency Building (5-7 minutes)

Include:
*Previously read books
*Books from Level _____
*Phonics Books

Word Study (8-10 minutes)

✓ **Blending "O Patterns" Review** *(Use the Blending Cards.)*
- Picture/Sound Sort Picture/Sound Sort
- Word Sorts –
  Group   Individual
✓ **Making Words Activity**

Make these words:
(Use the letter cards.)
grow, row, Roy, boy, bow, boat, goat, go, to, toy, tow, town, torn, worn

- Onset/Rime Activity
- Other: _____

Guided Reading (8-10 minutes)

✓ Phonics Book: _____ Book: _____
✓ Guided Reading Level: _____ Book: _____

Writing (5-7 minutes)

- Sound Boxes
- White Boards
- Writing Sort
- Dictation Sentences
✓ **Response Sentences** *Use a Comprehension Graphic Organizer.*

Guided Reading Level _____

DAY 2:

Fluency Building (5-7 minutes)

Include:
*Previously read books
*Books from Level _____
*Phonics Books

Word Study (8-10 minutes)

✓ **Blending "O Patterns" Review** *(Use the Blending Cards.)*
- Picture/Sound Sort
- Word Sorts –
  Group   Individual
- Making Words Activity
- Onset/Rime Activity
✓ **Other: Writing Sort**

(Use words from the Blending Cards and the 3-Column Writing Sort.)
<u>oi</u>   <u>ou</u>   <u>or</u>

Guided Reading (8-10 minutes)

✓ Phonics Book: _____ Book: _____
✓ Guided Reading Level: _____ Book: _____

Writing (5-7 minutes)

- Sound Boxes
- White Boards
- Writing Sort
- Dictation Sentences
✓ **Response Sentences** *Use a Comprehension Graphic Organizer.*

©The Reading Teacher's Plan Book

Review Week 14: "O Patterns" (cont.)
Use with activities on pages 320-322.

DAY 3:

Fluency Building (5-7 minutes)

Include:
* *Previously read books*
* *Books from Level* ____
* *Phonics Books*

Word Study (8-10 minutes)

✓ **Blending "O Patterns" Review** *(Use the Blending Cards.)*
* Picture/Sound Sort
* Word Sorts –
   * Group   Individual
* Making Words Activity
* Onset/Rime Activity
✓ Other: **Word Hunt** *(Use the Word Windows and Writing Mats.)*

Guided Reading (8-10 minutes)

✓ Phonics Book: ____ Book: ____
✓ Guided Reading Level: ____ Book: ____

Writing (5-7 minutes)

* Sound Boxes
* White Boards
* Writing Sort
* Dictation Sentences
✓ **Response Sentences** *Use a Comprehension Graphic Organizer.*

Guided Reading Level ____

DAY 4:

Fluency Building (5-7 minutes)

Include:
* *Previously read books*
* *Books from Level* ____
* *Phonics Books*

Word Study (8-10 minutes)

✓ **Blending "O Patterns" Review** *(Use the Blending Cards.)*
* Picture/Sound Sort
* Word Sorts –
   * Group   Individual
* Making Words Activity
* Onset/Rime Activity
✓ Other: **Dictation Sentences**

Dictation Sentences:
1. *The crowd shouted loudly for their team.*
2. *I wore my coat and mittens in the snow.*
3. *Boil the noodles for nine minutes.*

Guided Reading (8-10 minutes)

✓ Phonics Book: ____ Book: ____
✓ Guided Reading Level: ____ Book: ____

Writing (5-7 minutes)

* Sound Boxes
* White Boards
* Writing Sort
* Dictation Sentences
✓ **Response Sentences** *Use a Comprehension Graphic Organizer.*

©The Reading Teacher's Plan Book

Review Week 15: "U Patterns"
Use with activities on pages 323-326.

DAY 1:

Fluency Building
(5-7 minutes)

Include:
*Previously read books
*Books from Level _____
*Phonics Books

Word Study
(8-10 minutes)

✓ **Blending "U Patterns" Review** *(Use the Blending Cards.)*
 • Picture/Sound Sort
 • Word Sorts –
  Group   Individual
✓ **Making Words Activity**

Make these words:
(Use the letter cards.)
blue, clue, cue, cub, cube, tube, tub, but, bun, burn, turn

 • Onset/Rime Activity
 • Other: _____

Guided Reading
(8-10 minutes)

✓ Phonics Book: _____
✓ Guided Reading Level: _____ Book: _____

Writing
(5-7 minutes)

 • Sound Boxes
 • White Boards
 • Writing Sort
 • Dictation Sentences
✓ **Response Sentences** *Use a Comprehension Graphic Organizer.*

Guided Reading Level _____

DAY 2:

Fluency Building
(5-7 minutes)

Include:
*Previously read books
*Books from Level _____
*Phonics Books

Word Study
(8-10 minutes)

✓ **Blending "U Patterns" Review** *(Use the Blending Cards.)*
 • Picture/Sound Sort
 • Word Sorts –
  Group   Individual
 • Making Words Activity
 • Onset/Rime Activity
✓ **Other: Writing Sort**

(Use words from the Blending Cards and the 3-Column Writing Sort.)

 <u>ue</u>   <u>u-e</u>
 <u>ur</u>

Guided Reading
(8-10 minutes)

✓ Phonics Book: _____
✓ Guided Reading Level: _____ Book: _____

Writing
(5-7 minutes)

 • Sound Boxes
 • White Boards
 • Writing Sort
 • Dictation Sentences
✓ **Response Sentences** *Use a Comprehension Graphic Organizer.*

©The Reading Teacher's Plan Book

Review Week 15: "U Patterns" (cont.)
Use with activities on pages 323-326.

DAY 3:

Fluency Building (5-7 minutes)

Include:
*Previously read books
*Books from Level ____
*Phonics Books

Word Study (8-10 minutes)

✓ Blending "U Patterns" Review *(Use the Blending Cards.)*
- Picture/Sound Sort
- Word Sorts –
  Group   Individual
- Making Words Activity
- Onset/Rime Activity
✓ Other: **Word Hunt** *(Use Word Hunt Cube, Mats, and bingo chips.)*

Guided Reading (8-10 minutes)

✓ Phonics Book: _____ Book: _____
✓ Guided Reading Level: _____ Book: _____

Writing (5-7 minutes)

- Sound Boxes
- White Boards
- Writing Sort
- Dictation Sentences
✓ **Response Sentences** *Use a Comprehension Graphic Organizer.*

Guided Reading Level ____

DAY 4:

Fluency Building (5-7 minutes)

Include:
*Previously read books
*Books from Level ____
*Phonics Books

Word Study (8-10 minutes)

✓ Blending "U Patterns" Review *(Use the Blending Cards.)*
- Picture/Sound Sort
- Word Sorts –
  Group   Individual
- Making Words Activity
- Onset/Rime Activity
✓ Other: **Dictation Sentences**

<u>Dictation Sentences:</u>
1. I will get a new swimming suit in June.
2. Turn around at the curb.
3. The glue was spurting out of the bottle.

Guided Reading (8-10 minutes)

✓ Phonics Book: _____ Book: _____
✓ Guided Reading Level: _____ Book: _____

Writing (5-7 minutes)

- Sound Boxes
- White Boards
- Writing Sort
- Dictation Sentences
✓ **Response Sentences** *Use a Comprehension Graphic Organizer.*

©The Reading Teacher's Plan Book

ADVANCED WEEKS MATERIALS LIST

Advanced Week 1: Syllabication – Double Consonants (Use the Breaking Words into Syllables Chart, p. 399.)
    Double Consonants Lesson Plan
    Double Consonants Group Word Sort Cards, pgs. 327-328
    Double Consonants Syllable Match-Up Cards, pgs. 329-330
    3-Column Writing Sort, p. 381
    Comprehension Strategy Chart, p. 400
    Comprehension Graphic Organizers, pgs. 385-390

Advanced Week 2: Syllabication – Consonant + le (Use the Syllable Patterns Chart, p. 398.)
    Consonant + le Lesson Plan
    Consonant + le Group Word Sort Cards, pgs. 331-332
    Consonant + le Syllable Match-Up Cards, pgs. 333-334
    Consonant + le Individual Sort Cards, p. 335
    3-Column Writing Sort, p. 381
    Comprehension Strategy Chart, p. 400
    Comprehension Graphic Organizers, pgs. 385-390

Advanced Week 3: Syllabication – Suffixes (Use the Breaking Words into Syllables Chart, p. 399.)
    Suffixes Lesson Plan
    Suffixes Group Word Sort Cards, pgs. 336-337
    Suffixes Word Hunt Cube, Mats, & Bingo Chips, pgs. 338-339
    Suffixes Individual Sort Cards, p. 340
    Comprehension Strategy Chart, p. 400
    Comprehension Graphic Organizers, pgs. 385-390

Advanced Week 4: Syllabication – Prefixes (Use the Breaking Words into Syllables Chart, p. 399.)
    Prefixes Lesson Plan
    Prefixes Group Word Sort Cards, pgs. 341-342
    Prefixes Word Hunt Cube, Mats, and Bingo Chips, pgs. 343-344
    Prefixes Individual Sort Cards, p. 345
    3-Column Writing Sort, p. 381
    Comprehension Strategy Chart, p. 400
    Comprehension Graphic Organizers, pgs. 385-390

Advanced Week 5: Syllabication – Closed Syllables (Use the Syllable Patterns Chart, p. 398.)
    Closed Syllables Lesson Plan
    Closed Syllables Group Sort Cards, pgs. 346-347
    Closed Syllables Syllable Match-Up Cards, pgs. 348-349

©The Reading Teacher's Plan Book

Closed Syllables Individual Sort Cards, p. 350
Comprehension Strategy Chart, p. 400
Comprehension Graphic Organizers, pgs. 385-390

Advanced Week 6: Syllabication – Open Syllables (Use the Syllable Patterns Chart, p. 398.)
Open Syllables Lesson Plan
Open Syllables Group Sort Cards, pgs. 351-352
Open Syllables Syllable Match-Up Cards, pgs. 353-354
Open Syllables Individual Sort Cards, p. 355
2-Column Writing Sort, p. 380
Comprehension Strategy Chart, p. 400
Comprehension Graphic Organizers, pgs. 385-390

Advanced Week 7: Syllabication – Silent E Pattern (Use the Syllable Patterns Chart, p. 398.)
Silent E Pattern Lesson Plan
Silent E Pattern Group Sort Cards, pgs. 356-357
Silent E Pattern Syllable Match-Up Cards, pgs. 358-359
Silent E Pattern Individual Sort Cards, p. 360
Comprehension Strategy Chart, p. 400
Comprehension Graphic Organizers, pgs. 385-390

Advanced Week 8: Syllabication – Vowel Team Patterns (Use the Syllable Patterns Chart, p. 398.)
Vowel Team Patterns Lesson Plan
Vowel Team Patterns Group Sort Cards, pgs. 361-362
Vowel Team Patterns Syllable Match-Up Cards, pgs. 363-364
Vowel Team Patterns Word Hunt Cube, Mats, & Bingo Chips, pgs. 365-366
Vowel Team Patterns Individual Sort Cards, p. 367
Comprehension Strategy Chart, p. 400
Comprehension Graphic Organizers, pgs. 385-390

Advanced Week 9: Syllabication – Bossy R Patterns (Use the Syllable Patterns Chart, p. 398.)
Bossy R Patterns Lesson Plan
Bossy R Patterns Group Sort Cards, pgs. 368-369
Bossy R Patterns Syllable Match-Up Cards, pgs. 370-371
Bossy R Patterns Individual Sort Cards, p. 372
3-Column Writing Sort, p. 381
Comprehension Strategy Chart, p. 400
Comprehension Graphic Organizers, pgs. 385-390

Advanced Week 10: Syllabication – Dividing Words into Syllables (Use the Breaking Words into Syllables Chart, p. 399)

    Dividing Words into Syllables Lesson Plan
    Dividing Words into Syllables Group Sort Cards, pgs. 373-374
    Dividing Words into Syllables Word Hunt Cube, Mats, & Bingo Chips, pgs. 375-376
    Word Windows, pgs. 383-384
    Dividing Words into Syllables Writing Mats, p. 377
    Dividing Words into Syllables Individual Sort Cards, p. 378
    Comprehension Strategy Chart, p. 400
    Comprehension Graphic Organizers, pgs. 385-390

Advanced Week 1: Syllabication – Double Consonants
Use with activities on pages 327-330.

DAY 1:

**Fluency Building
(5-7 minutes)**

☐ Reread previously read books
☐ Read new books on an Independent Level – Level ____
☐ Timed Fluency Passage

**Word Study
(8-10 minutes)**

✓ *Review Breaking Words into Syllables Chart (#4)*
✓ *Blending* **Double Consonant Words** *(Use Group Word Sort Cards.)*
✓ **Word Sorts – Double Consonant Words**
- Word Sorts – Group   Individual
- Making Words Activity   Syllable Match-Up
- Making Words
✓ Writing Sort
- Dictation Sentences
- Other:

**Guided Reading: Comprehension and Writing
(15 minutes)**

Guided Reading Level: ____
Book: ____

✓ Review Strategy Chart
✓ Preview the story
  ✓ What I already know
  ✓ Questions or Predictions – what might happen, what I might learn
✓ Read today's portion of the story
✓ Use Strategy Chart – start with checking predictions or questions
✓ Graphic Organizer or Written Response

Guided Reading Level ____

DAY 2:

**Fluency Building
(5-7 minutes)**

☐ Reread previously read books
☐ Read new books on an Independent Level – Level ____
☐ Timed Fluency Passage

**Word Study
(8-10 minutes)**

✓ *Review Breaking Words into Syllables Chart (#4)*
✓ *Blending* **Double Consonant Words** *(Use Group Word Sort Cards.)*
- Word Sorts –
  Group   Individual
- Making Words Activity   Syllable Match-Up
- Making Words
✓ **Writing Sort**   *(Use words from the Group Sort Cards and the 3-Column Writing Sort.)*
- Dictation Sentences   double t   double n   double p
- Other:

**Guided Reading: Comprehension and Writing
(15 minutes)**

Guided Reading Level: ____
Book: ____

✓ Review Strategy Chart
✓ Preview the story
  ✓ What I already know
  ✓ Questions or Predictions – what might happen, what I might learn
✓ Read today's portion of the story
✓ Use Strategy Chart – start with checking predictions or questions
✓ Graphic Organizer or Written Response

©The Reading Teacher's Plan Book

Advanced Week 1: Syllabication – Double Consonants (cont.)
Use with activities on pages 327-330.

DAY 3:

Fluency Building (5-7 minutes)

☐ Reread previously read books
☐ Read new books on an Independent Level – Level _____
☐ Timed Fluency Passage

Word Study (8-10 minutes)

✓ *Review Breaking Words into Syllables Chart (#4)*
✓ Blending **Double Consonant Words** *(Use Group Word Sort Cards.)*
- Word Sorts –
    Group   Individual
- **Making Words Activity** *(Use the Syllable Match-Up Cards.)*
    Making Words   **Syllable Match-Up**
- Writing Sort
- Dictation Sentences
- Other: _____

Guided Reading: Comprehension and Writing (15 minutes)

Guided Reading Level: _____
Book: _____

✓ Review Strategy Chart
✓ Preview the story
  ✓ What I already know
  ✓ Questions or Predictions – what might happen, what I might learn
✓ Read today's portion of the story
✓ Use Strategy Chart – start with checking predictions or questions
✓ Graphic Organizer or Written Response

Guided Reading Level _____

DAY 4:

Fluency Building (5-7 minutes)

☐ Reread previously read books
☐ Read new books on an Independent Level – Level _____
☐ Timed Fluency Passage

Word Study (8-10 minutes)

✓ *Review Breaking Words into Syllables Chart (#4)*
✓ Blending **Double Consonant Words** *(Use Group Word Sort Cards.)*
- Word Sorts –
    Group   Individual
- Making Words Activity
    Making Words
- Writing Sort
- **Dictation Sentences**
- Other: _____

Dictation Sentences:
1. *Come see our new litter of kittens!*
2. *Can we dig a tunnel in the sand?*
3. *Mix the cake batter a little longer.*

Guided Reading: Comprehension and Writing (15 minutes)

Guided Reading Level: _____
Book: _____

✓ Review Strategy Chart
✓ Preview the story
  ✓ What I already know
  ✓ Questions or Predictions – what might happen, what I might learn
✓ Read today's portion of the story
✓ Use Strategy Chart – start with checking predictions or questions
✓ Graphic Organizer or Written Response

©The Reading Teacher's Plan Book

Advanced Week 2: Syllabication – Consonant + le
Use with activities on pages 331-335.

DAY 1:

Fluency Building (5-7 minutes)

- ☐ Reread previously read books
- ☐ Read new books on an Independent Level – Level _____
- ☐ Timed Fluency Passage

Word Study (8-10 minutes)

- ✓ *Review Syllable Patterns Chart (Pattern #6)*
- ✓ **Blending Consonant + le Words** *(Use Group Word Sort Cards.)*
- ✓ Word Sorts – **ble, gle, tle words**
  - Group   Individual
- • Making Words Activity   Syllable Match-Up
  - Making Words
  - Writing Sort
- • Dictation Sentences
- • Other:

Guided Reading: Comprehension and Writing (15 minutes)

Guided Reading Level: _____
Book: _____

- ✓ Review Strategy Chart
- ✓ Preview the story
  - ✓ What I already know
  - ✓ Questions or Predictions – what might happen, what I might learn
- ✓ Read today's portion of the story
- ✓ Use Strategy Chart – start with checking predictions or questions
- ✓ Graphic Organizer or Written Response

Guided Reading Level _____

DAY 2:

Fluency Building (5-7 minutes)

- ☐ Reread previously read books
- ☐ Read new books on an Independent Level – Level _____
- ☐ Timed Fluency Passage

Word Study (8-10 minutes)

- ✓ *Review Syllable Patterns Chart (Pattern #6)*
- ✓ **Blending Consonant + le Words** *(Use Group Word Sort Cards.)*
- • Word Sorts –
  - Group   Individual
- ✓ **Making Words Activity** *(Use the Syllable Match-Up Cards.)*
  - Making Words   **Syllable Match-Up**
  - Writing Sort
- • Dictation Sentences
- • Other:

Guided Reading: Comprehension and Writing (15 minutes)

Guided Reading Level: _____
Book: _____

- ✓ Review Strategy Chart
- ✓ Preview the story
  - ✓ What I already know
  - ✓ Questions or Predictions – what might happen, what I might learn
- ✓ Read today's portion of the story
- ✓ Use Strategy Chart – start with checking predictions or questions
- ✓ Graphic Organizer or Written Response

©The Reading Teacher's Plan Book

Advanced Week 2: Syllabication – Consonant + le (cont.)
Use with activities on pages 331-335.

DAY 3:

Fluency Building (5-7 minutes)

☐ Reread previously read books
☐ Read new books on an Independent Level – Level _____
☐ Timed Fluency Passage

Word Study (8-10 minutes)

✓ *Review Syllable Patterns Chart (Pattern #6)*
✓ *Blending Consonant + le Words (Use Group Word Sort Cards.)*
• Word Sorts –
  Group   Individual
• Making Words Activity
• Making Words   Syllable Match-Up
✓ Writing Sort   *(Use words from the Group Sort Cards and the 3-Column Writing Sort.)*
• Dictation Sentences   -tle   -ble   -gle
• Other:

Guided Reading: Comprehension and Writing (15 minutes)

Guided Reading Level: _____
Book: _____

✓ Review Strategy Chart
✓ Preview the story
  ✓ What I already know
  ✓ Questions or Predictions – what might happen, what I might learn
✓ Read today's portion of the story
✓ Use Strategy Chart – start with checking predictions or questions
✓ Graphic Organizer or Written Response

Guided Reading Level _____

DAY 4:

Fluency Building (5-7 minutes)

☐ Reread previously read books
☐ Read new books on an Independent Level – Level _____
☐ Timed Fluency Passage

Word Study (8-10 minutes)

✓ *Review Syllable Patterns Chart (Pattern #6)*
✓ *Blending Consonant + le Words (Use Group Word Sort Cards.)*
✓ *Word Sorts – Consonant + le Words*
  Group   Individual *(Use Individual Sort Cards.)*
• Making Words Activity
• Making Words   Syllable Match-Up
• Writing Sort
• Dictation Sentences
• Other:

Guided Reading: Comprehension and Writing (15 minutes)

Guided Reading Level: _____
Book: _____

✓ Review Strategy Chart
✓ Preview the story
  ✓ What I already know
  ✓ Questions or Predictions – what might happen, what I might learn
✓ Read today's portion of the story
✓ Use Strategy Chart – start with checking predictions or questions
✓ Graphic Organizer or Written Response

©The Reading Teacher's Plan Book

Advanced Week 3: Syllabication – Suffixes
Use with activities on pages 336-340.

DAY 1:

Fluency Building
(5-7 minutes)

- ☐ Reread previously read books
- ☐ Read new books on an Independent Level – Level _____
- ☐ Timed Fluency Passage

Word Study
(8-10 minutes)

- ✓ *Review Breaking Words into Syllables Chart (#1)*
- ✓ *Blending* <u>*Suffixes*</u> *(Use Group Word Sort Cards.)*
- ✓ <u>Word Sorts</u> – <u>Suffixes</u>
  - **Group**   Individual
- • Making Words Activity
- • Making Words   Syllable Match-Up
- • Writing Sort
- • Dictation Sentences
- • Other: _____

Guided Reading: Comprehension and Writing
(15 minutes)

Guided Reading Level: _____
Book: _____

- ✓ Review Strategy Chart
- ✓ Preview the story
  - ✓ What I already know
  - ✓ Questions or Predictions – what might happen, what I might learn
- ✓ Read today's portion of the story
- ✓ Use Strategy Chart – start with checking predictions or questions
- ✓ Graphic Organizer or Written Response

Guided Reading Level _____

DAY 2:

Fluency Building
(5-7 minutes)

- ☐ Reread previously read books
- ☐ Read new books on an Independent Level – Level _____
- ☐ Timed Fluency Passage

Word Study
(8-10 minutes)

- ✓ *Review Breaking Words into Syllables Chart (#1)*
- ✓ *Blending* <u>*Suffixes*</u> *(Use Group Word Sort Cards.)*
- • Word Sorts –
  - Group   Individual
- • Making Words Activity
- • Making Words   Syllable Match-Up
- • Writing Sort
- • Dictation Sentences
- ✓ **Other:** <u>**Word Hunt**</u> *(Use Word Hunt Cube, Mats, and bingo chips)*

Guided Reading: Comprehension and Writing
(15 minutes)

Guided Reading Level: _____
Book: _____

- ✓ Review Strategy Chart
- ✓ Preview the story
  - ✓ What I already know
  - ✓ Questions or Predictions – what might happen, what I might learn
- ✓ Read today's portion of the story
- ✓ Use Strategy Chart – start with checking predictions or questions
- ✓ Graphic Organizer or Written Response

©The Reading Teacher's Plan Book

Advanced Week 3: Syllabication – Suffixes (cont.)
Use with activities on pages 336-340.

DAY 3:

Fluency Building (5-7 minutes)

☐ Reread previously read books
☐ Read new books on an Independent Level – Level _____
☐ Timed Fluency Passage

Word Study (8-10 minutes)

✓ *Review Breaking Words into Syllables Chart (#1)*
✓ **Blending Suffixes** *(Use Group Word Sort Cards.)*
• Word Sorts –
   Group   Individual
• Making Words Activity
• Making Words   **Dictation Sentences:**
• Writing Sort   *1. The rock rolled quickly down the hill.*
✓ **Dictation Sentences** *2. We will be careful when crossing the street.*
• Other: *3. Our soccer game was scoreless.*

Guided Reading: Comprehension and Writing (15 minutes)

Guided Reading Level: _____
Book: _____

✓ Review Strategy Chart
✓ Preview the story
   ✓ What I already know
   ✓ Questions or Predictions – what might happen, what I might learn
✓ Read today's portion of the story
✓ Use Strategy Chart – start with checking predictions or questions
✓ Graphic Organizer or Written Response

Guided Reading Level _____

DAY 4:

Fluency Building (5-7 minutes)

☐ Reread previously read books
☐ Read new books on an Independent Level – Level _____
☐ Timed Fluency Passage

Word Study (8-10 minutes)

✓ *Review Breaking Words into Syllables Chart (#1)*
✓ **Blending Suffixes** *(Use Group Word Sort Cards.)*
✓ **Word Sorts – Suffixes**
   Group   **Individual** *(Use Individual Sort Cards.)*
• Making Words Activity
• Making Words   Syllable Match-Up
• Writing Sort
• Dictation Sentences
• Other:

Guided Reading: Comprehension and Writing (15 minutes)

Guided Reading Level: _____
Book: _____

✓ Review Strategy Chart
✓ Preview the story
   ✓ What I already know
   ✓ Questions or Predictions – what might happen, what I might learn
✓ Read today's portion of the story
✓ Use Strategy Chart – start with checking predictions or questions
✓ Graphic Organizer or Written Response

©The Reading Teacher's Plan Book

Advanced Week 4: Syllabication – Prefixes
Use with activities on pages 341-345.

DAY 1:

Fluency Building (5-7 minutes)

☐ Reread previously read books
☐ Read new books on an Independent Level – Level _____
☐ Timed Fluency Passage

Word Study (8-10 minutes)

✓ *Review Breaking Words into Syllables Chart (#2)*
✓ *Blending **Prefixes** (Use Group Word Sort Cards.)*
✓ **Word Sorts – Prefixes**
  - **Group**   Individual
- Making Words Activity
- Making Words   Syllable Match-Up
- Writing Sort
- Dictation Sentences
- Other:

Guided Reading: Comprehension and Writing (15 minutes)

Guided Reading Level: _____
Book: _____

✓ Review Strategy Chart
✓ Preview the story
  ✓ What I already know
  ✓ Questions or Predictions – what might happen, what I might learn
✓ Read today's portion of the story
✓ Use Strategy Chart – start with checking predictions or questions
✓ Graphic Organizer or Written Response

Guided Reading Level _____

DAY 2:

Fluency Building (5-7 minutes)

☐ Reread previously read books
☐ Read new books on an Independent Level – Level _____
☐ Timed Fluency Passage

Word Study (8-10 minutes)

✓ *Review Breaking Words into Syllables Chart (#2)*
✓ *Blending **Prefixes** (Use Group Word Sort Cards.)*
- Word Sorts –
  - Group   Individual
- Making Words Activity
- Making Words   Syllable Match-Up
- Writing Sort
- Dictation Sentences
✓ **Other: Word Hunt** *(Use Word Hunt Cube, Mats, and bingo chips)*

Guided Reading: Comprehension and Writing (15 minutes)

Guided Reading Level: _____
Book: _____

✓ Review Strategy Chart
✓ Preview the story
  ✓ What I already know
  ✓ Questions or Predictions – what might happen, what I might learn
✓ Read today's portion of the story
✓ Use Strategy Chart – start with checking predictions or questions
✓ Graphic Organizer or Written Response

©The Reading Teacher's Plan Book

Advanced Week 4: Syllabication – Prefixes (cont.)
Use with activities on pages 341-345.

DAY 3:

Fluency Building (5-7 minutes)

☐ Reread previously read books
☐ Read new books on an Independent Level – Level _____
☐ Timed Fluency Passage

Word Study (8-10 minutes)

- ✓ *Review Breaking Words into Syllables Chart (#2)*
- ✓ *Blending* **Prefixes** *(Use Group Word Sort Cards.)*
- • Word Sorts –
  - Group   Individual
- • Making Words Activity
- • Making Words   Syllable Match-Up
- ✓ **Writing Sort**   *(Use words from the Group Sort Cards and the 3-Column Writing Sort.)*
- • Dictation Sentences   mis-   re-   un-
- • Other:

Guided Reading: Comprehension and Writing (15 minutes)

Guided Reading Level: _____
Book: _____

- ✓ Review Strategy Chart
- ✓ Preview the story
  - ✓ What I already know
  - ✓ Questions or Predictions – what might happen, what I might learn
- ✓ Read today's portion of the story
- ✓ Use Strategy Chart – start with checking predictions or questions
- ✓ Graphic Organizer or Written Response

Guided Reading Level _____

DAY 4:

Fluency Building (5-7 minutes)

☐ Reread previously read books
☐ Read new books on an Independent Level – Level _____
☐ Timed Fluency Passage

Word Study (8-10 minutes)

- ✓ *Review Breaking Words into Syllables Chart (#2)*
- ✓ *Blending* **Prefixes** *(Use Group Word Sort Cards.)*
- ✓ **Word Sorts – Prefixes**
  - Group   **Individual** *(Use Individual Sort Cards.)*
- • Making Words Activity
- • Making Words   Syllable Match-Up
- • Writing Sort
- • Dictation Sentences
- • Other:

Guided Reading: Comprehension and Writing (15 minutes)

Guided Reading Level: _____
Book: _____

- ✓ Review Strategy Chart
- ✓ Preview the story
  - ✓ What I already know
  - ✓ Questions or Predictions – what might happen, what I might learn
- ✓ Read today's portion of the story
- ✓ Use Strategy Chart – start with checking predictions or questions
- ✓ Graphic Organizer or Written Response

©The Reading Teacher's Plan Book

Advanced Week 5: Syllabication – Closed Syllables
Use with activities on pages 346-350.

DAY 1:

Guided Reading Level _____

DAY 2:

Fluency Building (5-7 minutes)

- ☐ Reread previously read books
- ☐ Read new books on an Independent Level – Level _____
- ☐ Timed Fluency Passage

Word Study (8-10 minutes)

- ✓ *Review Syllable Patterns Chart (Pattern #1 – Contrast with Pattern #2)*
- ✓ **Blending Closed/Open Syllables** *(Use Group Word Sort Cards.)*
- ✓ **Word Sorts – Closed/Open Syllables**
  - Group   Individual
- • Making Words Activity
  - Making Words   Syllable Match-Up
- • Writing Sort
- • Dictation Sentences
- • Other:

Guided Reading: Comprehension and Writing (15 minutes)

Guided Reading Level: _____
Book: _____

- ✓ Review Strategy Chart
- ✓ Preview the story
  - ✓ What I already know
  - ✓ Questions or Predictions – what might happen, what I might learn
- ✓ Read today's portion of the story
- ✓ Use Strategy Chart – start with checking predictions or questions
- ✓ Graphic Organizer or Written Response

Fluency Building (5-7 minutes)

- ☐ Reread previously read books
- ☐ Read new books on an Independent Level – Level _____
- ☐ Timed Fluency Passage

Word Study (8-10 minutes)

- ✓ *Review Syllable Patterns Chart (Pattern #1 – Contrast with Pattern #2)*
- ✓ **Blending Closed/Open Syllables** *(Use Group Word Sort Cards.)*
- ✓ Word Sorts –
  - Group   Individual
- • **Making Words Activity** *(Use the Syllable Match-Up Cards.)*
  - Making Words   Syllable Match-Up
- • Writing Sort
- • Dictation Sentences
- • Other:

Guided Reading: Comprehension and Writing (15 minutes)

Guided Reading Level: _____
Book: _____

- ✓ Review Strategy Chart
- ✓ Preview the story
  - ✓ What I already know
  - ✓ Questions or Predictions – what might happen, what I might learn
- ✓ Read today's portion of the story
- ✓ Use Strategy Chart – start with checking predictions or questions
- ✓ Graphic Organizer or Written Response

©The Reading Teacher's Plan Book

Advanced Week 5: Syllabication – Closed Syllables (cont.)
Use with activities on pages 346-350.

DAY 3:

Fluency Building (5-7 minutes)

☐ Reread previously read books
☐ Read new books on an Independent Level – Level _____
☐ Timed Fluency Passage

Word Study (8-10 minutes)

✓ *Review Syllable Patterns Chart (Pattern #1 – Contrast with Pattern #2)*
✓ **Blending Closed/Open Syllables** (*Use Group Word Sort Cards.*)
- Word Sorts –
   Group   Individual
- Making Words Activity
- Making Words   ***Dictation Sentences:***
- Writing Sort   *1. Let's pack napkins in our picnic lunch.*
- **Dictation Sentences** *2. We go fishing in the river by our cabin.*
- Other: *3. I will paint this sunset for the art contest.*

Guided Reading: Comprehension and Writing (15 minutes)

Guided Reading Level: _____
Book: _____

✓ Review Strategy Chart
✓ Preview the story
   ✓ What I already know
   ✓ Questions or Predictions – what might happen, what I might learn
✓ Read today's portion of the story
✓ Use Strategy Chart – start with checking predictions or questions
✓ Graphic Organizer or Written Response

Guided Reading Level _____

DAY 4:

Fluency Building (5-7 minutes)

☐ Reread previously read books
☐ Read new books on an Independent Level – Level _____
☐ Timed Fluency Passage

Word Study (8-10 minutes)

✓ *Review Syllable Patterns Chart (Pattern #1 – Contrast with Pattern #2)*
✓ **Blending Closed/Open Syllables** (*Use Group Word Sort Cards.*)
✓ **Word Sorts – Closed/Open Syllables**   Individual (*Use Individual Sort Cards.*)
- Group
- Making Words Activity
- Making Words   Syllable Match-Up
- Writing Sort
- Dictation Sentences
- Other:

Guided Reading: Comprehension and Writing (15 minutes)

Guided Reading Level: _____
Book: _____

✓ Review Strategy Chart
✓ Preview the story
   ✓ What I already know
   ✓ Questions or Predictions – what might happen, what I might learn
✓ Read today's portion of the story
✓ Use Strategy Chart – start with checking predictions or questions
✓ Graphic Organizer or Written Response

©The Reading Teacher's Plan Book

Advanced Week 6: Syllabication – Open Syllables
Use with activities on pages 351-355.

DAY 1:

Fluency Building (5-7 minutes)

☐ Reread previously read books
☐ Read new books on an Independent Level – Level _____
☐ Timed Fluency Passage

Word Study (8-10 minutes)

✓ *Review Syllable Patterns Chart (Pattern #2 – Contrast with Pattern #1)*
✓ *Blending* <u>Open/Closed Syllables</u> *(Use Group Word Sort Cards.)*
✓ *Word Sorts –* <u>**Open Syllables**</u>
- **Group**   Individual
- Making Words Activity   Syllable Match-Up
- Making Words
- Writing Sort
- Dictation Sentences
- Other:

Guided Reading: Comprehension and Writing (15 minutes)

Guided Reading Level: _____
Book: _____

✓ Review Strategy Chart
✓ Preview the story
  ✓ What I already know
  ✓ Questions or Predictions – what might happen, what I might learn
✓ Read today's portion of the story
✓ Use Strategy Chart – start with checking predictions or questions
✓ Graphic Organizer or Written Response

Guided Reading Level _____

DAY 2:

Fluency Building (5-7 minutes)

☐ Reread previously read books
☐ Read new books on an Independent Level – Level _____
☐ Timed Fluency Passage

Word Study (8-10 minutes)

✓ *Review Syllable Patterns Chart (Pattern #2 – Contrast with Pattern #1)*
✓ *Blending* <u>Open/Closed Syllables</u> *(Use Group Word Sort Cards.)*
- Word Sorts –
- Group   Individual
- **Making Words Activity** *(Use the Syllable Match-Up Cards.)* <u>**Syllable Match-Up**</u>
- Making Words
- Writing Sort
- Dictation Sentences
- Other:

Guided Reading: Comprehension and Writing (15 minutes)

Guided Reading Level: _____
Book: _____

✓ Review Strategy Chart
✓ Preview the story
  ✓ What I already know
  ✓ Questions or Predictions – what might happen, what I might learn
✓ Read today's portion of the story
✓ Use Strategy Chart – start with checking predictions or questions
✓ Graphic Organizer or Written Response

©The Reading Teacher's Plan Book

Advanced Week 6: Syllabication – Open Syllables (cont.)
Use with activities on pages 351-355.

DAY 3:

Fluency Building (5-7 minutes)

☐ Reread previously read books
☐ Read new books on an Independent Level – Level _____
☐ Timed Fluency Passage

Word Study (8-10 minutes)

✓ *Review Syllable Patterns Chart (Pattern #2 – Contrast with Pattern #1)*
✓ *Blending Open/Closed Syllables (Use Group Word Sort Cards.)*
✓ Word Sorts –
   • Group   Individual
   • Making Words Activity
   • Making Words   Syllable Match-Up
✓ **Writing Sort**   *(Use words from the Group Sort Cards and the 2-Column Writing Sort.)*
   • Dictation Sentences   *open   closed*
   • Other:

Guided Reading: Comprehension and Writing (15 minutes)

Guided Reading Level: _____
Book: _____

✓ Review Strategy Chart
✓ Preview the story
   ✓ What I already know
   ✓ Questions or Predictions – what might happen, what I might learn
✓ Read today's portion of the story
✓ Use Strategy Chart – start with checking predictions or questions
✓ Graphic Organizer or Written Response

Guided Reading Level _____

DAY 4:

Fluency Building (5-7 minutes)

☐ Reread previously read books
☐ Read new books on an Independent Level – Level _____
☐ Timed Fluency Passage

Word Study (8-10 minutes)

✓ *Review Syllable Patterns Chart (Pattern #2 – Contrast with Pattern #1)*
✓ *Blending Open/Closed Syllables (Use Group Word Sort Cards.)*
✓ **Word Sorts – Open/Closed Syllables**
   • Group   **Individual** *(Use Individual Sort Cards.)*
   • Making Words Activity
   • Making Words   Syllable Match-Up
   • Writing Sort
   • Dictation Sentences
   • Other:

Guided Reading: Comprehension and Writing (15 minutes)

Guided Reading Level: _____
Book: _____

✓ Review Strategy Chart
✓ Preview the story
   ✓ What I already know
   ✓ Questions or Predictions – what might happen, what I might learn
✓ Read today's portion of the story
✓ Use Strategy Chart – start with checking predictions or questions
✓ Graphic Organizer or Written Response

©The Reading Teacher's Plan Book

Advanced Week 7: Syllabication – Silent E Pattern
Use with activities on pages 356-360.

Guided Reading Level _____

DAY 1: _____

Fluency Building (5-7 minutes)

- ☐ Reread previously read books
- ☐ Read new books on an Independent Level – Level _____
- ☐ Timed Fluency Passage

Word Study (8-10 minutes)

- ✓ *Review Syllable Patterns Chart (Pattern #3)*
- ✓ Blending <u>Silent E Pattern Syllables</u> *(Use Group Word Sort Cards.)*
- ✓ Word Sorts – <u>Silent E Pattern Syllables</u>
  - Group ___ Individual ___
- • Making Words Activity   Syllable Match-Up
- • Making Words
- • Writing Sort
- • Dictation Sentences
- • Other:

Guided Reading: Comprehension and Writing (15 minutes)

Guided Reading Level: _____
Book: _____

- ✓ Review Strategy Chart
- ✓ Preview the story
  - ✓ What I already know
  - ✓ Questions or Predictions – what might happen, what I might learn
- ✓ Read today's portion of the story
- ✓ Use Strategy Chart – start with checking predictions or questions
- ✓ Graphic Organizer or Written Response

DAY 2: _____

Fluency Building (5-7 minutes)

- ☐ Reread previously read books
- ☐ Read new books on an Independent Level – Level _____
- ☐ Timed Fluency Passage

Word Study (8-10 minutes)

- ✓ *Review Syllable Patterns Chart (Pattern #3)*
- ✓ Blending <u>Silent E Pattern Syllables</u> *(Use Group Word Sort Cards.)*
- • Word Sorts –
  - Group ___   Individual ___
- ✓ **Making Words Activity** *(Use the Syllable Match-Up Cards.)*   **Syllable Match-Up**
- • Making Words
- • Writing Sort
- • Dictation Sentences
- • Other:

Guided Reading: Comprehension and Writing (15 minutes)

Guided Reading Level: _____
Book: _____

- ✓ Review Strategy Chart
- ✓ Preview the story
  - ✓ What I already know
  - ✓ Questions or Predictions – what might happen, what I might learn
- ✓ Read today's portion of the story
- ✓ Use Strategy Chart – start with checking predictions or questions
- ✓ Graphic Organizer or Written Response

©The Reading Teacher's Plan Book

Advanced Week 7: Syllabication – Silent E Pattern (cont.)

Use with activities on pages 356-360.

DAY 3:

Fluency Building (5-7 minutes)

☐ Reread previously read books
☐ Read new books on an Independent Level – Level _____
☐ Timed Fluency Passage

Word Study (8-10 minutes)

✓ *Review Syllable Patterns Chart (Pattern #3)*
✓ **Blending Silent E Pattern Syllables** *(Use Group Word Sort Cards.)*
- Word Sorts –
    Group   Individual
- Making Words Activity
- Making Words   *Dictation Sentences:*
- Writing Sort   1. Help me locate the reptile house at the zoo.
- **Dictation Sentences**   2. My homework is in my notebook.
- Other: 3. Shall we play inside or outside today?

Guided Reading: Comprehension and Writing (15 minutes)

Guided Reading Level: _____
Book: _____

✓ Review Strategy Chart
✓ Preview the story
    ✓ What I already know
    ✓ Questions or Predictions – what might happen, what I might learn
✓ Read today's portion of the story
✓ Use Strategy Chart – start with checking predictions or questions
✓ Graphic Organizer or Written Response

Guided Reading Level _____

DAY 4:

Fluency Building (5-7 minutes)

☐ Reread previously read books
☐ Read new books on an Independent Level – Level _____
☐ Timed Fluency Passage

Word Study (8-10 minutes)

✓ *Review Syllable Patterns Chart (Pattern #3)*
✓ **Blending Silent E Pattern Syllables** *(Use Group Word Sort Cards.)*
✓ **Word Sorts – Silent E Pattern Syllables** Individual *(Use Individual Sort Cards.)*
- Group
- Making Words Activity
- Making Words   Syllable Match-Up
- Writing Sort
- Dictation Sentences
- Other:

Guided Reading: Comprehension and Writing (15 minutes)

Guided Reading Level: _____
Book: _____

✓ Review Strategy Chart
✓ Preview the story
    ✓ What I already know
    ✓ Questions or Predictions – what might happen, what I might learn
✓ Read today's portion of the story
✓ Use Strategy Chart – start with checking predictions or questions
✓ Graphic Organizer or Written Response

©The Reading Teacher's Plan Book

Advanced Week 8: Syllabication – Vowel Team Patterns
Use with activities on pages 361-367.

DAY 1: _____

Fluency Building (5-7 minutes)

- ☐ Reread previously read books
- ☐ Read new books on an Independent Level – Level _____
- ☐ Timed Fluency Passage

Word Study (8-10 minutes)

- ✓ *Review Syllable Patterns Chart (Pattern #4)*
- ✓ *Blending Vowel Team Pattern Syllables (Use Group Word Sort Cards.)*
- ✓ *Word Sorts – Vowel Team Pattern Syllables*
  - **Group**   Individual
- • Making Words Activity   Syllable Match-Up
- • Making Words
- • Writing Sort
- • Dictation Sentences
- • Other:

Guided Reading: Comprehension and Writing (15 minutes)

Guided Reading Level: _____
Book: _____

- ✓ Review Strategy Chart
- ✓ Preview the story
  - ✓ What I already know
  - ✓ Questions or Predictions – what might happen, what I might learn
- ✓ Read today's portion of the story
- ✓ Use Strategy Chart – start with checking predictions or questions
- ✓ Graphic Organizer or Written Response

Guided Reading Level _____

DAY 2: _____

Fluency Building (5-7 minutes)

- ☐ Reread previously read books
- ☐ Read new books on an Independent Level – Level _____
- ☐ Timed Fluency Passage

Word Study (8-10 minutes)

- ✓ *Review Syllable Patterns Chart (Pattern #4)*
- ✓ *Blending Vowel Team Pattern Syllables (Use Group Word Sort Cards.)*
- ✓ Word Sorts –
  - Group   Individual
- ✓ **Making Words Activity** (*Use the Syllable Match-Up Cards.*)
  - Making Words   **Syllable Match-Up**
- • Writing Sort
- • Dictation Sentences
- • Other:

Guided Reading: Comprehension and Writing (15 minutes)

Guided Reading Level: _____
Book: _____

- ✓ Review Strategy Chart
- ✓ Preview the story
  - ✓ What I already know
  - ✓ Questions or Predictions – what might happen, what I might learn
- ✓ Read today's portion of the story
- ✓ Use Strategy Chart – start with checking predictions or questions
- ✓ Graphic Organizer or Written Response

©The Reading Teacher's Plan Book

Advanced Week 8: Syllabication – Vowel Team Patterns (cont.)
Use with activities on pages 361-367.

Guided Reading Level ____

DAY 3:

Fluency Building (5-7 minutes)

- ☐ Reread previously read books
- ☐ Read new books on an Independent Level – Level ____
- ☐ Timed Fluency Passage

Word Study (8-10 minutes)

- ✓ *Review Syllable Patterns Chart (Pattern #4)*
- ✓ *Blending Vowel Team Pattern Syllables (Use Group Word Sort Cards.)*
- • Word Sorts –
   Group   Individual
- • Making Words Activity
- • Making Words   Syllable Match-Up
- • Writing Sort
- • Dictation Sentences
- ✓ **Other: Word Hunt** *(Use Word Hunt Cube, Mats, and bingo chips)*

Guided Reading: Comprehension and Writing (15 minutes)

Guided Reading Level: ____
Book: ____

- ✓ Review Strategy Chart
- ✓ Preview the story
   - ✓ What I already know
   - ✓ Questions or Predictions – what might happen, what I might learn
- ✓ Read today's portion of the story
- ✓ Use Strategy Chart – start with checking predictions or questions
- ✓ Graphic Organizer or Written Response

DAY 4:

Fluency Building (5-7 minutes)

- ☐ Reread previously read books
- ☐ Read new books on an Independent Level – Level ____
- ☐ Timed Fluency Passage

Word Study (8-10 minutes)

- ✓ *Review Syllable Patterns Chart (Pattern #4)*
- ✓ *Blending Vowel Team Pattern Syllables (Use Group Word Sort Cards.)*
- ✓ **Word Sorts – Vowel Team Pattern Syllables**
   Group   **Individual** *(Use Individual Sort Cards.)*
- • Making Words Activity
- • Making Words   Syllable Match-Up
- • Writing Sort
- • Dictation Sentences
- • Other:

Guided Reading: Comprehension and Writing (15 minutes)

Guided Reading Level: ____
Book: ____

- ✓ Review Strategy Chart
- ✓ Preview the story
   - ✓ What I already know
   - ✓ Questions or Predictions – what might happen, what I might learn
- ✓ Read today's portion of the story
- ✓ Use Strategy Chart – start with checking predictions or questions
- ✓ Graphic Organizer or Written Response

©The Reading Teacher's Plan Book

Advanced Week 9: Syllabication – Bossy R Patterns
Use with activities on pages 368-372.

DAY 1: _____

Fluency Building
(5-7 minutes)

☐ Reread previously read books
☐ Read new books on an Independent Level – Level ____
☐ Timed Fluency Passage

Word Study
(8-10 minutes)

✓ *Review Syllable Patterns Chart (Pattern #5)*
✓ **Blending Bossy R Pattern Syllables** *(Use Group Word Sort Cards.)*
✓ **Word Sorts – Bossy R Pattern Syllables**
  • Group   Individual
  • Making Words Activity   Syllable Match-Up
  • Making Words
  • Writing Sort
  • Dictation Sentences
  • Other:

Guided Reading: Comprehension and Writing
(15 minutes)

Guided Reading Level: _____
Book: _____

✓ Review Strategy Chart
✓ Preview the story
  ✓ What I already know
  ✓ Questions or Predictions – what might happen, what I might learn
✓ Read today's portion of the story
✓ Use Strategy Chart – start with checking predictions or questions
✓ Graphic Organizer or Written Response

Guided Reading Level _____

DAY 2: _____

Fluency Building
(5-7 minutes)

☐ Reread previously read books
☐ Read new books on an Independent Level – Level ____
☐ Timed Fluency Passage

Word Study
(8-10 minutes)

✓ *Review Syllable Patterns Chart (Pattern #5)*
✓ **Blending Bossy R Pattern Syllables** *(Use Group Word Sort Cards.)*
• Word Sorts –
  Group   Individual
✓ **Making Words Activity** *(Use the Syllable Match-Up Cards.)*
  • Making Words   Syllable Match-Up
  • Writing Sort
  • Dictation Sentences
  • Other:

Guided Reading: Comprehension and Writing
(15 minutes)

Guided Reading Level: _____
Book: _____

✓ Review Strategy Chart
✓ Preview the story
  ✓ What I already know
  ✓ Questions or Predictions – what might happen, what I might learn
✓ Read today's portion of the story
✓ Use Strategy Chart – start with checking predictions or questions
✓ Graphic Organizer or Written Response

©The Reading Teacher's Plan Book

Advanced Week 9: Syllabication – Bossy R Patterns (cont.)
Use with activities on pages 368-372.

DAY 3:

Fluency Building (5-7 minutes)

☐ Reread previously read books
☐ Read new books on an Independent Level – Level _____
☐ Timed Fluency Passage

Word Study (8-10 minutes)

✓ *Review Syllable Patterns Chart (Pattern #5)*
✓ *Blending Bossy R Pattern Syllables (Use Group Word Sort Cards.)*
• Word Sorts –
  Group   Individual
• Making Words Activity
  Making Words   Syllable Match-Up
✓ Writing Sort   *(Use words from the Group Sort Cards and the 3-Column Writing Sort.)*
• Dictation Sentences   ar   ur   or
• Other:

Guided Reading: Comprehension and Writing (15 minutes)

Guided Reading Level: _____
Book: _____

✓ Review Strategy Chart
✓ Preview the story
  ✓ What I already know
  ✓ Questions or Predictions – what might happen, what I might learn
✓ Read today's portion of the story
✓ Use Strategy Chart – start with checking predictions or questions
✓ Graphic Organizer or Written Response

Guided Reading Level _____

DAY 4:

Fluency Building (5-7 minutes)

☐ Reread previously read books
☐ Read new books on an Independent Level – Level _____
☐ Timed Fluency Passage

Word Study (8-10 minutes)

✓ *Review Syllable Patterns Chart (Pattern #5)*
✓ *Blending Bossy R Pattern Syllables (Use Group Word Sort Cards.)*
✓ *Word Sorts – Bossy R Pattern Syllables*
  Group   Individual *(Use Individual Sort Cards.)*
• Making Words Activity
  Making Words   Syllable Match-Up
• Writing Sort
• Dictation Sentences
• Other:

Guided Reading: Comprehension and Writing (15 minutes)

Guided Reading Level: _____
Book: _____

✓ Review Strategy Chart
✓ Preview the story
  ✓ What I already know
  ✓ Questions or Predictions – what might happen, what I might learn
✓ Read today's portion of the story
✓ Use Strategy Chart – start with checking predictions or questions
✓ Graphic Organizer or Written Response

©The Reading Teacher's Plan Book

Advanced Week 10: Syllabication – Dividing Words into Syllables
Use with activities on pages 373-378.

DAY 1:

Fluency Building (5-7 minutes)

- ☐ Reread previously read books
- ☐ Read new books on an Independent Level – Level _____
- ☐ Timed Fluency Passage

Word Study (8-10 minutes)

- ✓ *Review Breaking Words into Syllables Chart*
- ✓ *Blending Dividing Words into Syllables* (*Use Group Word Sort Cards.*)
- ✓ **Word Sorts – Dividing Words into Syllables**
  - **Group**   Individual
- • Making Words Activity
- • Making Words   Syllable Match-Up
- • Writing Sort
- • Dictation Sentences
- • Other: _____

Guided Reading: Comprehension and Writing (15 minutes)

Guided Reading Level: _____
Book: _____

- ✓ Review Strategy Chart
- ✓ Preview the story
  - ✓ What I already know
  - ✓ Questions or Predictions – what might happen, what I might learn
- ✓ Read today's portion of the story
- ✓ Use Strategy Chart – start with checking predictions or questions
- ✓ Graphic Organizer or Written Response

Guided Reading Level _____

DAY 2:

Fluency Building (5-7 minutes)

- ☐ Reread previously read books
- ☐ Read new books on an Independent Level – Level _____
- ☐ Timed Fluency Passage

Word Study (8-10 minutes)

- ✓ *Review Breaking Words into Syllables Chart*
- ✓ *Blending Dividing Words into Syllables* (*Use Group Word Sort Cards.*)
- • Word Sorts –
  - Group   Individual
- • Making Words Activity
- • Making Words   Syllable Match-Up
- • Writing Sort
- • Dictation Sentences
- ✓ **Other: Word Hunt** (*Use Word Hunt Cube, Mats, and bingo chips*)

Guided Reading: Comprehension and Writing (15 minutes)

Guided Reading Level: _____
Book: _____

- ✓ Review Strategy Chart
- ✓ Preview the story
  - ✓ What I already know
  - ✓ Questions or Predictions – what might happen, what I might learn
- ✓ Read today's portion of the story
- ✓ Use Strategy Chart – start with checking predictions or questions
- ✓ Graphic Organizer or Written Response

©The Reading Teacher's Plan Book

Advanced Week 10: Syllabication – Dividing Words into Syllables (cont.)   *Guided Reading Level* ___

Use with activities on pages 373-378.

DAY 3:   DAY 4:

Fluency Building (5-7 minutes)

- ☐ Reread previously read books
- ☐ Read new books on an Independent Level – Level ___
- ☐ Timed Fluency Passage

Word Study (8-10 minutes)

- ✓ *Review Breaking Words into Syllables Chart*
- ✓ *Blending Dividing Words into Syllables* (*Use Group Word Sort Cards.*)
- • Word Sorts –
      Group   Individual
- • Making Words Activity
- • Making Words   Syllable Match-Up
- • Writing Sort
- • Dictation Sentences
- ✓ **Other:** *Word Hunt* (*Use the Word Windows and Writing Mats.*)

Guided Reading: Comprehension and Writing (15 minutes)

Guided Reading Level: ___
Book: ___

- ✓ Review Strategy Chart
- ✓ Preview the story
  - ✓ What I already know
  - ✓ Questions or Predictions – what might happen, what I might learn
- ✓ Read today's portion of the story
- ✓ Use Strategy Chart – start with checking predictions or questions
- ✓ Graphic Organizer or Written Response

Fluency Building (5-7 minutes)

- ☐ Reread previously read books
- ☐ Read new books on an Independent Level – Level ___
- ☐ Timed Fluency Passage

Word Study (8-10 minutes)

- ✓ *Review Breaking Words into Syllables Chart*
- ✓ *Blending Dividing Words into Syllables* (*Use Group Word Sort Cards.*)
- ✓ **Word Sorts – Dividing Words into Syllables**
      Group   **Individual** (*Use Individual Sort Cards.*)
- • Making Words Activity
- • Making Words   Syllable Match-Up
- • Writing Sort
- • Dictation Sentences
- • Other:

Guided Reading: Comprehension and Writing (15 minutes)

Guided Reading Level: ___
Book: ___

- ✓ Review Strategy Chart
- ✓ Preview the story
  - ✓ What I already know
  - ✓ Questions or Predictions – what might happen, what I might learn
- ✓ Read today's portion of the story
- ✓ Use Strategy Chart – start with checking predictions or questions
- ✓ Graphic Organizer or Written Response

©The Reading Teacher's Plan Book

Teaching Week 1: Short A Families at, an, ap
Group Sort Cards (Page 1 of 2)

at	an	ap
bat	can	cap
cat	fan	clap
fat	man	flap
hat	pan	lap

Copy onto cardstock. Laminate and cut into individual cards. Follow directions on page 8.

Teaching Week 1: Short A Families at, an, ap
Group Sort Cards (Page 2 of 2)

mat	plan	map
pat	ran	nap
rat	tan	sap
sat	than	tap
that	van	trap

Copy onto cardstock. Laminate and cut into individual cards. Follow directions on page 8.

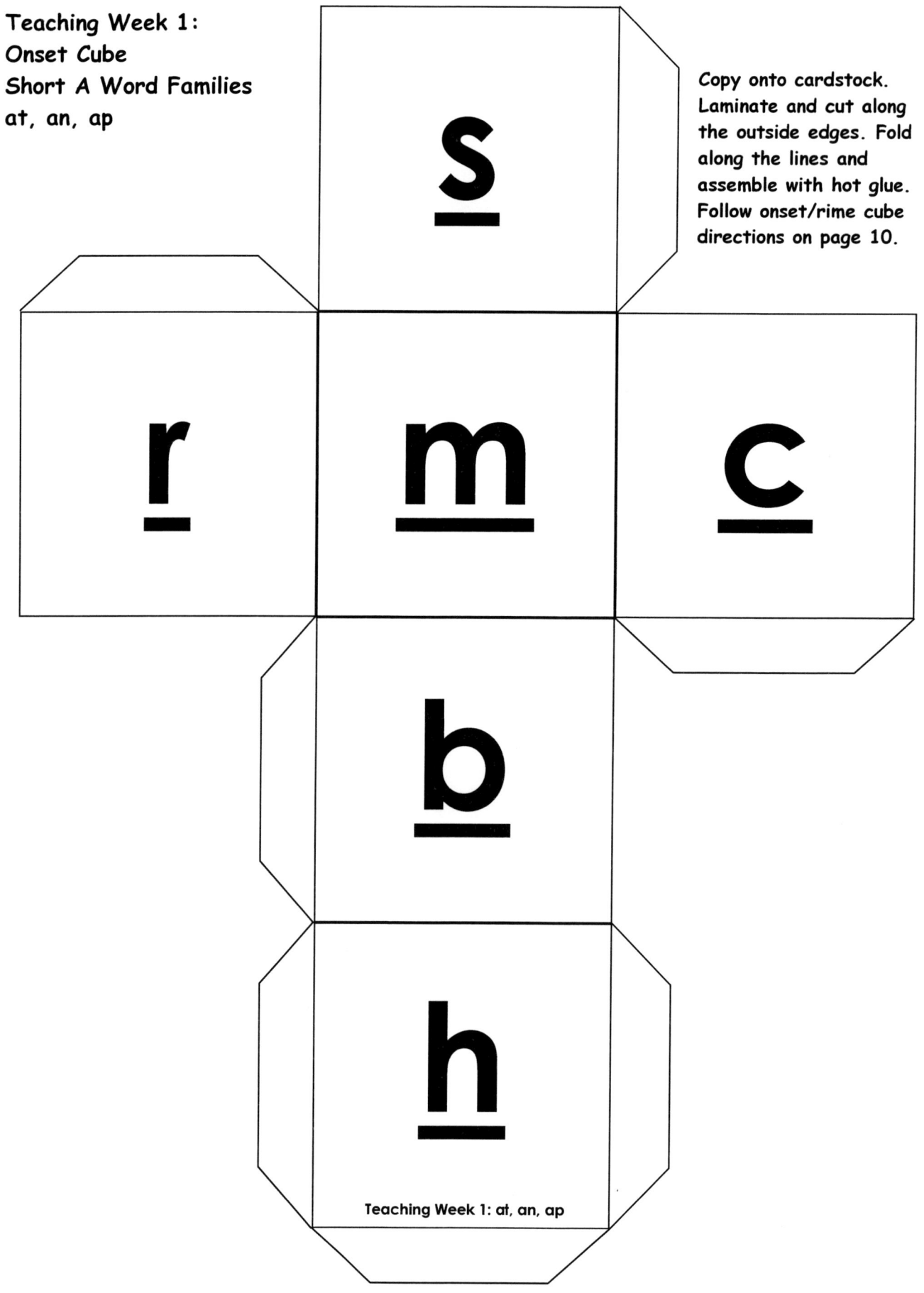

Teaching Week 1:
Onset Cube
Short A Word Families
at, an, ap

Copy onto cardstock. Laminate and cut along the outside edges. Fold along the lines and assemble with hot glue. Follow onset/rime cube directions on page 10.

s

r **m** **c**

b

h

Teaching Week 1: at, an, ap

122 ©The Reading Teacher's Plan Book

Teaching Week 1:
Rime Cube
Short A Word Families
at, an, ap

Copy onto cardstock. Laminate and cut along the outside edges. Fold along the lines and assemble with hot glue. Follow onset/rime cube directions on page 10.

ap

at an an

at

ap

Teaching Week 1: at, an, ap

Teaching Week 1: Short A Families -- at, an, ap
Making Words Letter Cards

a	c	n	p	t	r
a	c	n	p	t	r
a	c	n	p	t	r
a	c	n	p	t	r
a	c	n	p	t	r
a	c	n	p	t	r

Make these words: can, pan, pat, cat, rat, ran, rap, trap Copy onto cardstock. Use one row of letters per student. Cut into individual letter cards. Follow directions on page 9.

Teaching Week 1: Short A Families at, an, ap
Individual Sort Cards

at	an	ap
cat	can	cap
mat	fan	lap
pat	man	nap
rat	ran	sap
sat	van	tap

Copy a set of Individual Sort Cards for each student. Cut into individual cards. Follow directions on p. 9.

Teaching Week 2: Short I Families it, in, ig
Group Sort Cards (Page 1 of 2)

it	in	ig
bit	bin	big
fit	chin	dig
hit	fin	fig
kit	kin	jig

Copy onto cardstock. Laminate and cut into individual cards. Follow directions on page 8.

Teaching Week 2: Short I Families it, in, ig
Group Sort Cards (Page 2 of 2)

lit	pin	pig
pit	spin	rig
quit	thin	twig
sit	tin	wig
	win	zig

Copy onto cardstock. Laminate and cut into individual cards. Follow directions on page 8.

**Teaching Week 2:
Onset Cube
Short I Word Families
it, in, ig**

Copy onto cardstock. Laminate and cut along the outside edges. Fold along the lines and assemble with hot glue. Follow onset/rime cube directions on page 10.

f

sk   p   b

w

sp

Teaching Week 2: it, in, ig

128 ©The Reading Teacher's Plan Book

**Teaching Week 2:
Rime Cube
Short I Word Families
it, in, ig**

it

ig   **in**   **ig**

it

in

Copy onto cardstock. Laminate and cut along the outside edges. Fold along the lines and assemble with hot glue. Follow onset/rime cube directions on page 10.

Teaching Week 2: it, in, ig

©The Reading Teacher's Plan Book

Teaching Week 2: Short I Families – it, in, ig
Making Words Letter Cards

i	t	n	g	b	p	f	w
i	t	n	g	b	p	f	w
i	t	n	g	b	p	f	w
i	t	n	g	b	p	f	w
i	t	n	g	b	p	f	w
i	t	n	g	b	p	f	w

Make these words: pig, big, bit, fit, fin, pin, win, twin, twig Copy onto cardstock. Use one row of letters per student. Cut into individual letter cards. Follow directions on page 9.

©The Reading Teacher's Plan Book

Teaching Week 2: Short I Families it, in, ig
Individual Sort Cards

it	in	ig
bit	bin	big
fit	fin	dig
hit	pin	fig
lit	thin	jig
pit	win	twig

Copy a set of Individual Sort Cards for each student. Cut into individual cards. Follow directions on p. 9.

Teaching Week 3: Short O Families ot, op, ob
Group Sort Cards (Page 1 of 2)

ot	op	ob
cot	bop	blob
got	cop	cob
hot	drop	gob
jot	hop	job

Copy onto cardstock. Laminate and cut into individual cards. Follow directions on page 8.

©The Reading Teacher's Plan Book

Teaching Week 3: Short O Families ot, op, ob
Group Sort Cards (Page 2 of 2)

lot	mop	lob
not	pop	mob
pot	shop	rob
rot	stop	slob
shot	top	sob

Copy onto cardstock. Laminate and cut into individual cards. Follow directions on page 8.

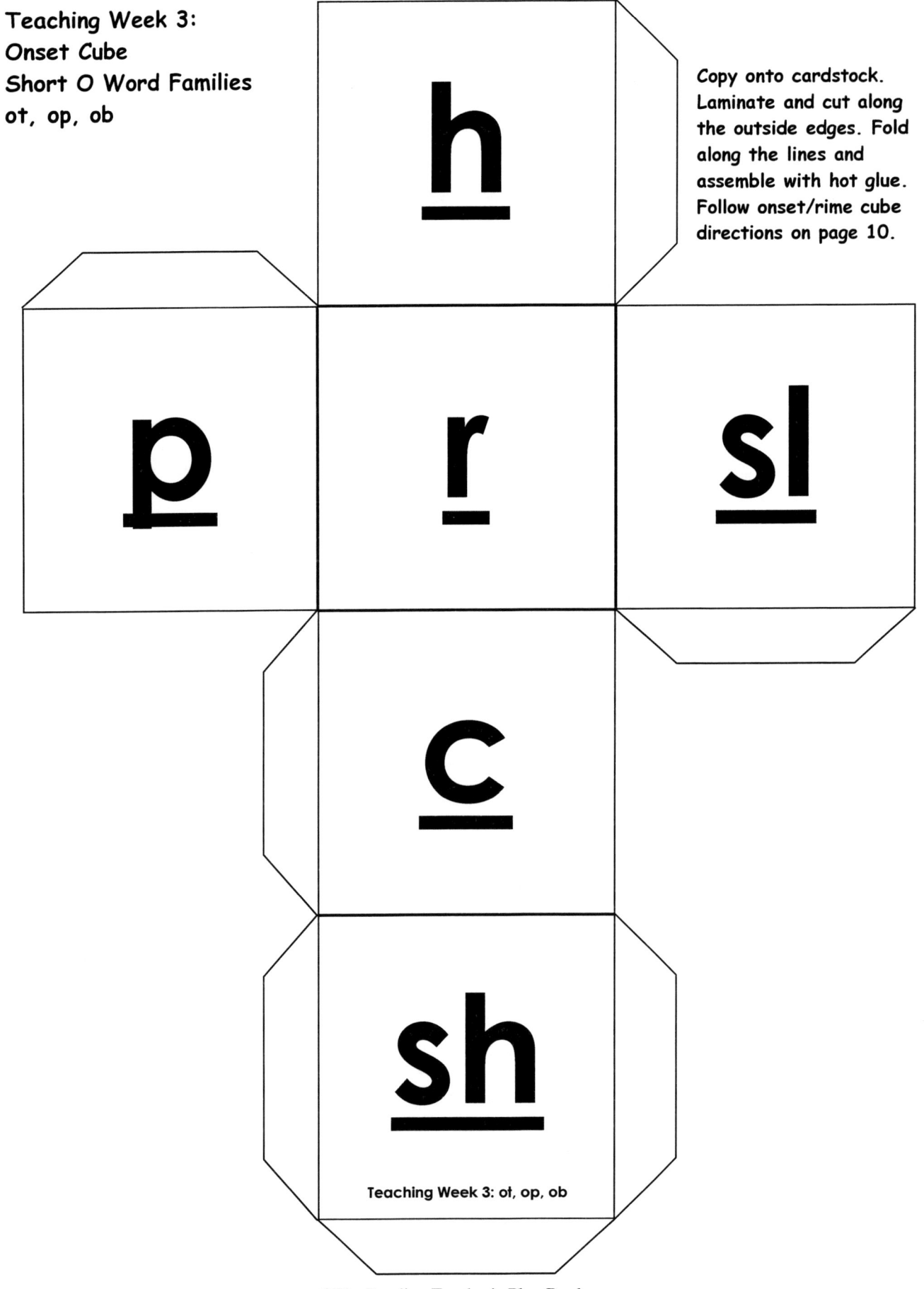

**Teaching Week 3:
Onset Cube
Short O Word Families
ot, op, ob**

Copy onto cardstock. Laminate and cut along the outside edges. Fold along the lines and assemble with hot glue. Follow onset/rime cube directions on page 10.

h

p   r   sl

c

sh

Teaching Week 3: ot, op, ob

Teaching Week 3:
Rime Cube
Short O Word Families
ot, op, ob

Copy onto cardstock. Laminate and cut along the outside edges. Fold along the lines and assemble with hot glue. Follow onset/rime cube directions on page 10.

ot

ot   op   ob

ob

op

Teaching Week 3: ot, op, ob

Teaching Week 3: Short O Families – ot, op, ob
Making Words Letter Cards

o	t	p	s	h	r	c	b
o	t	p	s	h	r	c	b
o	t	p	s	h	r	c	b
o	t	p	s	h	r	c	b
o	t	p	s	h	r	c	b
o	t	p	s	h	r	c	b

Make these words: hot, rot, rob, cob, cop, hop, top, stop Copy onto cardstock. Use one row of letters per student. Cut into individual letter cards. Follow directions on page 9.

Teaching Week 3: Short O Families ot, op, ob
Individual Sort Cards

ot	op	ob
cot	hop	cob
got	mop	job
hot	shop	mob
lot	stop	rob
rot	top	slob

Copy a set of Individual Sort Cards for each student. Cut into individual cards. Follow directions on p. 9.

Teaching Week 4: Short E Families et, ed, en
Group Sort Cards (Page 1 of 2)

et	ed	en
get	bed	Ben
jet	fed	den
let	fled	hen
met	led	men

Copy onto cardstock. Laminate and cut into individual cards. Follow directions on page 8.

Teaching Week 4: Short E Families et, ed, en
Group Sort Cards (Page 2 of 2)

net	red	pen
pet	shed	ten
set	sled	then
vet	Ted	when
wet	wed	

Copy onto cardstock. Laminate and cut into individual cards. Follow directions on page 8.

Teaching Week 4:
Onset Cube
Short E Word Families
et, ed, en

Copy onto cardstock. Laminate and cut along the outside edges. Fold along the lines and assemble with hot glue. Follow onset/rime cube directions on page 10.

m

sl l b

p

v

Teaching Week 4: et, ed, en

Teaching Week 4:
Rime Cube
Short E Word Families
et, ed, en

Copy onto cardstock. Laminate and cut along the outside edges. Fold along the lines and assemble with hot glue. Follow onset/rime cube directions on page 10.

et

et   ed   en

en

ed

Teaching Week 4: et, ed, en

©The Reading Teacher's Plan Book

Teaching Week 4: Short E Families – et, ed, en
Making Words Letter Cards

e	d	n	t	p	m	s	l
e	d	n	t	p	m	s	l
e	d	n	t	p	m	s	l
e	d	n	t	p	m	s	l
e	d	n	t	p	m	s	l
e	d	n	t	p	m	s	l

Make these words: ten, pen, men, met, pet, let, led, sled Copy onto cardstock. Use one row of letters per student. Cut into individual letter cards. Follow directions on page 9.

Teaching Week 4: Short E Families et, ed, en
Individual Sort Cards

et	ed	en
get	bed	den
jet	fed	hen
let	red	men
met	sled	ten
pet	wed	then

Copy a set of Individual Sort Cards for each student. Cut into individual cards. Follow directions on p. 9.

Teaching Week 5: Short U Families ut, un, ug
Group Sort Cards (Page 1 of 2)

ut	un	ug
but	bun	bug
cut	fun	dug
gut	pun	hug
hut	run	jug

Copy onto cardstock. Laminate and cut into individual cards. Follow directions on page 8.

Teaching Week 5: Short U Families ut, un, ug
Group Sort Cards (Page 2 of 2)

nut	sun	lug
rut	spun	mug
shut		rug
		slug
		tug

Copy onto cardstock. Laminate and cut into individual cards. Follow directions on page 8.

Teaching Week 5:
Onset Cube
Short U Word Families
ut, un, ug

Copy onto cardstock. Laminate and cut along the outside edges. Fold along the lines and assemble with hot glue. Follow onset/rime cube directions on page 10.

m

b r h

c

sh

Teaching Week 5: ut, un, ug

**Teaching Week 5:
Rime Cube
Short U Word Families
ut, un, ug**

ut

ut   ug   un

un

ug

Teaching Week 5: ut, un, ug

Copy onto cardstock. Laminate and cut along the outside edges. Fold along the lines and assemble with hot glue. Follow onset/rime cube directions on page 10.

©The Reading Teacher's Plan Book

Teaching Week 5: Short U Families – ut, un, ug
Making Words Letter Cards

u	g	n	t	b	h	s	r
u	g	n	t	b	h	s	r
u	g	n	t	b	h	s	r
u	g	n	t	b	h	s	r
u	g	n	t	b	h	s	r
u	g	n	t	b	h	s	r

Make these words: **bug, rug, run, sun, bun, but, nut, hut, shut** Copy onto cardstock. Use one row of letters per student. Cut into individual letter cards. Follow directions on page 9.

Teaching Week 5: Short U Families ut, un, ug
Individual Sort Cards

ut	un	ug
but	bun	dug
cut	fun	hug
hut	pun	jug
nut	run	rug
shut	sun	slug

Copy a set of Individual Sort Cards for each student. Cut into individual cards. Follow directions on p. 9.

Teaching Week 6a: ack, ick, ock, uck
Group Sort Cards (Page 1 of 2)

ack	ick	ock
back	brick	block
black	flick	clock
lack	kick	dock
pack	lick	flock

Copy onto cardstock. Laminate and cut into individual cards. Follow directions on page 8.

Teaching Week 6a: ack, ick, ock, uck
Group Sort Cards (Page 2 of 2)

uck	rack	stick
buck	sack	rock
cluck	shack	sock
duck	pick	stuck
luck	quick	tuck

Copy onto cardstock. Laminate and cut into individual cards. Follow directions on page 8.

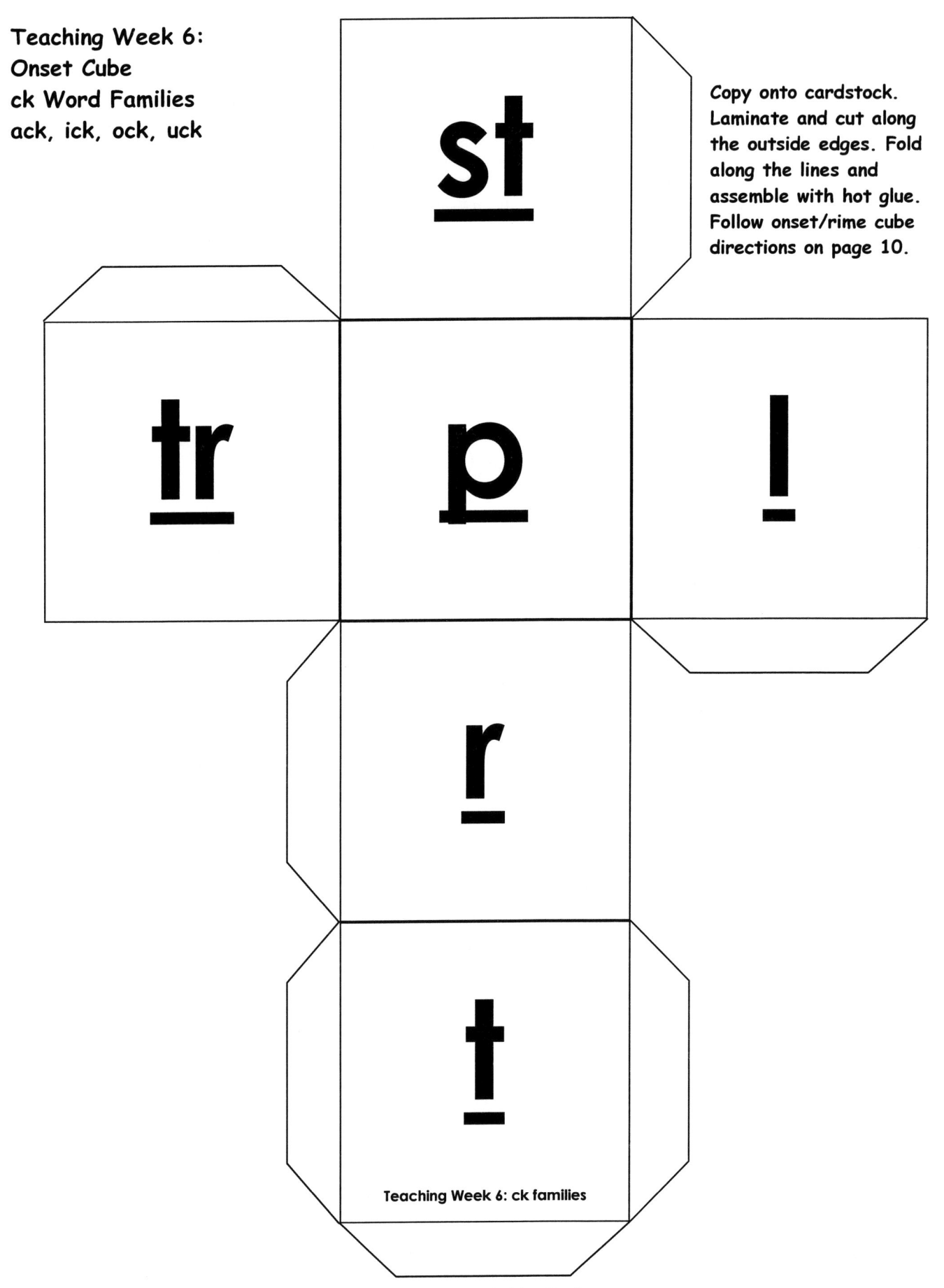

**Teaching Week 6:
Onset Cube
ck Word Families
ack, ick, ock, uck**

Copy onto cardstock. Laminate and cut along the outside edges. Fold along the lines and assemble with hot glue. Follow onset/rime cube directions on page 10.

st

tr   p   l

r

t

Teaching Week 6: ck families

**Teaching Week 6:
Rime Cube
ck Word Families
ack, ick, ock, uck**

ack

ick   uck   ock

ack

ick

Teaching Week 6: ck families

Copy onto cardstock. Laminate and cut along the outside edges. Fold along the lines and assemble with hot glue. Follow onset/rime cube directions on page 10.

©The Reading Teacher's Plan Book

Teaching Week 6b: ch, sh, th
Group Sort Cards (Page 1 of 2)

ch	sh	th
chat	shack	than
chess	shed	that
chick	shell	then
chimp	ship	thick

Copy onto cardstock. Laminate and cut into individual cards. Follow directions on page 8.

Teaching Week 6b: ch, sh, th
Group Sort Cards (Page 2 of 2)

chin	shop	thin
chop	shock	this
chug	shut	thump

Copy onto cardstock. Laminate and cut into individual cards. Follow directions on page 8.

Teaching Week 6: ch, sh, th Picture Sort

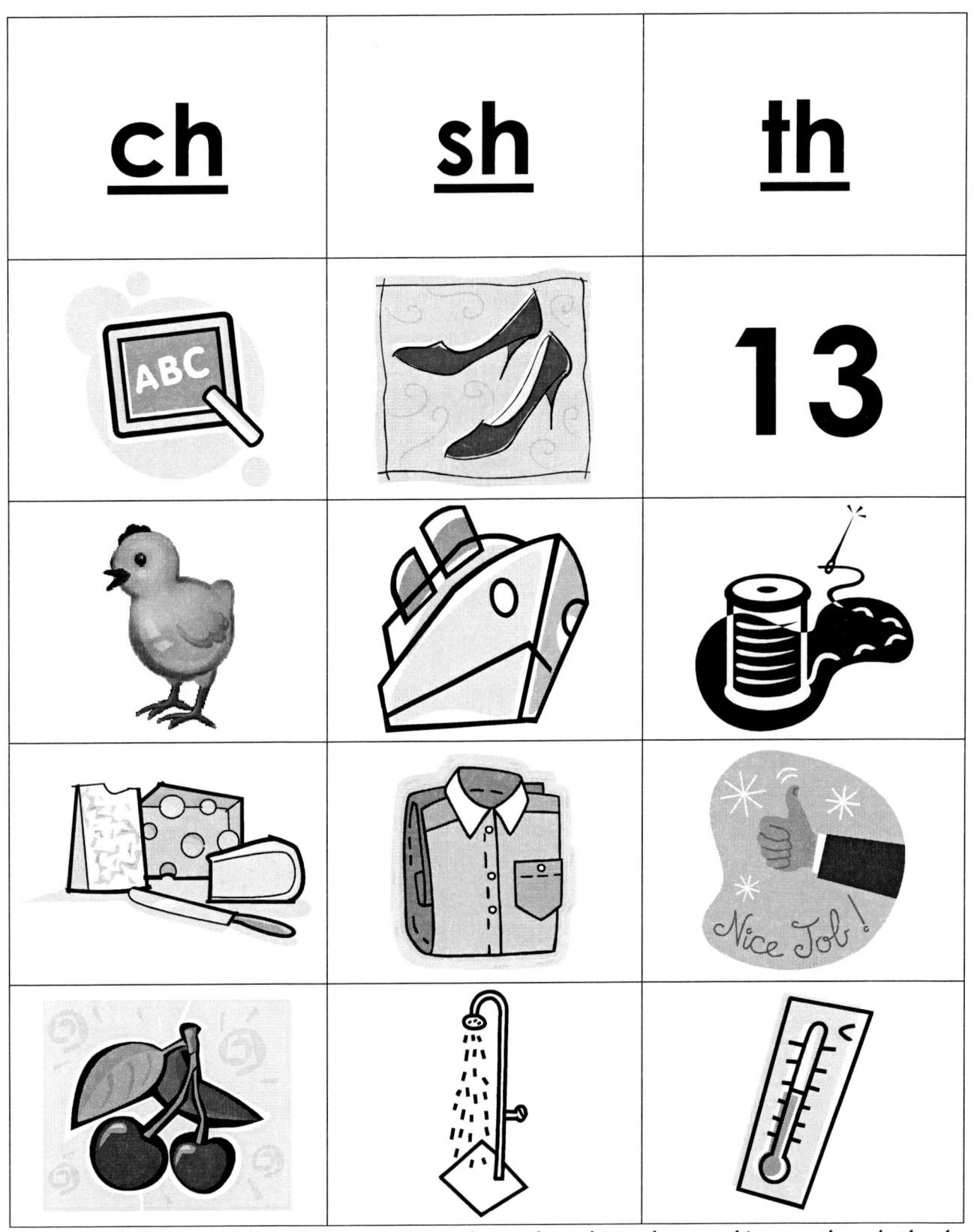

ch	sh	th

Pictures: chalkboard, chick, cheese, cherries, shoes, ship, shirt, shower, thirteen, thread, thumb, thermometer Copy onto cardstock. Laminate and cut into individual cards. Follow directions on page 8.

156 ©The Reading Teacher's Plan Book

Teaching Week 7: Long A with Silent E
Group Sort Cards (Page 1 of 2)

short a	a-e	
branch	bake	
cat	came	
clap	date	
dad	game	

Copy onto cardstock. Laminate and cut into individual cards. Follow directions on page 8.

Teaching Week 7: Long A with Silent E
Group Sort Cards (Page 2 of 2)

flag	late	
grand	make	
mash	name	
plant	race	
trap	shake	

Copy onto cardstock. Laminate and cut into individual cards. Follow directions on page 8.

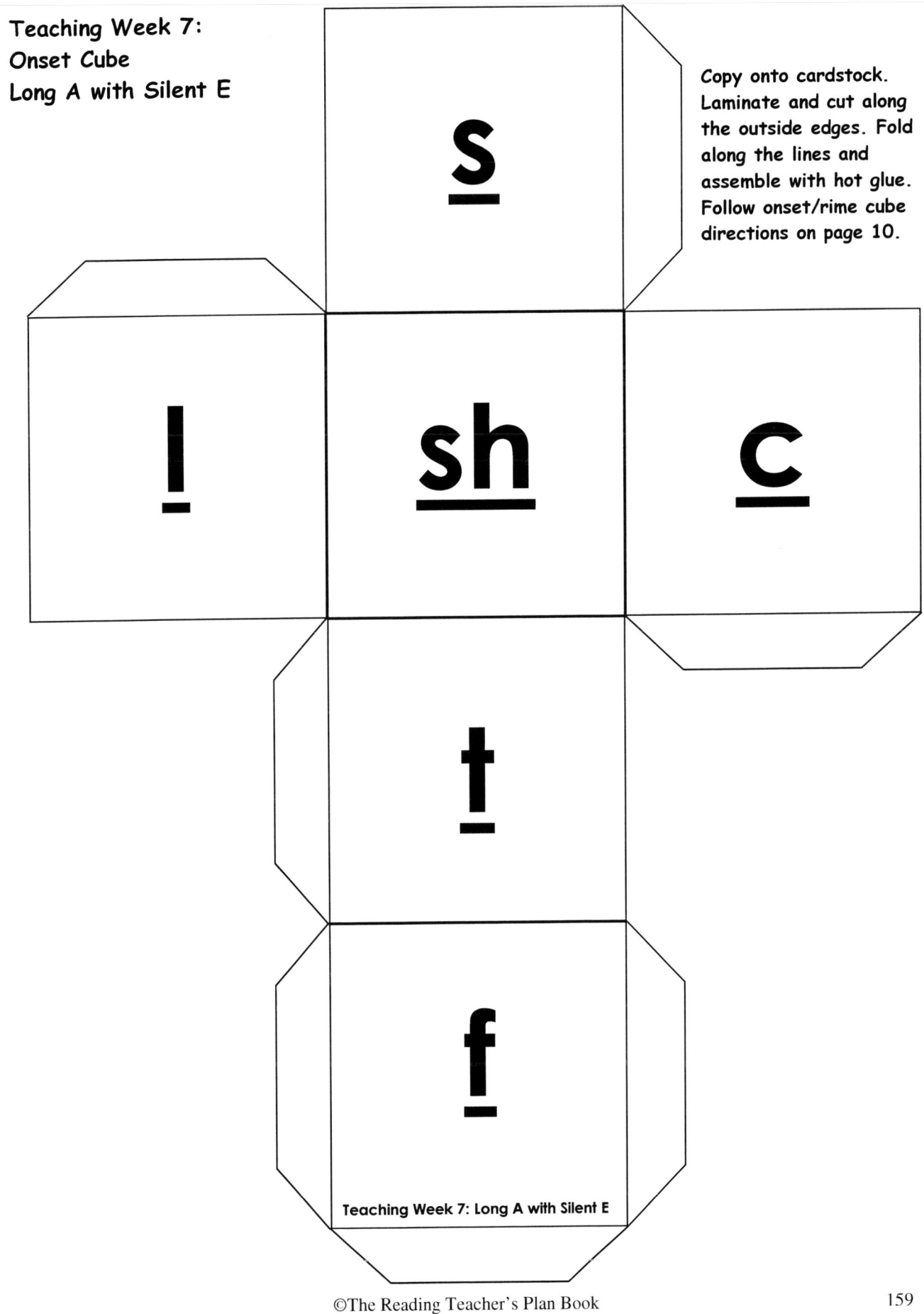

Teaching Week 7:
Onset Cube
Long A with Silent E

Copy onto cardstock. Laminate and cut along the outside edges. Fold along the lines and assemble with hot glue. Follow onset/rime cube directions on page 10.

s

l sh c

t

f

Teaching Week 7: Long A with Silent E

©The Reading Teacher's Plan Book

**Teaching Week 7:
Rime Cube
Long A with Silent E**

Copy onto cardstock. Laminate and cut along the outside edges. Fold along the lines and assemble with hot glue. Follow onset/rime cube directions on page 10.

ape

ake   ame   ape

ake

ame

Teaching Week 7: Long A with Silent E

©The Reading Teacher's Plan Book

Teaching Week 7: Short A/Long A Picture Sort

short a sound	long a sound	

Pictures: ant, axe, cat, flag, grapes, cape, game, flame, apple, ape, hat, rake
Copy onto cardstock. Laminate and cut into individual cards. Follow directions on page 8.

©The Reading Teacher's Plan Book

Teaching Week 7: Long A with Silent E
Individual Sort Cards

short a	a-e	
cat	bake	plan
clap	came	ran
dad	game	name
flag	late	race
grand	make	shake

Copy a set of Individual Sort Cards for each student. Cut into individual cards. Follow directions on p. 9.

Teaching Week 8: Long I with Silent E
Group Sort Cards (Page 1 of 2)

short i	i-e	
chin	bike	
fin	fine	
flip	kite	
hint	mine	

Copy onto cardstock. Laminate and cut into individual cards. Follow directions on page 8.

©The Reading Teacher's Plan Book

Teaching Week 8: Long I with Silent E
Group Sort Cards (Page 2 of 2)

list	nice	
pinch	ride	
rid	spine	
spin	time	
twig	white	

Copy onto cardstock. Laminate and cut into individual cards. Follow directions on page 8.

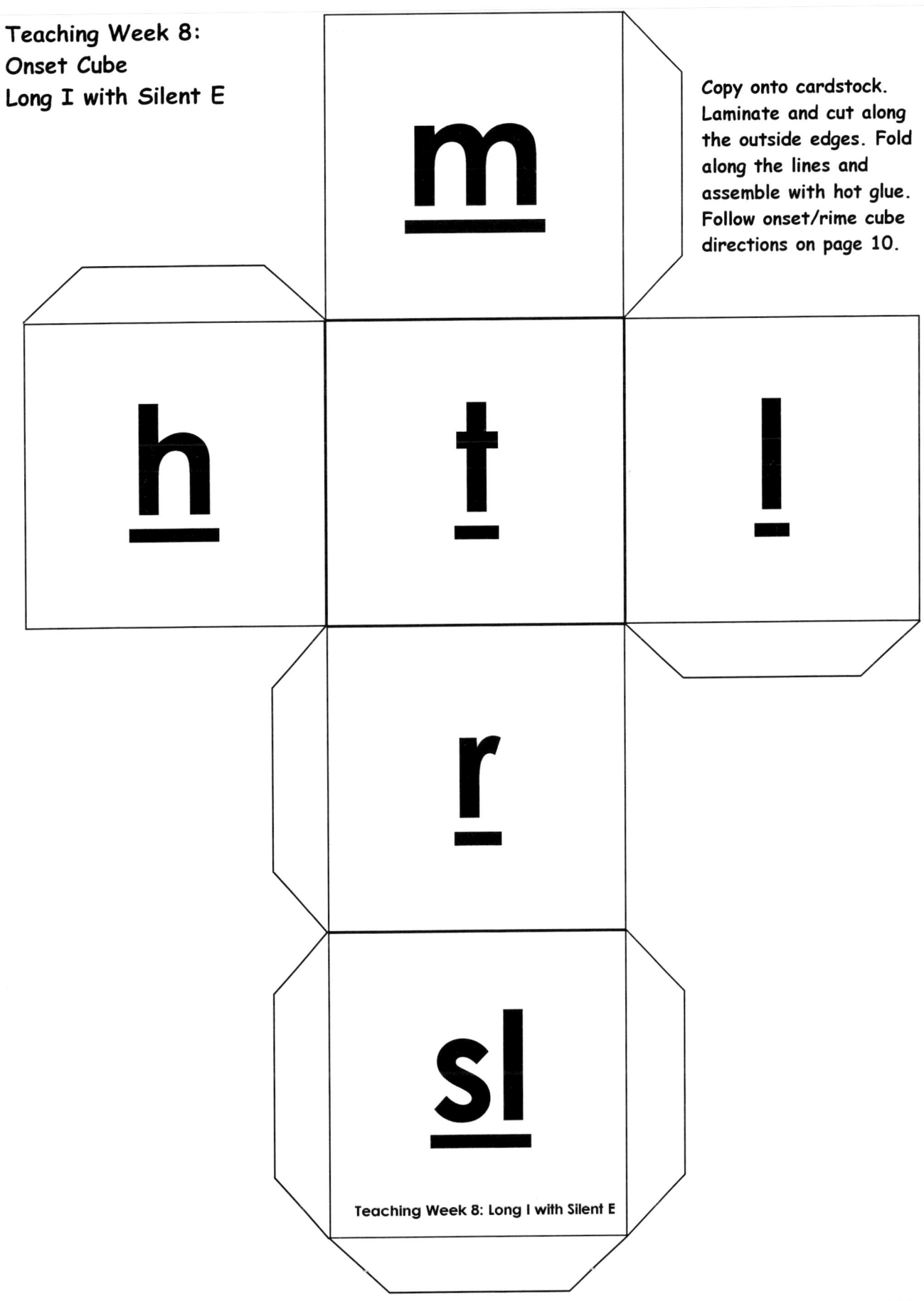

Teaching Week 8:
Onset Cube
Long I with Silent E

Copy onto cardstock. Laminate and cut along the outside edges. Fold along the lines and assemble with hot glue. Follow onset/rime cube directions on page 10.

m

h   t   l

r

sl

Teaching Week 8: Long I with Silent E

©The Reading Teacher's Plan Book

165

Teaching Week 8:
Rime Cube
Long I with Silent E

Copy onto cardstock. Laminate and cut along the outside edges. Fold along the lines and assemble with hot glue. Follow onset/rime cube directions on page 10.

ice

ike | ide | ice

ike

ide

Teaching Week 8: Long I with Silent E

166 ©The Reading Teacher's Plan Book

Teaching Week 8: Short I/Long I Picture Sort

short I sound	long I sound	

Pictures: igloo, iguana, pig, fish, ice cream, icicle, bike, hike, pin, bride, fins, dice
Copy onto cardstock. Laminate and cut into individual cards. Follow directions on page 8.

©The Reading Teacher's Plan Book

Teaching Week 8: Long I with Silent E
Making Words Letter Cards

a	e	i	c	f	p	m	n
a	e	i	c	f	p	m	n
a	e	i	c	f	p	m	n
a	e	i	c	f	p	m	n
a	e	i	c	f	p	m	n
a	e	i	c	f	p	m	n

Make these words: man, mane, cane, can, pan, pane, pine, pin, fin, fine, mine Copy onto cardstock. Use one row of letters per student. Cut into individual letter cards. Follow directions on p. 9.

Teaching Week 8: Long I with Silent E
Individual Sort Cards

short i	i-e	
chin	bike	spin
fin	fine	twig
flip	kite	ride
pinch	mine	spine
rid	nice	white

Copy a set of Individual Sort Cards for each student. Cut into individual cards. Follow directions on p. 9.

Teaching Week 9: Long O, U with Silent E
Group Sort Cards (Page 1 of 2)

o-e	u-e	a-e
broke	cube	cane
hole	cute	frame
note	fuse	gate
rode	huge	lake

Copy onto cardstock. Laminate and cut into individual cards. Follow directions on page 8.

Teaching Week 9: Long O, U with Silent E
Group Sort Cards (Page 2 of 2)

rope	June	make
smoke	mule	place
those	rule	shape
vote	tune	snake
woke	use	tape

Copy onto cardstock. Laminate and cut into individual cards. Follow directions on page 8.

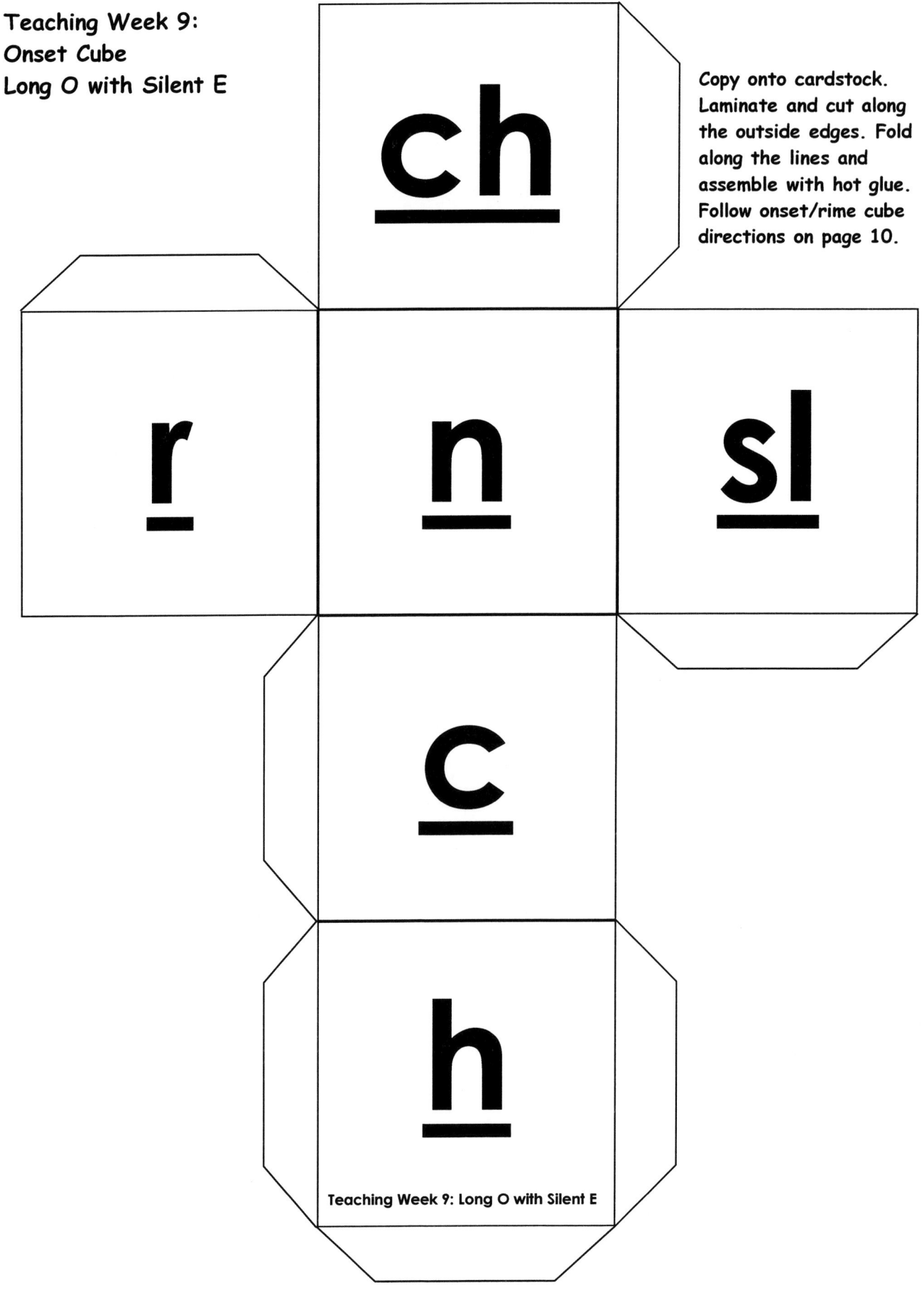

Teaching Week 9:
Onset Cube
Long O with Silent E

Copy onto cardstock. Laminate and cut along the outside edges. Fold along the lines and assemble with hot glue. Follow onset/rime cube directions on page 10.

ch

r   n   sl

c

h

Teaching Week 9: Long O with Silent E

172   ©The Reading Teacher's Plan Book

**Teaching Week 9:
Rime Cube
Long O with Silent E**

Copy onto cardstock. Laminate and cut along the outside edges. Fold along the lines and assemble with hot glue. Follow onset/rime cube directions on page 10.

ope

oke | **ose** | **ope**

oke

ose

Teaching Week 9: Long O with Silent E

©The Reading Teacher's Plan Book

**Teaching Week 9:
Onset Cube
Long U with Silent E**

Copy onto cardstock. Laminate and cut along the outside edges. Fold along the lines and assemble with hot glue. Follow onset/rime cube directions on page 10.

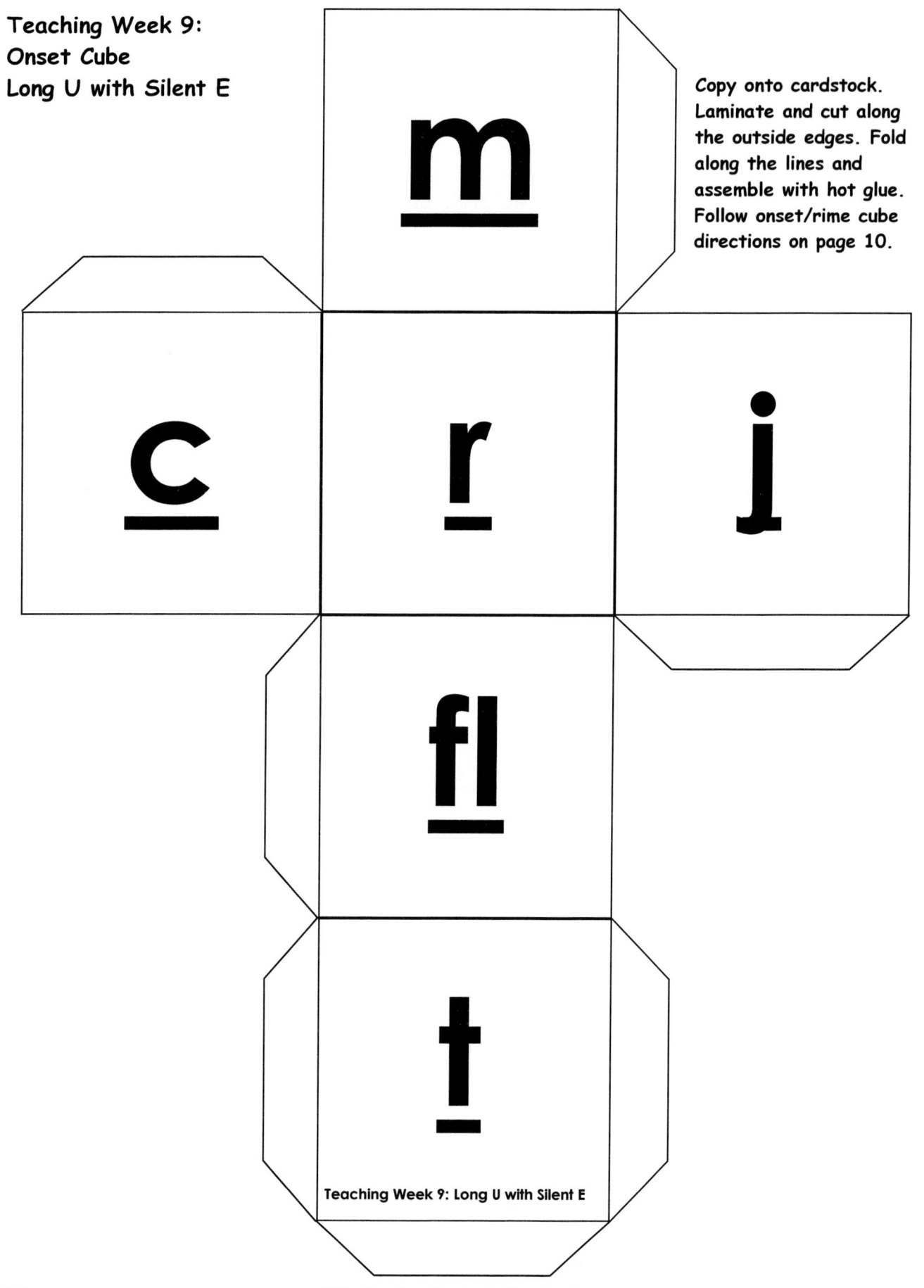

m

c　**r**　**j**

fl

t

Teaching Week 9: Long U with Silent E

174　　©The Reading Teacher's Plan Book

**Teaching Week 9:
Rime Cube
Long U with Silent E**

Copy onto cardstock. Laminate and cut along the outside edges. Fold along the lines and assemble with hot glue. Follow onset/rime cube directions on page 10.

ute

une | ule | ute

une

ule

Teaching Week 9: Long U with Silent E

©The Reading Teacher's Plan Book

Teaching Week 9: Short O/Long O Picture Sort

short o sound	long o sound	

Pictures: octopus, otter, pot, hop, overalls, open, phone, coat, pond, bone, knob, boat
Copy onto cardstock. Laminate and cut into individual cards. Follow directions on page 8.

Teaching Week 9: Short U/Long U Picture Sort

short u sound	long u sound	

Pictures: umbrella, up, sun, bug, unicorn, ukulele, mule, cube, lunch, Utah, cut, fuel
Copy onto cardstock. Laminate and cut into individual cards. Follow directions on page 8.

©The Reading Teacher's Plan Book

Teaching Week 9: Long O, U with Silent E
Making Words Letter Cards

o	u	e	h	c	p	b	t
o	u	e	h	c	p	b	t
o	u	e	h	c	p	b	t
o	u	e	h	c	p	b	t
o	u	e	h	c	p	b	t
o	u	e	h	c	p	b	t

Make these words: hop, hope, cope, cop, cup, cub, cube, cute, cut Copy onto cardstock. Use one row of letters per student. Cut into individual letter cards. Follow directions on page 9.

©The Reading Teacher's Plan Book

Teaching Week 9: Long O, U with Silent E
Individual Sort Cards

o-e	u-e	a-e
broke	cube	bake
hole	cute	came
note	huge	date
rode	June	lake
woke	mule	same

Copy a set of Individual Sort Cards for each student. Cut into individual cards. Follow directions on p. 9.

Teaching Week 10: Long A Vowel Patterns ai, ay
Group Sort Cards (Page 1 of 2)

short a	ai	ay
back	chain	bay
cat	drain	day
clap	gain	gray
flag	mail	hay

Copy onto cardstock. Laminate and cut into individual cards. Follow directions on page 8.

©The Reading Teacher's Plan Book

Teaching Week 10: Long A Vowel Patterns ai, ay
Group Sort Cards (Page 2 of 2)

grand	main	may
hat	rain	pay
plant	sail	play
ran	snail	stay
stack	plain	way

Copy onto cardstock. Laminate and cut into individual cards. Follow directions on page 8.

**Teaching Week 10:
Onset Cube
Long A Patterns**

Copy onto cardstock. Laminate and cut along the outside edges. Fold along the lines and assemble with hot glue. Follow onset/rime cube directions on page 10.

tr

pl   st   r

p

m

Teaching Week 10: Long A Patterns

**Teaching Week 10:
Rime Cube
Long A Patterns**

Copy onto cardstock. Laminate and cut along the outside edges. Fold along the lines and assemble with hot glue. Follow onset/rime cube directions on page 10.

ain

ay # ay # ail

ain

ail

Teaching Week 10: Long A Patterns

©The Reading Teacher's Plan Book

Teaching Week 10: Long A Vowel Patterns ai, ay
Making Words Letter Cards

a	i	y	t	r	l	p	m	n
a	i	y	t	r	l	p	m	n
a	i	y	t	r	l	p	m	n
a	i	y	t	r	l	p	m	n
a	i	y	t	r	l	p	m	n
a	i	y	t	r	l	p	m	n

Make these words: ran, rain, pain, pail, rail, mail, main, man, may, ray, pay, play Copy onto cardstock. Use one row of letters per student. Cut into individual letter cards. Follow directions on p. 9.

Teaching Week 10: Long A Vowel Patterns ai, ay
Individual Sort Cards

short a	ai	ay
back	mail	day
clap	rain	hay
hat	sail	may
ran	snail	play
stack	plain	stay

Copy a set of Individual Sort Cards for each student. Cut into individual cards. Follow directions on p. 9.

Teaching Week 11: Long E Vowel Patterns e, ee, ea
Group Sort Cards (Page 1 of 2)

e	ee	ea
be	bee	beach
he	beep	dear
me	deer	heat
she	feet	leap

Copy onto cardstock. Laminate and cut into individual cards. Follow directions on page 8.

Teaching Week 11: Long E Vowel Patterns e, ee, ea
Group Sort Cards (Page 2 of 2)

we	jeep	neat
	keep	rear
	meet	seat
	peek	weak
	sheet	year

Copy onto cardstock. Laminate and cut into individual cards. Follow directions on page 8.

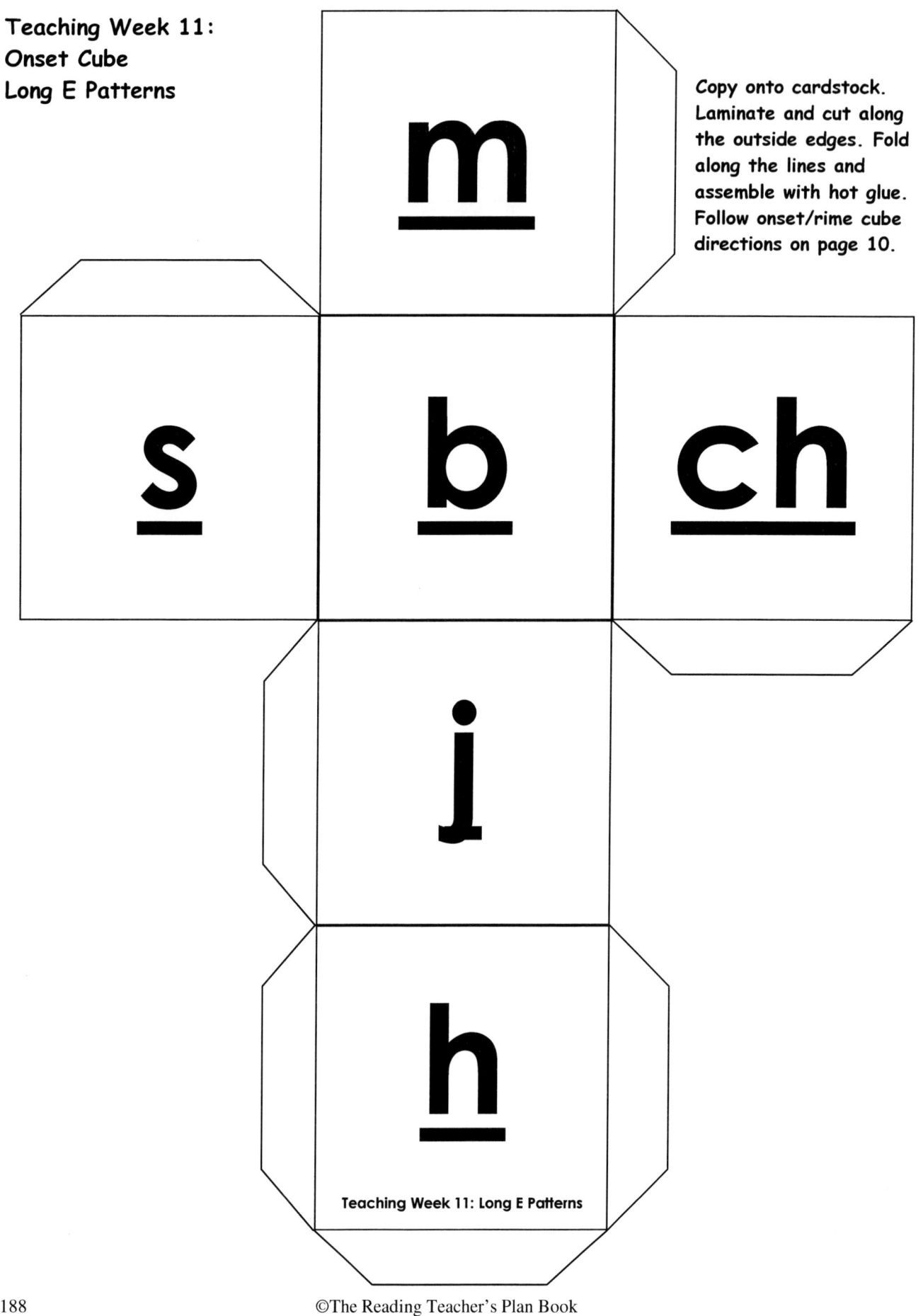

Teaching Week 11:
Onset Cube
Long E Patterns

Copy onto cardstock. Laminate and cut along the outside edges. Fold along the lines and assemble with hot glue. Follow onset/rime cube directions on page 10.

m

s b ch

j

h

Teaching Week 11: Long E Patterns

188 ©The Reading Teacher's Plan Book

**Teaching Week 11:
Rime Cube
Long E Patterns**

Copy onto cardstock. Laminate and cut along the outside edges. Fold along the lines and assemble with hot glue. Follow onset/rime cube directions on page 10.

eat

eep | ean | eep

eat

ean

Teaching Week 11: Long E Patterns

©The Reading Teacher's Plan Book

Teaching Week 11: Long E Vowel Patterns e, ee, ea
Making Words Letter Cards

e	e	a	b	g	t	h	s
e	e	a	b	g	t	h	s
e	e	a	b	g	t	h	s
e	e	a	b	g	t	h	s
e	e	a	b	g	t	h	s
e	e	a	b	g	t	h	s

Make these words: ***be, beg, bet, beat, heat, seat, sea, see, bee, beet, sheet, she*** Copy onto cardstock. Use one row of letters per student. Cut into individual letter cards. Follow directions on p. 9.

Teaching Week 11: Long E Vowel Patterns e, ee, ea
Individual Sort Cards

short e	ee	ea
beg	beep	beach
bell	feet	dear
red	jeep	leap
shed	meet	neat
when	sheet	seat

Copy a set of Individual Sort Cards for each student. Cut into individual cards. Follow directions on p. 9.

Teaching Week 12: Long O Vowel Patterns o, oa, ow
Group Sort Cards (Page 1 of 2)

o	oa	ow
go	boat	bow
no	coach	crow
so	coat	glow
	goat	grow

Copy onto cardstock. Laminate and cut into individual cards. Follow directions on page 8.

Teaching Week 12: Long O Vowel Patterns o, oa, ow
Group Sort Cards (Page 2 of 2)

	load	know
	loan	low
	moan	mow
	road	slow
	soak	snow

Copy onto cardstock. Laminate and cut into individual cards. Follow directions on page 8.

©The Reading Teacher's Plan Book

Teaching Week 12: Long O Vowel Patterns o, oa, ow
Onset/Rime Cards and Mat

b	oat
m	oan
fl	ow
g	ain
gr	eet

Copy one Onset/Rime Cards and Mat for each student. The cards are on the left, and the mat is on the right. Cut along the dotted lines to make individual cards. Paper clip one set of cards to each mat. Follow directions on page 10.

Teaching Week 12: Long O Vowel Patterns o, oa, ow
Making Words Letter Cards

a	o	w	s	g	t	b	l
a	o	w	s	g	t	b	l
a	o	w	s	g	t	b	l
a	o	w	s	g	t	b	l
a	o	w	s	g	t	b	l
a	o	w	s	g	t	b	l

***Make these words:** so, go, got, goat, boat, bow, blow, low, tow* Copy onto cardstock. Use one row of letters per student. Cut into individual letter cards. Follow directions on page 9.

Teaching Week 12: Long O Vowel Patterns o, oa, ow
Individual Sort Cards

short o	oa	ow
chop	boat	blow
got	coach	low
mop	goat	mow
rock	loan	slow
stop	road	snow

Copy a set of Individual Sort Cards for each student. Cut into individual cards. Follow directions on p. 9.

Teaching Week 13: Long I Vowel Patterns ie, igh, y
Group Sort Cards (Page 1 of 2)

ie	igh	y
die	bright	by
flies	flight	cry
fries	high	fly
lie	light	fry

Copy onto cardstock. Laminate and cut into individual cards. Follow directions on page 8.

Teaching Week 13: Long I Vowel Patterns ie, igh, y
Group Sort Cards (Page 2 of 2)

pie	might	my
tie	night	shy
tried	right	sly
	sight	try
	tight	why

Copy onto cardstock. Laminate and cut into individual cards. Follow directions on page 8.

Teaching Week 13: Long I Vowel Patterns ie, igh, y
Onset/Rime Cards and Mat

f<u>l</u>	ies
<u>b</u>	y
<u>m</u>	ight
<u>l</u>	ike
t<u>r</u>	ay

Copy one Onset/Rime Cards and Mat for each student. The cards are on the left, and the mat is on the right. Cut along the dotted lines to make individual cards. Paper clip one set of cards to each mat. Follow directions on page 10.

©The Reading Teacher's Plan Book

199

Teaching Week 13: Long I Vowel Patterns ie, igh, y
Making Words Letter Cards

e	i	y	t	s	l	p	m	g	h
e	i	y	t	s	l	p	m	g	h
e	i	y	t	s	l	p	m	g	h
e	i	y	t	s	l	p	m	g	h
e	i	y	t	s	l	p	m	g	h
e	i	y	t	s	l	p	m	g	h

Make these words: *tie, ties, pie, pies, lie, lies, light, sight, might, my, spy, sly* Copy onto cardstock. Use one row of letters per student. Cut into individual letter cards. Follow directions on p. 9.

Teaching Week 13: Long I Vowel Patterns ie, igh, y
Individual Sort Cards

ie	igh	short i
flies	bright	chin
lie	flight	drip
pie	might	flip
tie	night	swim
tried	right	trick

Copy a set of Individual Sort Cards for each student. Cut into individual cards. Follow directions on p. 9.

Teaching Week 14: "Spooky Sound" oo, ew, ue, u-e
Group Sort Cards (Page 1 of 2)

oo	ew	ue
boot	blew	blue
droop	brew	clue
food	chew	glue
moon	crew	true

Copy onto cardstock. Laminate and cut into individual cards. Follow directions on page 8.

Teaching Week 14: "Spooky Sound" oo, ew, ue
Group Sort Cards (Page 2 of 2)

noon	drew	u-e
pool	flew	duke
root	knew	flute
shoot	new	June
tool	stew	rule

Copy onto cardstock. Laminate and cut into individual cards. Follow directions on page 8.

Teaching Week 14: "Spooky Sound" oo, ew, ue, u-e
Onset/Rime Cards and Mat

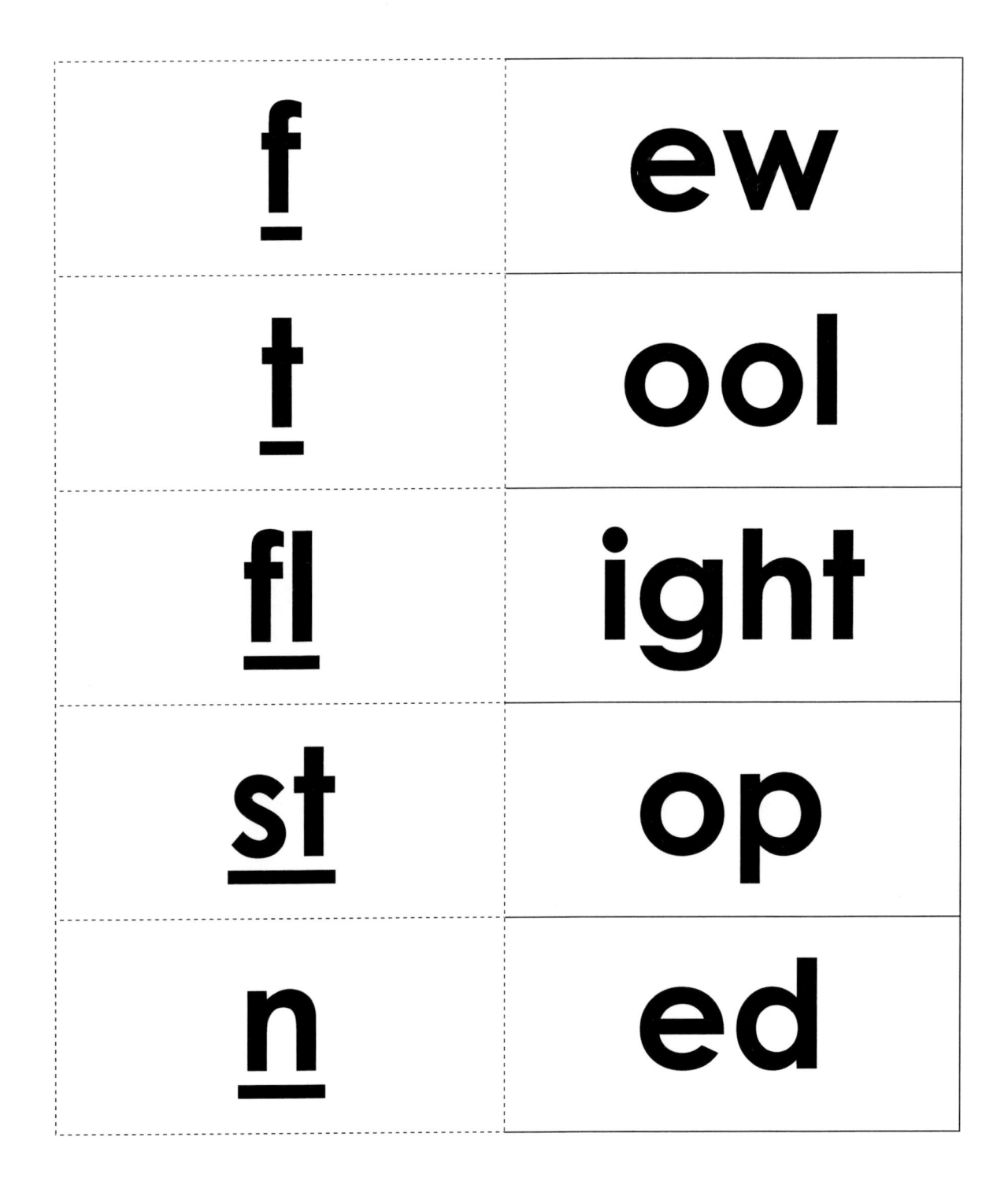

f	ew
t	ool
fl	ight
st	op
n	ed

Copy one Onset/Rime Cards and Mat for each student. The cards are on the left, and the mat is on the right. Cut along the dotted lines to make individual cards. Paper clip one set of cards to each mat. Follow directions on page 10.

Teaching Week 14: "Spooky Sound" oo, ew, ue, u-e
Making Words Letter Cards

e	o	o	u	r	l	t	s	b	w
e	o	o	u	r	l	t	s	b	w
e	o	o	u	r	l	t	s	b	w
e	o	o	u	r	l	t	s	b	w
e	o	o	u	r	l	t	s	b	w
e	o	o	u	r	l	t	s	b	w

Make these words: rule, tool, stool, boot, boost, stew, brew, blew, blue Copy onto cardstock. Use one row of letters per student. Cut into individual letter cards. Follow directions on page 9.

Teaching Week 14: "Spooky Sound" oo, ew, ue, u-e
Individual Sort Cards

oo	ew	ue
boot	blew	blue
food	chew	clue
moon	drew	glue
shoot	flew	Sue
tool	new	true

Copy a set of Individual Sort Cards for each student. Cut into individual cards. Follow directions on p. 9.

Teaching Week 15: "Hurt Sound" ou, ow
Group Sort Cards (Page 1 of 2)

ou	**ow**	**oo**
count	bow	boot
hound	brow	droop
loud	cow	food
mound	down	moon

Copy onto cardstock. Laminate and cut into individual cards. Follow directions on page 8.

Teaching Week 15: "Hurt Sound" ou, ow
Group Sort Cards (Page 2 of 2)

out	frown	pool
pound	gown	stool
pout	how	
round	now	
shout	plow	

Copy onto cardstock. Laminate and cut into individual cards. Follow directions on page 8.

Teaching Week 15: "Hurt Sound" ou, ow
Onset/Rime Cards and Mat

s<u>h</u>	out
<u>h</u>	ow*
<u>r</u>	ound
<u>p</u>	ot
<u>m</u>	ay

Copy one Onset/Rime Cards and Mat for each student. The cards are on the left, and the mat is on the right. Cut along the dotted lines to make individual cards. Paper clip one set of cards to each mat. Follow directions on page 10.

©The Reading Teacher's Plan Book

Teaching Week 15: "Hurt Sound" ou, ow
Making Words Letter Cards

o	u	w	s	h	t	n	d
o	u	w	s	h	t	n	d
o	u	w	s	h	t	n	d
o	u	w	s	h	t	n	d
o	u	w	s	h	t	n	d
o	u	w	s	h	t	n	d

Make these words: *out, shout, show, how, tow, town, down, now* Copy onto cardstock. Use one row of letters per student. Cut into individual letter cards. Follow directions on page 9.

Teaching Week 15: "Hurt Sound" ou, ow
Individual Sort Cards

ou	**ow**	**oo**
count	bow	boot
loud	cow	food
round	down	moon
shout	how	pool
sound	town	stool

Copy a set of Individual Sort Cards for each student. Cut into individual cards. Follow directions on p. 9.

Teaching Week 16: "Bossy R Sounds" ar, are, er, ir, ur, or
Group Sort Cards (Page 1 of 2)

ar	are	er/ir/ur
barn	bare	fern
card	care	her
dark	dare	perk
mark	mare	bird

Copy onto cardstock. Laminate and cut into individual cards. Follow directions on page 8.

Teaching Week 16: "Bossy R Sounds" ar, are, er, ir, ur, or
Group Sort Cards (Page 2 of 2)

<u>or</u>	share	dirt
born	stare	stir
cord	square	burn
fork	part	curb
short	shark	fur

Copy onto cardstock. Laminate and cut into individual cards. Follow directions on page 8.

Teaching Week 16: "Bossy R Sounds" ar, are, er, ir, ur, or
Onset/Rime Cards and Mat

c	ar
f	are
b	urn
st	ore
t	orn

Copy one Onset/Rime Cards and Mat for each student. The cards are on the left, and the mat is on the right. Cut along the dotted lines to make individual cards. Paper clip one set of cards to each mat. Follow directions on page 10.

Teaching Week 16: "Bossy R Sounds" ar, are, er, ir, ur, or
Making Words Letter Cards

a	e	o	u	c	m	n	r	t
a	e	o	u	c	m	n	r	t
a	e	o	u	c	m	n	r	t
a	e	o	u	c	m	n	r	t
a	e	o	u	c	m	n	r	t
a	e	o	u	c	m	n	r	t

Make these words: *tar, car, cart, care, mare, more, tore, torn, turn* Copy onto cardstock. Use one row of letters per student. Cut into individual letter cards. Follow directions on page 9.

Teaching Week 16: "Bossy R Sounds" ar, are, er, ir, ur, or
Individual Sort Cards

<u>ar</u>	<u>are</u>	<u>or</u>
barn	care	born
card	dare	cord
dark	mare	fork
part	share	pork
shark	stare	short

Copy a set of Individual Sort Cards for each student. Cut into individual cards. Follow directions on p. 9.

Teaching Week 17: "Whining Sound" aw, au, all
Group Sort Cards (Page 1 of 2)

aw	au	all
claw	caught	ball
crawl	haul	call
draw	Paul	fall
law	taught	hall

Copy onto cardstock. Laminate and cut into individual cards. Follow directions on page 8.

©The Reading Teacher's Plan Book

Teaching Week 17: "Whining Sound" aw, au, all
Group Sort Cards (Page 2 of 2)

lawn	<u>ar</u>	mall
paw	barn	small
saw	card	tall
straw	farm	wall
yawn	park	shark

Copy onto cardstock. Laminate and cut into individual cards. Follow directions on page 8.

Teaching Week 17: "Whining Sound" aw, au, all
Onset/Rime Cards and Mat

l	aw
m	all
y	awn
dr	ain
p	ark

Copy one Onset/Rime Cards and Mat for each student. The cards are on the left, and the mat is on the right. Cut along the dotted lines to make individual cards. Paper clip one set of cards to each mat. Follow directions on page 10.

Teaching Week 17: "Whining Sound" aw, au, all
Making Words Letter Cards

a	w	l	l	r	t	n	c
a	w	l	l	r	t	n	c
a	w	l	l	r	t	n	c
a	w	l	l	r	t	n	c
a	w	l	l	r	t	n	c
a	w	l	l	r	t	n	c

Make these words: tan, can, car, cart, call, tall, law, claw, raw, lawn Copy onto cardstock. Use one row of letters per student. Cut into individual letter cards. Follow directions on page 9.

Teaching Week 17: "Whining Sound" aw, au, all
Individual Sort Cards

<u>aw</u>	<u>al</u>l	<u>ar</u>
claw	ball	barn
draw	call	card
lawn	fall	farm
paw	small	park
straw	tall	shark

Copy a set of Individual Sort Cards for each student. Cut into individual cards. Follow directions on p. 9.

©The Reading Teacher's Plan Book

Teaching Week 18: "Bouncy Sound" oi, oy "Boxing Sound" oo
Group Sort Cards (Page 1 of 2)

oi	oy	oo
boil	boy	book
coil	coy	brook
coin	joy	cook
foil	loyal	good

Copy onto cardstock. Laminate and cut into individual cards. Follow directions on page 8.

Teaching Week 18: "Bouncy Sound" oi, oy "Boxing Sound" oo
Group Sort Cards (Page 2 of 2)

join	ploy	hook
noise	Roy	look
oil	royal	shook
soil	soy	took
spoil	toy	wood

Copy onto cardstock. Laminate and cut into individual cards. Follow directions on page 8.

©The Reading Teacher's Plan Book

Teaching Week 18: "Bouncy Sound" oi, oy, "Boxing Sound" oo
Onset/Rime Cards and Mat

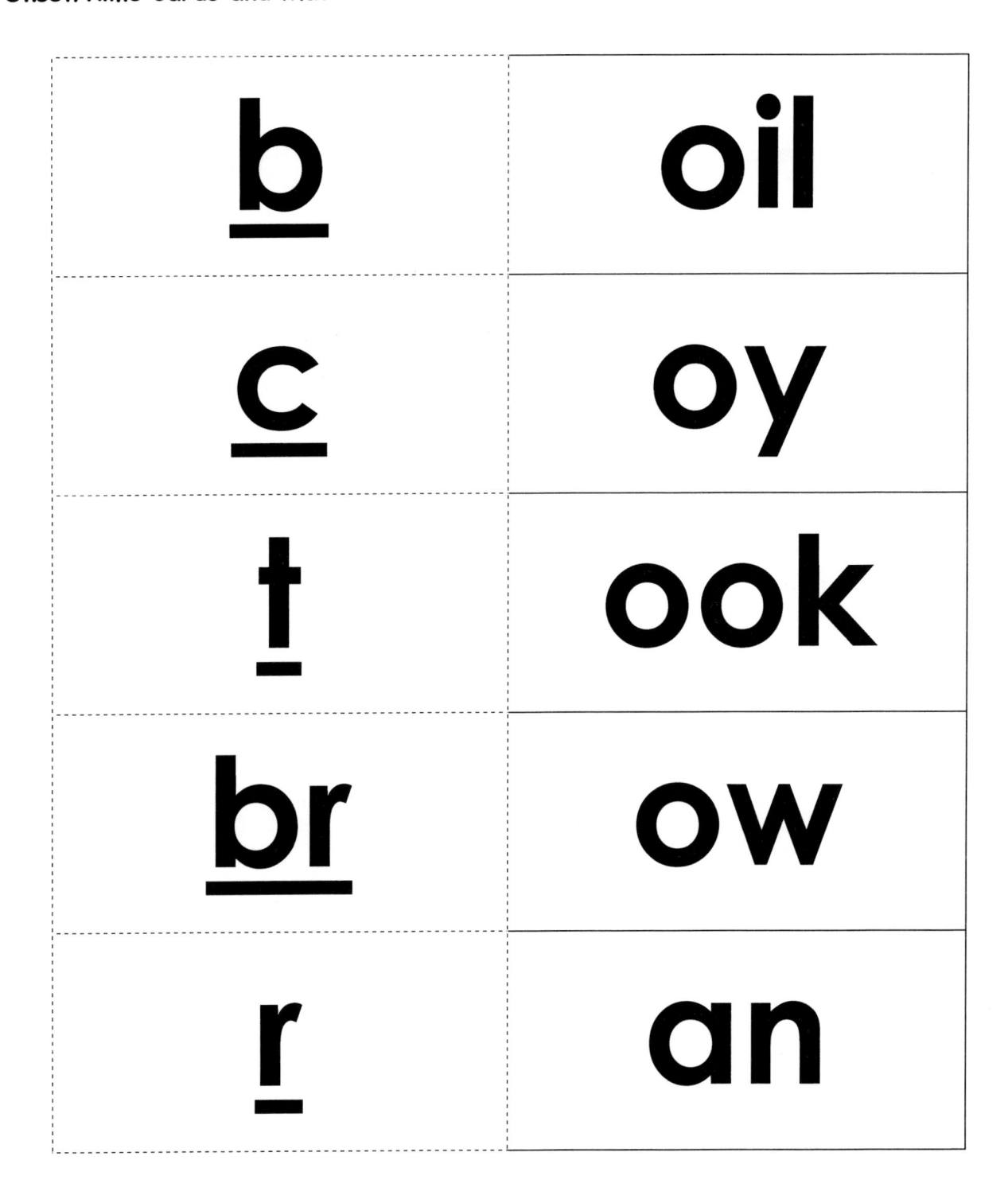

<u>b</u>	oil
<u>c</u>	oy
<u>t</u>	ook
<u>br</u>	ow
<u>r</u>	an

Copy one Onset/Rime Cards and Mat for each student. The cards are on the left, and the mat is on the right. Cut along the dotted lines to make individual cards. Paper clip one set of cards to each mat. Follow directions on page 10.

Teaching Week 18: "Bouncy Sound" oi, oy
Making Words Letter Cards

o	i	y	b	l	t	j	n	c
o	i	y	b	l	t	j	n	c
o	i	y	b	l	t	j	n	c
o	i	y	b	l	t	j	n	c
o	i	y	b	l	t	j	n	c
o	i	y	b	l	t	j	n	c

Make these words: boy, boil, toil, toy, joy, join, coin, coil, coy Copy onto cardstock. Use one row of letters per student. Cut into individual letter cards. Follow directions on page 9.

©The Reading Teacher's Plan Book

Teaching Week 18: "Bouncy Sound" oi, oy "Boxing Sound" oo
Individual Sort Cards

oi	oy	oo
boil	boy	book
coin	joy	good
join	ploy	look
noise	Roy	shook
oil	toy	wood

Copy a set of Individual Sort Cards for each student. Cut into individual cards. Follow directions on p. 9.

Teaching Week 19a: Sounds of "ed" -- /t/ /d/ /ed/
Group Sort Cards (Page 1 of 2)

ed says /t/	ed says /d/	ed says /ed/
asked	buzzed	added
baked	closed	chanted
bumped	framed	ended
clapped	grabbed	landed

Copy onto cardstock. Laminate and cut into individual cards. Follow directions on page 8.

©The Reading Teacher's Plan Book

Teaching Week 19a: Sounds of "ed" -- /t/ /d/ /ed/
Group Sort Cards (Page 2 of 2)

mixed	hummed	melted
passed	named	planted
placed	robbed	skated
sliced	smiled	traded
wished	used	voted

Copy onto cardstock. Laminate and cut into individual cards. Follow directions on page 8.

Teaching Week 19b: Endings -ed, -ing, -er
Blending Cards (Page 1 of 2)

-ed	-ing	-er
acted	catching	banker
blamed	drawing	builder
bumped	ending	catcher
chanted	floating	closer

Copy onto cardstock. Laminate and cut into individual cards. Follow directions on page 7 for Blending Practice.

Teaching Week 19b: Endings –ed, -ing, -er
Blending Cards (Page 2 of 2)

filled	jumping	dreamer
helped	painting	farmer
lifted	running	jogger
phoned	sleeping	singer
sliced	walking	washer

Copy onto cardstock. Laminate and cut into individual cards. Follow directions on page 7 for Blending Practice.

Teaching Week 19: "Endings" Word Hunt Writing Mats

Word Hunt Writing Mat

-ed	-ing	-er

Word Hunt Writing Mat

-ed	-ing	-er

Copy a Writing Mat for each student. Use with Word Windows (pgs. 383-384). Follow directions on p. 11.

Teaching Week 19: Endings –ed, -ing, -er
Individual Sort Cards

-ed	-ing	-er
acted	drawing	closer
bumped	ending	dreamer
chanted	jumping	farmer
filled	running	singer
helped	walking	washer

Copy a set of Individual Sort Cards for each student. Cut into individual cards. Follow directions on p. 9.

Teaching 20: Compound Words
Blending Cards (Page 1 of 2)

anywhere	clubhouse	downtown
baseball	doorbell	driveway
birthday	downhill	football
butterfly	downstream	handstand
campfire	downstairs	homework

Copy onto cardstock. Laminate and cut into individual cards. Follow directions on page 7 for Blending Practice.

Teaching Week 20: Compound Words
Blending Cards (Page 2 of 2)

hotdog	overhead	springtime
lighthouse	overlook	sunset
mailbox	sidewalk	uphill
nowhere	somewhere	upset
overcast	spaceship	upstairs

Copy onto cardstock. Laminate and cut into individual cards. Follow directions on page 7 for Blending Practice.

Teaching Week 20: Compound Words
Compound Word Match-Up (page 1 of 2)

broom	stick	foot	ball
sun	set	down	hill
butter	fly	birth	day

Copy onto cardstock. Laminate. Cut each strip into four cards and clip together. Keep sets separate. Follow directions for "Syllable Match-Up" on page 9.

©The Reading Teacher's Plan Book

Teaching Week 20: Compound Words
Compound Word Match-Up (page 2 of 2)

hot	dog	drive	way
jelly	fish	hair	cut
door	bell	rose	bud

Copy onto cardstock. Laminate. Cut each strip into four cards and clip together. Keep sets separate. Follow directions for "Syllable Match-Up" on page 9.

©The Reading Teacher's Plan Book

**Teaching Week 20:
Word Hunt Cube
"Compound Words"**

Copy onto cardstock. Laminate and cut along the outside edges. Fold along the lines and assemble with hot glue. Use with "Compound Words" Word Hunt Mats. Follow Word Hunt directions on page 11.

over

under | up | down

where

ball

Teaching Week 20: Compound Words

©The Reading Teacher's Plan Book

Teaching Week 20: "Compound Words" Word Hunt Mats

overlook	anywhere	downtown
downtown	uphill	somewhere
baseball	understand	overdone

upset	football	overall
anywhere	upstream	overhead
underground	downstream	underline

underwater	everywhere	downstairs
overcast	upstairs	basketball
nowhere	softball	downhill

Copy a mat for each student. (Three mats are provided.) Provide an assortment of bingo chips. Use with "Compound Word" Word Hunt Cube. Follow directions on page 11.

Review Week 1: Short A, I, O
Group Sort Cards (Page 1 of 2)

a	i	o
bat	bit	chop
can	chin	cob
flag	dig	drop
hat	fish	fox

Copy onto cardstock. Laminate and cut into individual cards. Follow directions on page 8.

©The Reading Teacher's Plan Book

Review Week 1: Short A, I, O
Group Sort Cards (Page 2 of 2)

map	hit	hog
pan	pig	mop
rat	swim	rob
snap	tip	shop
that	win	top

Copy onto cardstock. Laminate and cut into individual cards. Follow directions on page 8.

Review Week 1: Short A, I, O
Making Words Letter Cards

a	i	o	l	p	s	t
a	i	o	l	p	s	t
a	i	o	l	p	s	t
a	i	o	l	p	s	t
a	i	o	l	p	s	t
a	i	o	l	p	s	t

***Make these words:** pat, sat, sit, spit, spot, pot, lot, lit, lip, slip, slap, lap, tap, top* Copy onto cardstock. Use one row of letters per student. Cut into individual letter cards. Follow directions on p. 9.

Review Week 1: Short Vowels A, I, O
Onset/Rime Cards and Mat

<u>t</u>	an
<u>sl</u>	ap
<u>ch</u>	in
<u>r</u>	ip
<u>m</u>	op

Copy one Onset/Rime Cards and Mat for each student. The cards are on the left, and the mat is on the right. Cut along the dotted lines to make individual cards. Paper clip one set of cards to each mat. Follow directions on page 10.

Review Week 1: Short A, I, O
Individual Sort Cards

a	i	o
bat	chin	drop
can	dig	fox
flag	hit	mop
map	swim	shop
snap	win	top

Copy a set of Individual Sort Cards for each student. Cut into individual cards. Follow directions on p. 9.

Review Week 2: Short E, U
Group Sort Cards (Page 1 of 2)

e	**u**	
bed	bun	
fell	club	
get	dug	
hen	hug	

Copy onto cardstock. Laminate and cut into individual cards. Follow directions on page 8.

244 ©The Reading Teacher's Plan Book

Review Week 2: Short E, U
Group Sort Cards (Page 2 of 2)

men	jump	
net	nut	
pet	run	
sled	shut	
then	tug	

Copy onto cardstock. Laminate and cut into individual cards. Follow directions on page 8.

©The Reading Teacher's Plan Book

Review Week 2: Short E, U
Making Words Letter Cards

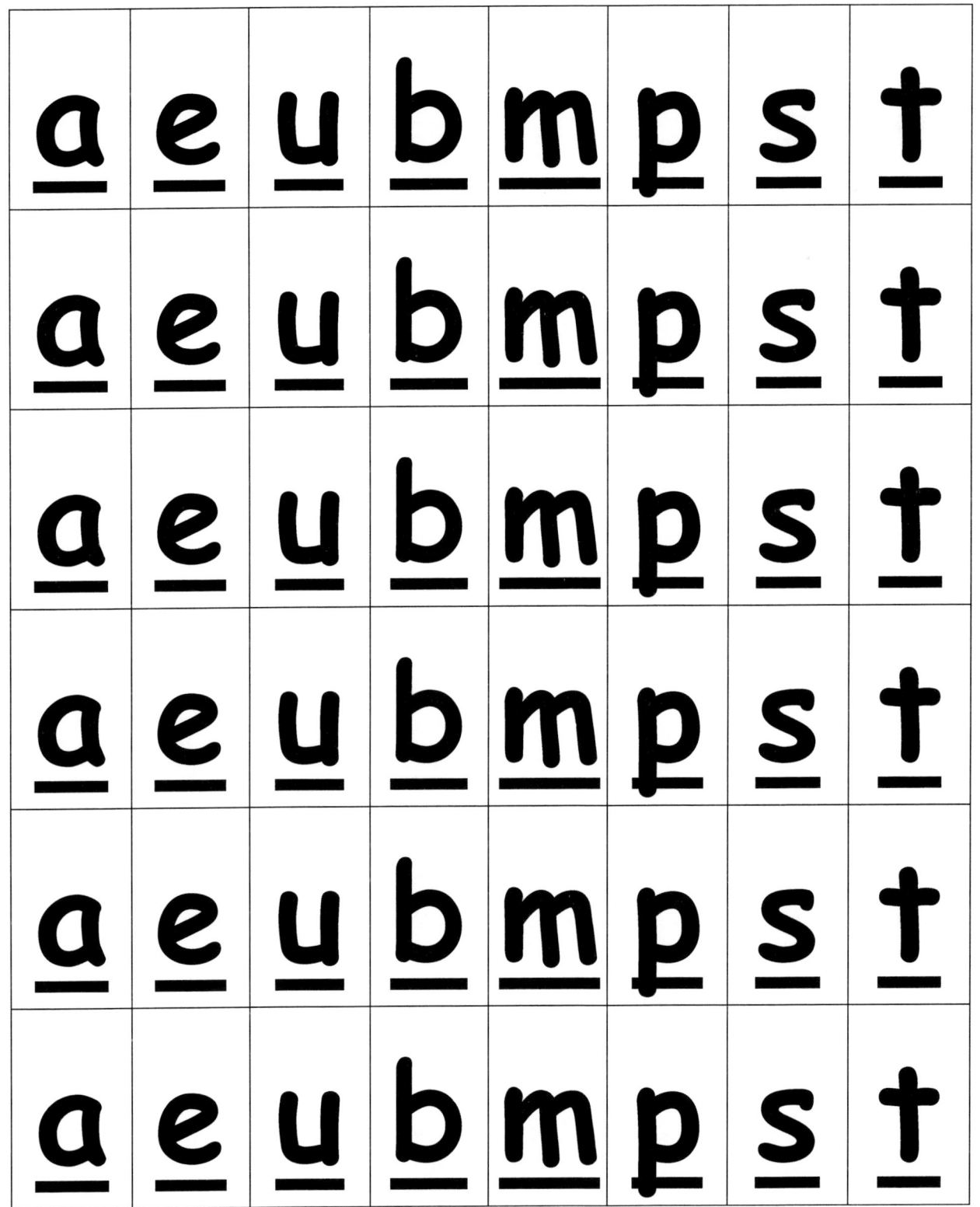

a	e	u	b	m	p	s	t
a	e	u	b	m	p	s	t
a	e	u	b	m	p	s	t
a	e	u	b	m	p	s	t
a	e	u	b	m	p	s	t
a	e	u	b	m	p	s	t

Make these words: pet, bet, best, pest, past, mast, must, stump, bump Copy onto cardstock. Use one row of letters per student. Cut into individual letter cards. Follow directions on page 9.

Review Week 2: Short Vowels E, U
Onset/Rime Cards and Mat

<u>b</u>	ed
<u>p</u>	est
<u>m</u>	en
<u>r</u>	un
<u>j</u>	ump

Copy one Onset/Rime Cards and Mat for each student. The cards are on the left, and the mat is on the right. Cut along the dotted lines to make individual cards. Paper clip one set of cards to each mat. Follow directions on page 10.

Review Week 2: Short E, U
Individual Sort Cards

<u>a</u>	<u>e</u>	<u>u</u>
clap	bed	bun
hat	fell	club
pan	get	run
rat	sled	shut
that	hen	tug

Copy a set of Individual Sort Cards for each student. Cut into individual cards. Follow directions on p. 9.

Review Week 3: Short Vowels
Blending Cards

check	grand	shop
chip	jump	slug
clock	mash	thin
drag	pond	trick
fled	sell	truck

Copy onto cardstock. Laminate and cut into individual cards. Follow directions on page 7 for Blending Practice.

Review Week 3: Short Vowel Review
Onset/Rime Cards and Mat

r	an
b	ed
ch	ip
sl	op
m	ug

Copy one Onset/Rime Cards and Mat for each student. The cards are on the left, and the mat is on the right. Cut along the dotted lines to make individual cards. Paper clip one set of cards to each mat. Follow directions on page 10.

Review Week 3: Short Vowels
Making Words Letter Cards

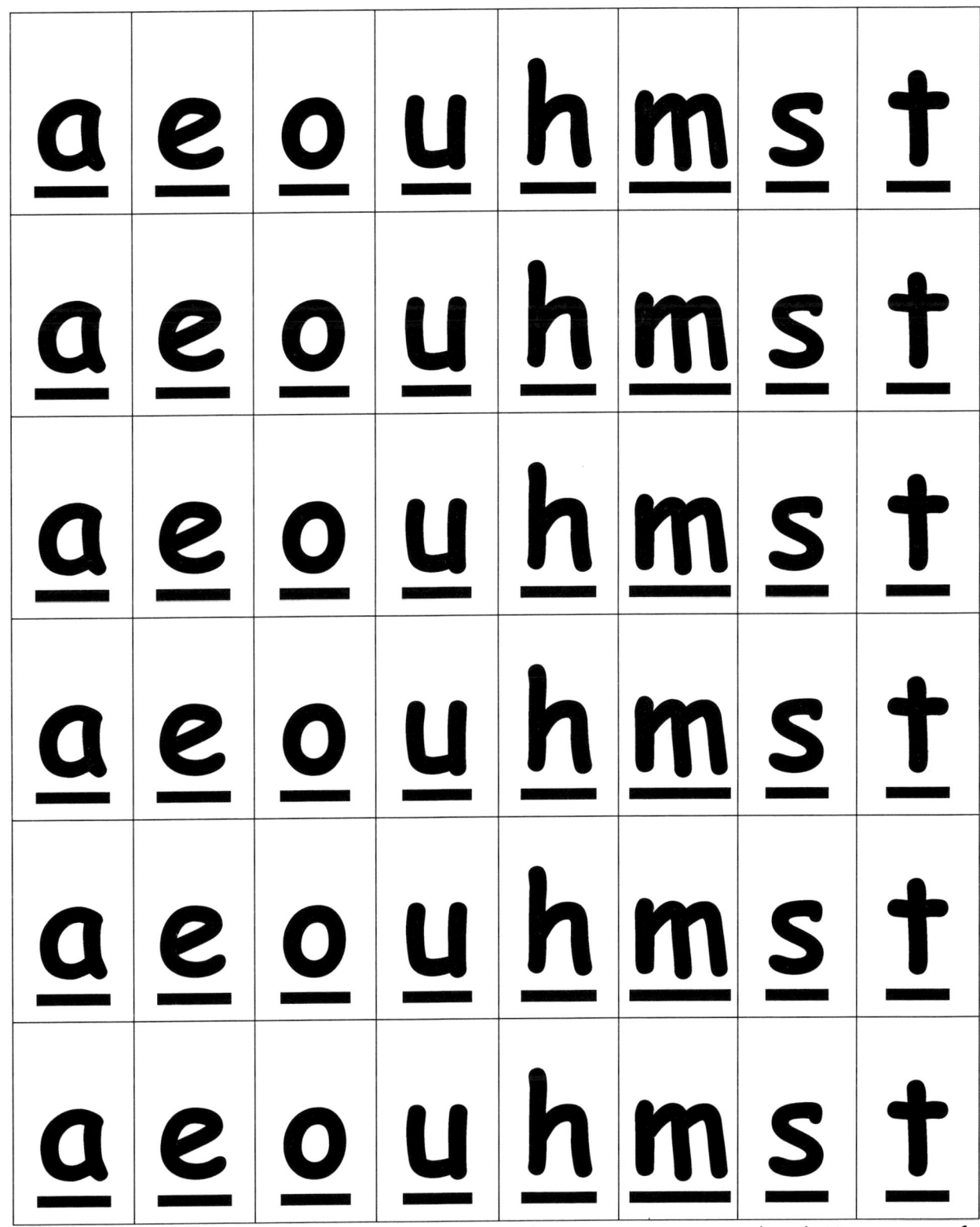

a	e	o	u	h	m	s	t
a	e	o	u	h	m	s	t
a	e	o	u	h	m	s	t
a	e	o	u	h	m	s	t
a	e	o	u	h	m	s	t
a	e	o	u	h	m	s	t

Make these words: met, mat, hat, hot, shot, shut, hut, hum Copy onto cardstock. Use one row of letters per student. Cut into individual letter cards. Follow directions on page 9.

Review Week 3: Short Vowels
Individual Sort Cards

a	e	o
drag	best	clock
grand	check	drop
jam	fled	hot
mash	sell	pond
sand	vest	shop

Copy a set of Individual Sort Cards for each student. Cut into individual cards. Follow directions on p. 9.

Review Week 3: Short Vowels Echo Game (page 1 of 3)

ham	hat	him
hit	hut	hum
ham	hat	him
hit	hut	hum

Copy onto cardstock. Laminate and cut into individual cards. There are two matching sets of cards per page. Clip each set of cards together. Follow directions on p. 10.

©The Reading Teacher's Plan Book

Review Week 3: Short Vowels Echo Game (page 2 of 3)

tan	ten	tin
top	tap	tip
tan	ten	tin
top	tap	tip

Copy onto cardstock. Laminate and cut into individual cards. There are two matching sets of cards per page. Clip each set of cards together. Follow directions on p. 10.

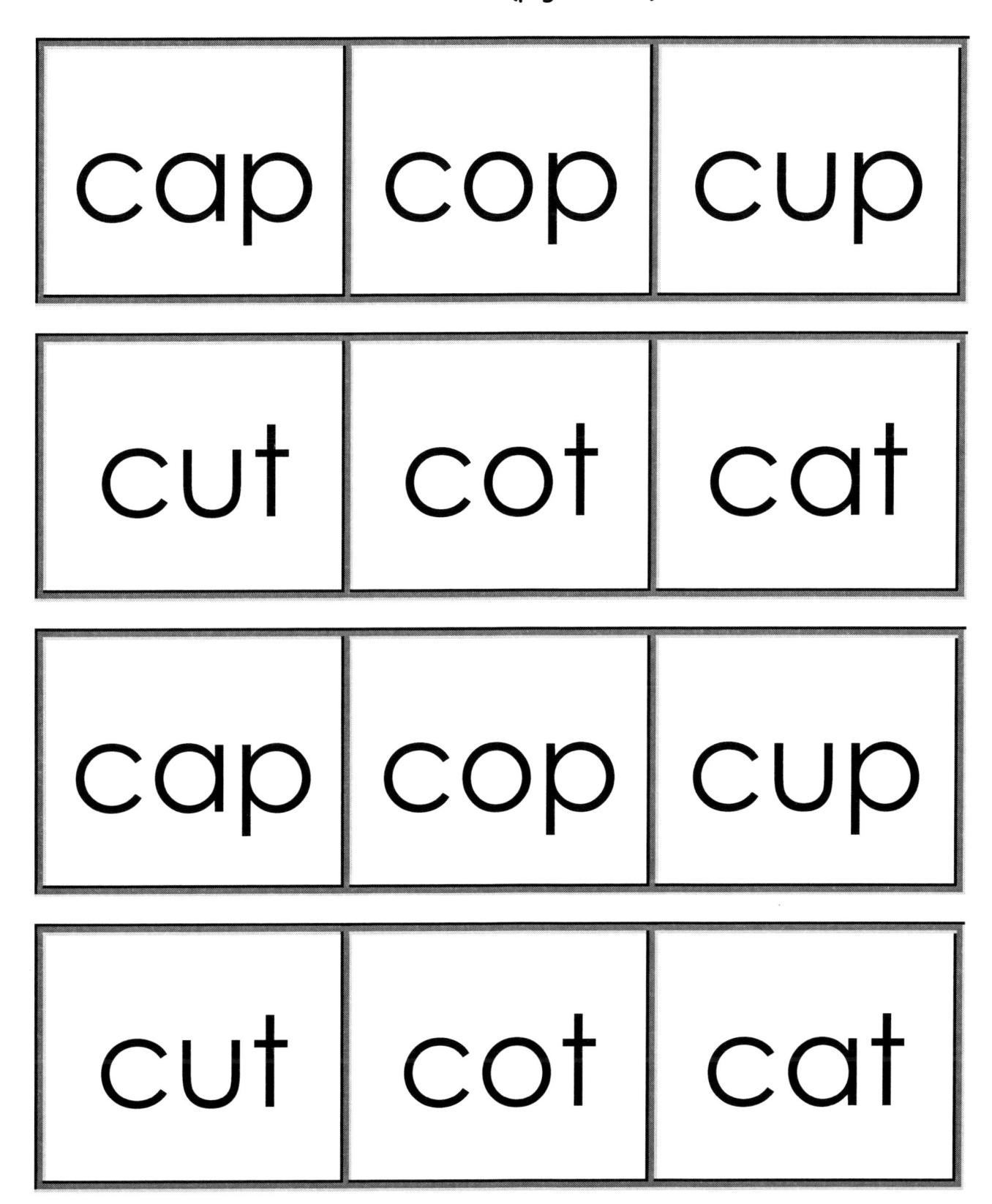

Review Week 3: Short Vowels Echo Game (page 3 of 3)

cap	cop	cup
cut	cot	cat
cap	cop	cup
cut	cot	cat

Copy onto cardstock. Laminate and cut into individual cards. There are two matching sets of cards per page. Clip each set of cards together. Follow directions on p. 10.

©The Reading Teacher's Plan Book

Review Week 3: Short Vowels Slinky Words

Slinky Words: jump, chick, lock, crash, flag, sun, sled, bells
Copy onto cardstock. Laminate and cut into individual cards. Follow directions on page 14.

Review Week 4: Short Vowels
Blending Cards

bell	drop	send
block	dump	shut
chin	glob	stick
crash	hand	stump
dress	lamp	wish

Copy onto cardstock. Laminate and cut into individual cards. Follow directions on page 7 for Blending Practice.

©The Reading Teacher's Plan Book

Review Week 4: Short Vowel Review
Onset/Rime Cards and Mat

sh	ack
b	ell
t	in
sl	op
m	ug

Copy one Onset/Rime Cards and Mat for each student. The cards are on the left, and the mat is on the right. Cut along the dotted lines to make individual cards. Paper clip one set of cards to each mat. Follow directions on page 10.

Review Week 4: Short Vowels
Making Words Letter Cards

a	e	i	c	d	l	p	s
a	e	i	c	d	l	p	s
a	e	i	c	d	l	p	s
a	e	i	c	d	l	p	s
a	e	i	c	d	l	p	s
a	e	i	c	d	l	p	s

Make these words: led, sled, slid, slip, slap, clap, clip, lip Copy onto cardstock. Use one row of letters per student. Cut into individual letter cards. Follow directions on page 9.

Review Week 4: Short Vowels
Individual Sort Cards

e	i	u
bell	chin	bun
dress	list	dump
nest	spill	hunt
send	stick	shut
spell	wish	stump

Copy a set of Individual Sort Cards for each student. Cut into individual cards. Follow directions on p. 9.

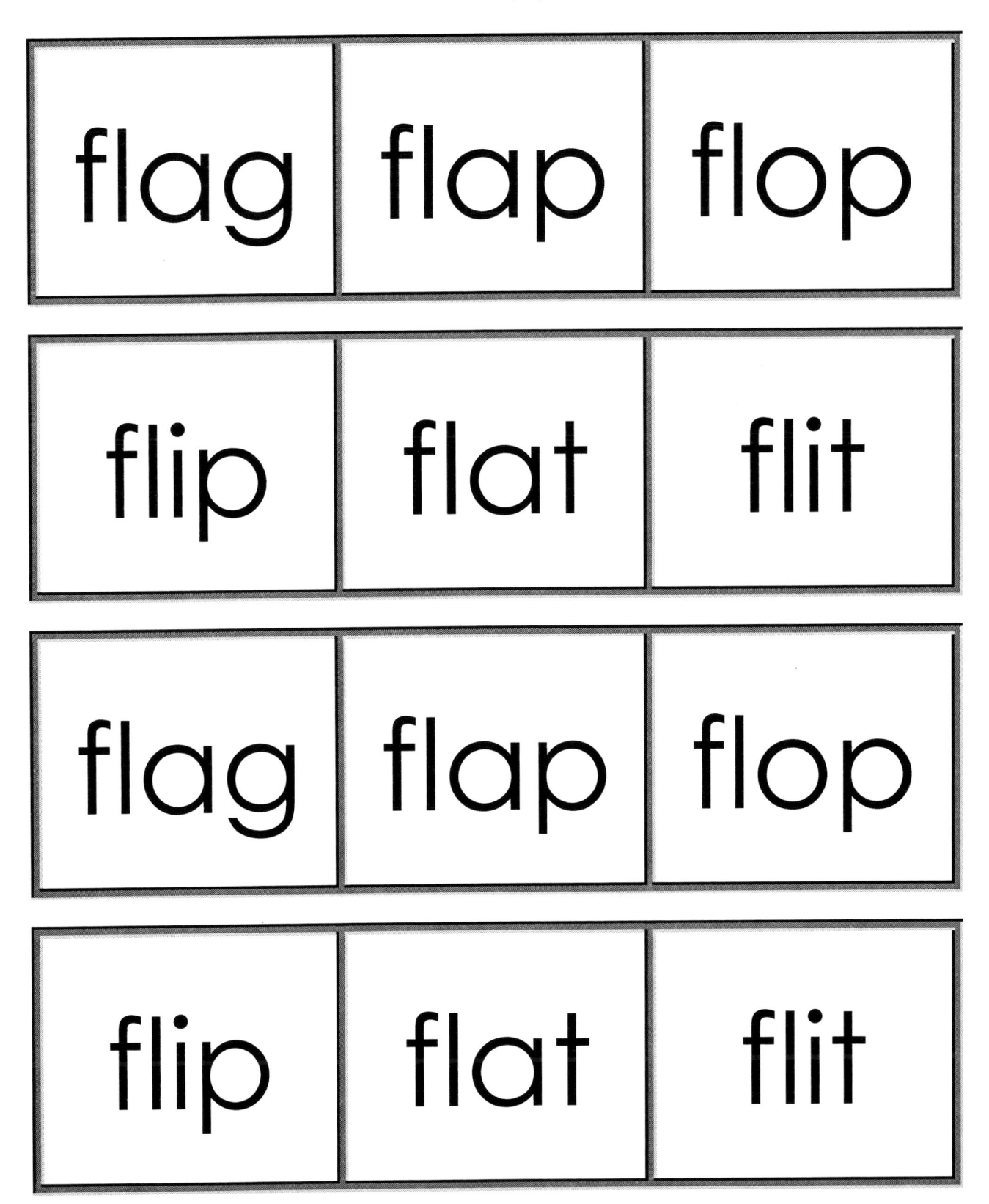

Review Week 4: Short Vowels Echo Game (page 1 of 3)

flag	flap	flop
flip	flat	flit
flag	flap	flop
flip	flat	flit

Copy onto cardstock. Laminate and cut into individual cards. There are two matching sets of cards per page. Clip each set of cards together. Follow directions on p. 10.

©The Reading Teacher's Plan Book

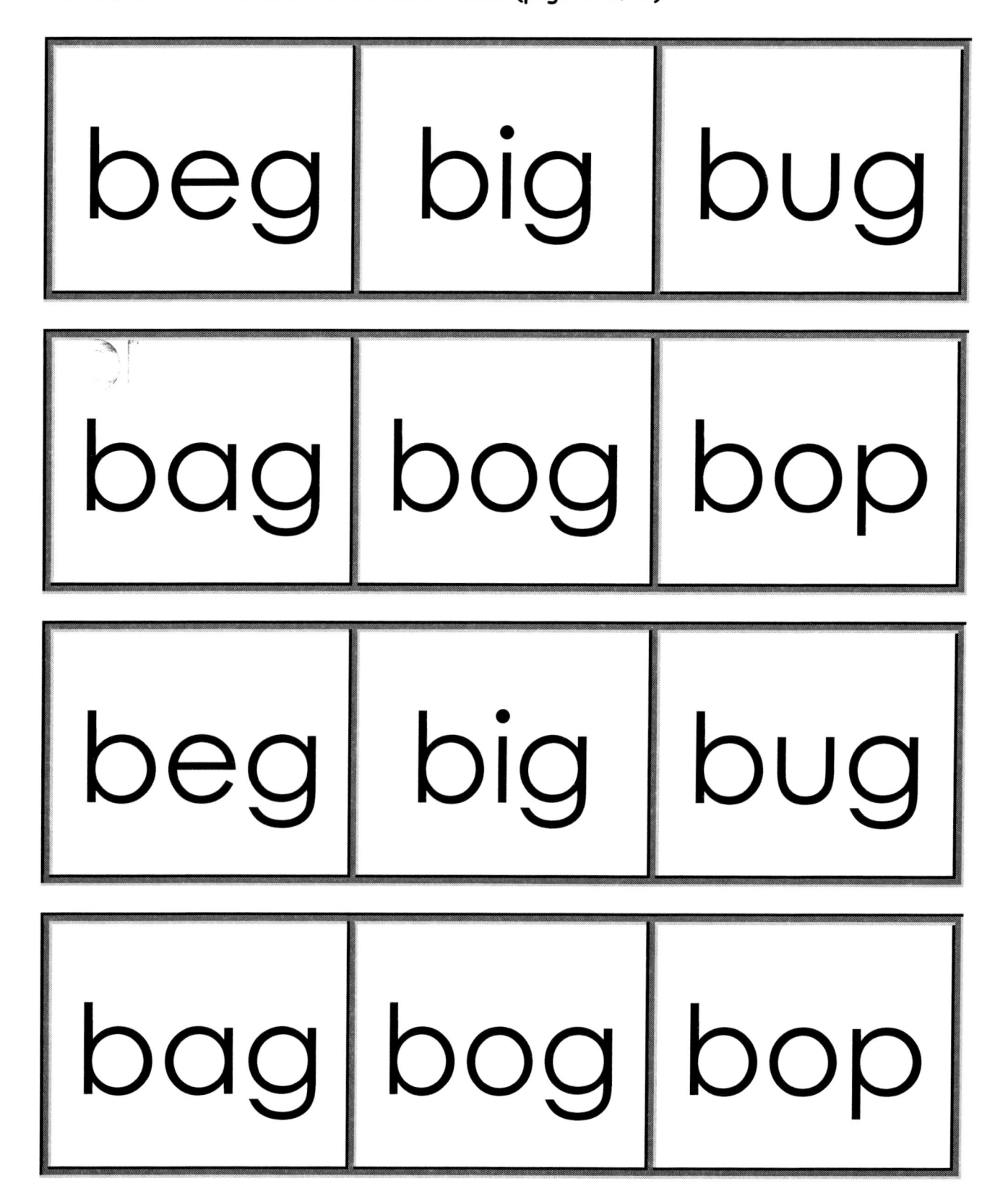

Review Week 4: Short Vowels Echo Game (page 2 of 3)

beg	big	bug
bag	bog	bop
beg	big	bug
bag	bog	bop

Copy onto cardstock. Laminate and cut into individual cards. There are two matching sets of cards per page. Clip each set of cards together. Follow directions on p. 10.

©The Reading Teacher's Plan Book

Review Week 4: Short Vowels Echo Game (page 3 of 3)

men	man	met
mat	map	mop
men	man	met
mat	map	mop

Copy onto cardstock. Laminate and cut into individual cards. There are two matching sets of cards per page. Clip each set of cards together. Follow directions on p. 10.

©The Reading Teacher's Plan Book

Review Week 4: Short Vowels Review Slinky Words

***Slinky Words:** sand, mop, fish, clock, cut, shell, nest, brush*
Copy onto cardstock. Laminate and cut into individual cards. Follow directions on page 14.

Review Week 5: Short Vowels
Blending Cards

chop	mend	slob
cluck	pinch	splash
desk	pump	stamp
dish	shell	stomp
math	slick	thump

Copy onto cardstock. Laminate and cut into individual cards. Follow directions on page 7 for Blending Practice.

Review Week 5: Short Vowel Review
Onset/Rime Cards and Mat

t**h**	at
h	en
cl	ick
p	ock
r	ug

Copy one Onset/Rime Cards and Mat for each student. The cards are on the left, and the mat is on the right. Cut along the dotted lines to make individual cards. Paper clip one set of cards to each mat. Follow directions on page 10.

Review Week 5: Short Vowels
Making Words Letter Cards

a	o	u	g	h	l	p	s	t
a	o	u	g	h	l	p	s	t
a	o	u	g	h	l	p	s	t
a	o	u	g	h	l	p	s	t
a	o	u	g	h	l	p	s	t
a	o	u	g	h	l	p	s	t

Make these words: shop, hop, hot, shot, shut, hut, hug, tug, tag, tap, lap, slap Copy onto cardstock. Use one row of letters per student. Cut into individual letter cards. Follow directions on p. 9.

©The Reading Teacher's Plan Book

Review Week 5: Short Vowels
Individual Sort Cards

a	o	u
brand	chop	cluck
class	knot	dust
math	rock	hush
splash	slob	plug
tack	stomp	thump

Copy a set of Individual Sort Cards for each student. Cut into individual cards. Follow directions on p. 9.

Review Week 5: Short Vowels Echo Game (page 1 of 3)

slap	slip	slop
slit	sit	sat
slap	slip	slop
slit	sit	sat

Copy onto cardstock. Laminate and cut into individual cards. There are two matching sets of cards per page. Clip each set of cards together. Follow directions on p. 10.

Review Week 5: Short Vowels Echo Game (page 2 of 3)

pat	pet	pit
pot	pig	peg
pat	pet	pit
pot	pig	peg

Copy onto cardstock. Laminate and cut into individual cards. There are two matching sets of cards per page. Clip each set of cards together. Follow directions on p. 10.

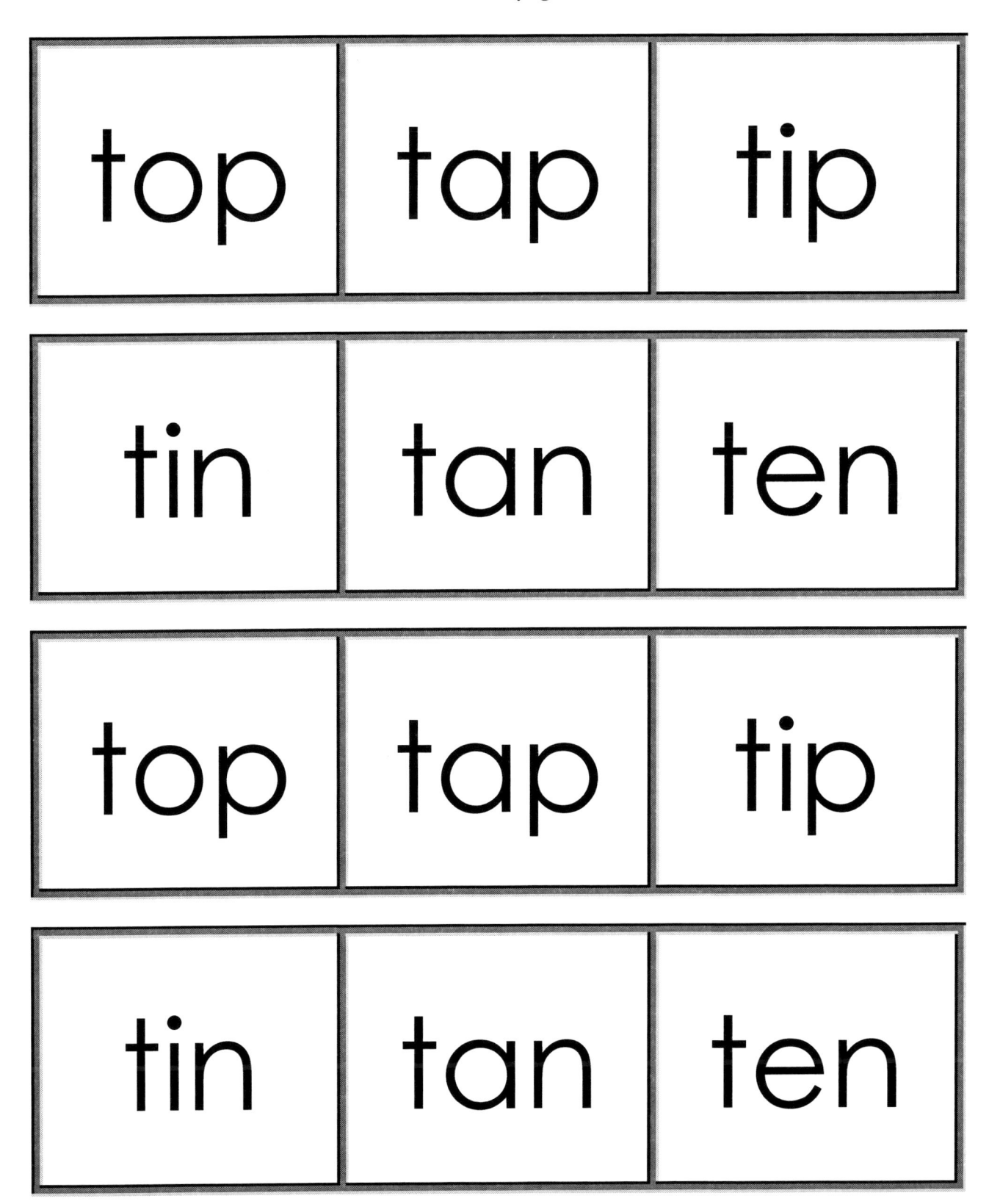

Review Week 5: Short Vowels Echo Game (page 3 of 3)

top	tap	tip
tin	tan	ten
top	tap	tip
tin	tan	ten

Copy onto cardstock. Laminate and cut into individual cards. There are two matching sets of cards per page. Clip each set of cards together. Follow directions on p. 10.

©The Reading Teacher's Plan Book

Review Week 5: Short Vowels Review/ Slinky Words

Slinky Words: swim, map, twins, pen, lunch, pond, truck, check
Copy onto cardstock. Laminate and cut into individual cards. Follow directions on page 14.

272 ©The Reading Teacher's Plan Book

Review Week 6: Long Vowels/Silent E
Blending Cards

bake	mule	shine
chose	nose	slide
cute	ride	smile
hope	rode	tune
made	shake	whale

Copy onto cardstock. Laminate and cut into individual cards. Follow directions on page 7 for Blending Practice.

Review Week 6: Long Vowels/Silent E
Onset/Rime Cards and Mat

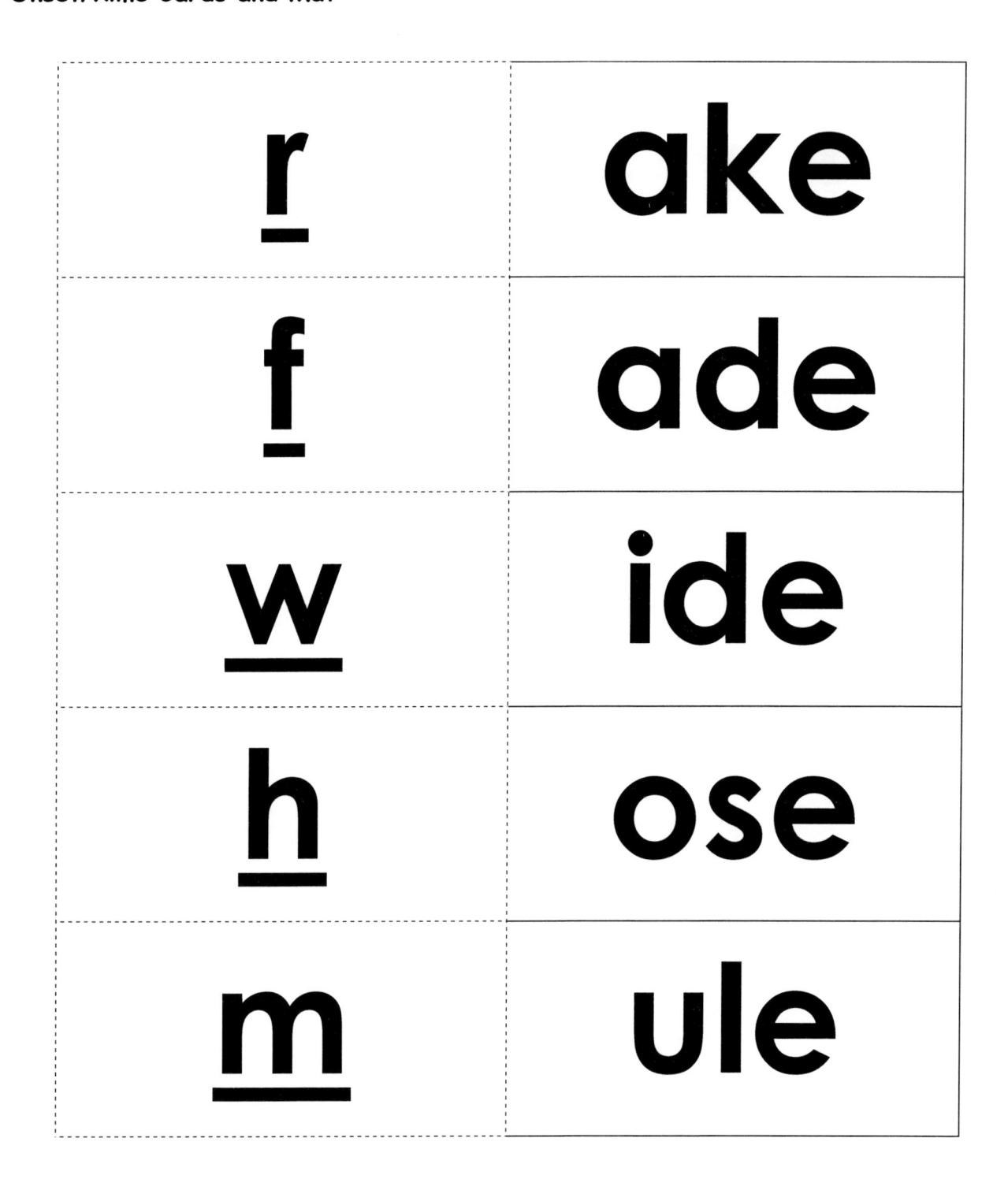

r	ake
f	ade
w	ide
h	ose
m	ule

Copy one Onset/Rime Cards and Mat for each student. The cards are on the left, and the mat is on the right. Cut along the dotted lines to make individual cards. Paper clip one set of cards to each mat. Follow directions on page 10.

Review Week 6: Long Vowels/Silent E
Making Words Letter Cards

a	e	e	i	f	m	n	p	t
a	e	e	i	f	m	n	p	t
a	e	e	i	f	m	n	p	t
a	e	e	i	f	m	n	p	t
a	e	e	i	f	m	n	p	t
a	e	e	i	f	m	n	p	t

Make these words: *Pete, pet, pen, pin, pine, fine, mine, mane, man, pan, pane* Copy onto cardstock. Use one row of letters per student. Cut into individual letter cards. Follow directions on p. 9.

Review Week 6: Long Vowels/Silent E
Individual Sort Cards

a-e	i-e	o-e
bake	bike	chose
made	ride	hope
plane	shine	nose
shake	smile	rode
whale	while	woke

Copy a set of Individual Sort Cards for each student. Cut into individual cards. Follow directions on p. 9.

Review Week 6: Long Vowels/Silent E Echo Game (page 1 of 3)

male	mile	mole
mule	mine	mane
male	mile	mole
mule	mine	mane

Copy onto cardstock. Laminate and cut into individual cards. There are two matching sets of cards per page. Clip each set of cards together. Follow directions on p. 10.

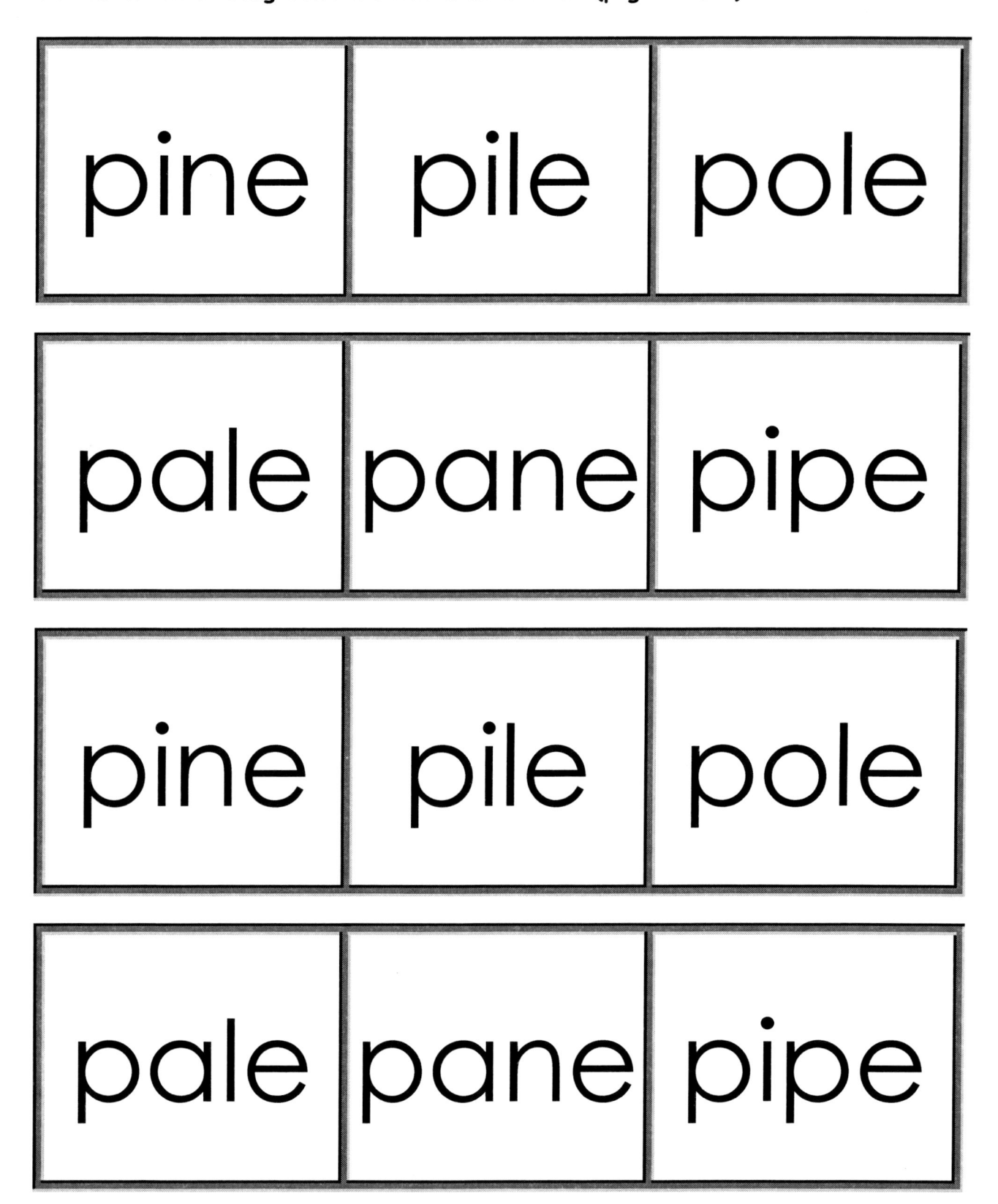

Review Week 6: Long Vowels/Silent E Echo Game (page 2 of 3)

pine	pile	pole
pale	pane	pipe
pine	pile	pole
pale	pane	pipe

Copy onto cardstock. Laminate and cut into individual cards. There are two matching sets of cards per page. Clip each set of cards together. Follow directions on p. 10.

Review Week 6: Long Vowels/Silent E Echo Game (page 3 of 3)

rise	rose	rode
rope	ripe	ride
rise	rose	rode
rope	ripe	ride

Copy onto cardstock. Laminate and cut into individual cards. There are two matching sets of cards per page. Clip each set of cards together. Follow directions on p. 10.

©The Reading Teacher's Plan Book

Review Week 7: Long Vowels/Silent E
Blending Cards

bike	nice	space
cage	page	spike
flake	place	stage
hike	race	twice
make	slice	wake

Copy onto cardstock. Laminate and cut into individual cards. Follow directions on page 7 for Blending Practice.

Review Week 7: Long Vowels/Silent E
Onset/Rime Cards and Mat

<u>m</u>	ake
<u>l</u>	ike
<u>p</u>	ace
<u>r</u>	ice
<u>st</u>	age

Copy one Onset/Rime Cards and Mat for each student. The cards are on the left, and the mat is on the right. Cut along the dotted lines to make individual cards. Paper clip one set of cards to each mat. Follow directions on page 10.

Review Week 7: Long Vowels/Silent E
Making Words Letter Cards

a	e	i	c	g	k	l	m	p
a	e	i	c	g	k	l	m	p
a	e	i	c	g	k	l	m	p
a	e	i	c	g	k	l	m	p
a	e	i	c	g	k	l	m	p
a	e	i	c	g	k	l	m	p

Make these words: mice, Mike, make, lake, lace, place, pace, page, cage, cake Copy onto cardstock. Use one row of letters per student. Cut into individual letter cards. Follow directions on p. 9.

Review Week 7: Long Vowels/Silent E
Individual Sort Cards

ace	ice	age
face	dice	cage
lace	mice	page
place	nice	rage
race	rice	stage
space	slice	wage

Copy a set of Individual Sort Cards for each student. Cut into individual cards. Follow directions on p. 9.

Review Week 7: Long Vowels/Silent E Echo Game (page 1 of 3)

race	rage	rake
rice	rate	rise
race	rage	rake
rice	rate	rise

Copy onto cardstock. Laminate and cut into individual cards. There are two matching sets of cards per page. Clip each set of cards together. Follow directions on p. 10.

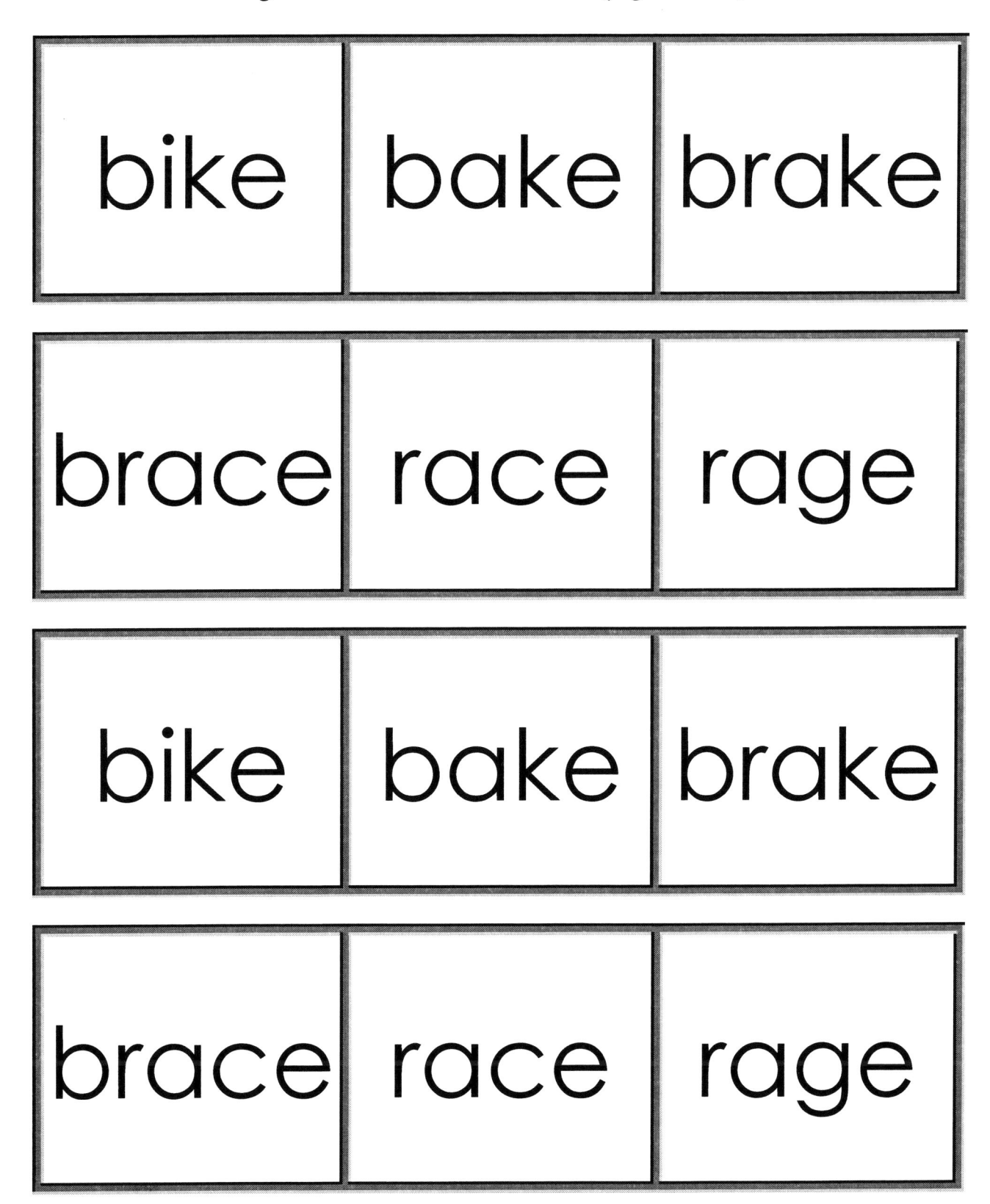

Review Week 7: Long Vowels/Silent E Echo Game (page 2 of 3)

bike	bake	brake
brace	race	rage
bike	bake	brake
brace	race	rage

Copy onto cardstock. Laminate and cut into individual cards. There are two matching sets of cards per page. Clip each set of cards together. Follow directions on p. 10.

Review Week 7: Long Vowels/Silent E Echo Game (page 3 of 3)

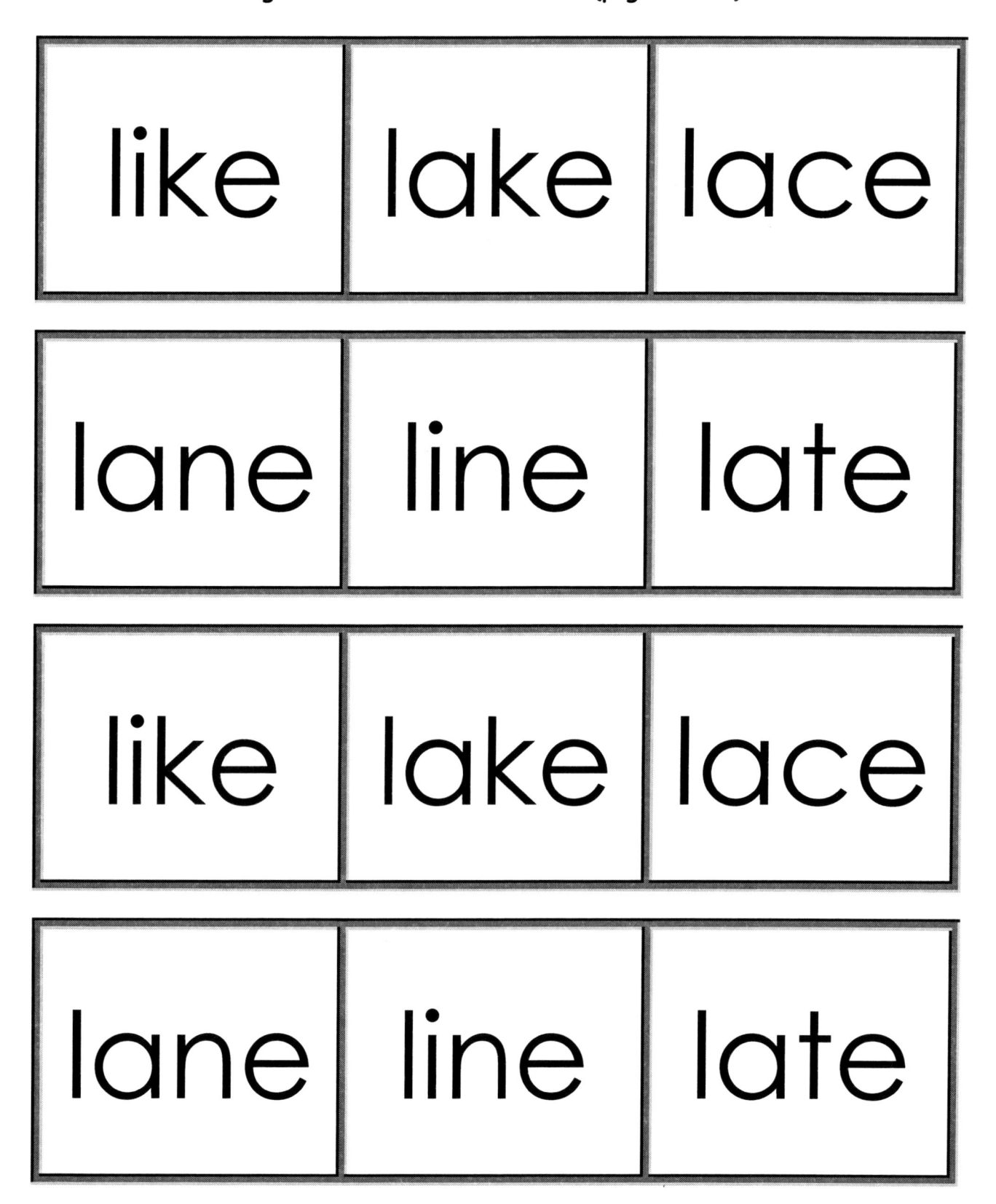

like	lake	lace
lane	line	late
like	lake	lace
lane	line	late

Copy onto cardstock. Laminate and cut into individual cards. There are two matching sets of cards per page. Clip each set of cards together. Follow directions on p. 10.

Review Week 8: Long Vowel Patterns
Blending Cards

clay	lies	snow
cried	meet	spray
flow	peek	sweet
grow	pie	tie
keep	show	tray

Copy onto cardstock. Laminate and cut into individual cards. Follow directions on page 7 for Blending Practice.

©The Reading Teacher's Plan Book

Review Week 8: Long Vowel Patterns
Onset/Rime Cards and Mat

<u>m</u>	ay
<u>b</u>	eet
<u>l</u>	ies
<u>gr</u>	ow
<u>fl</u>	oat

Copy one Onset/Rime Cards and Mat for each student. The cards are on the left, and the mat is on the right. Cut along the dotted lines to make individual cards. Paper clip one set of cards to each mat. Follow directions on page 10.

Review Week 8: Long Vowel Patterns
Individual Sort Cards

ay	ee	ie
clay	keep	cried
day	peek	lies
spray	sweet	pie
tray	ow	tie
flow	grow	snow

Copy a set of Individual Sort Cards for each student. Cut into individual cards. Follow directions on p. 9.

©The Reading Teacher's Plan Book

Review Week 8: Long Vowels Echo Game (page 1 of 3)

seal	seat	seed
seem	seek	seep
seal	seat	seed
seem	seek	seep

Copy onto cardstock. Laminate and cut into individual cards. There are two matching sets of cards per page. Clip each set of cards together. Follow directions on p. 10.

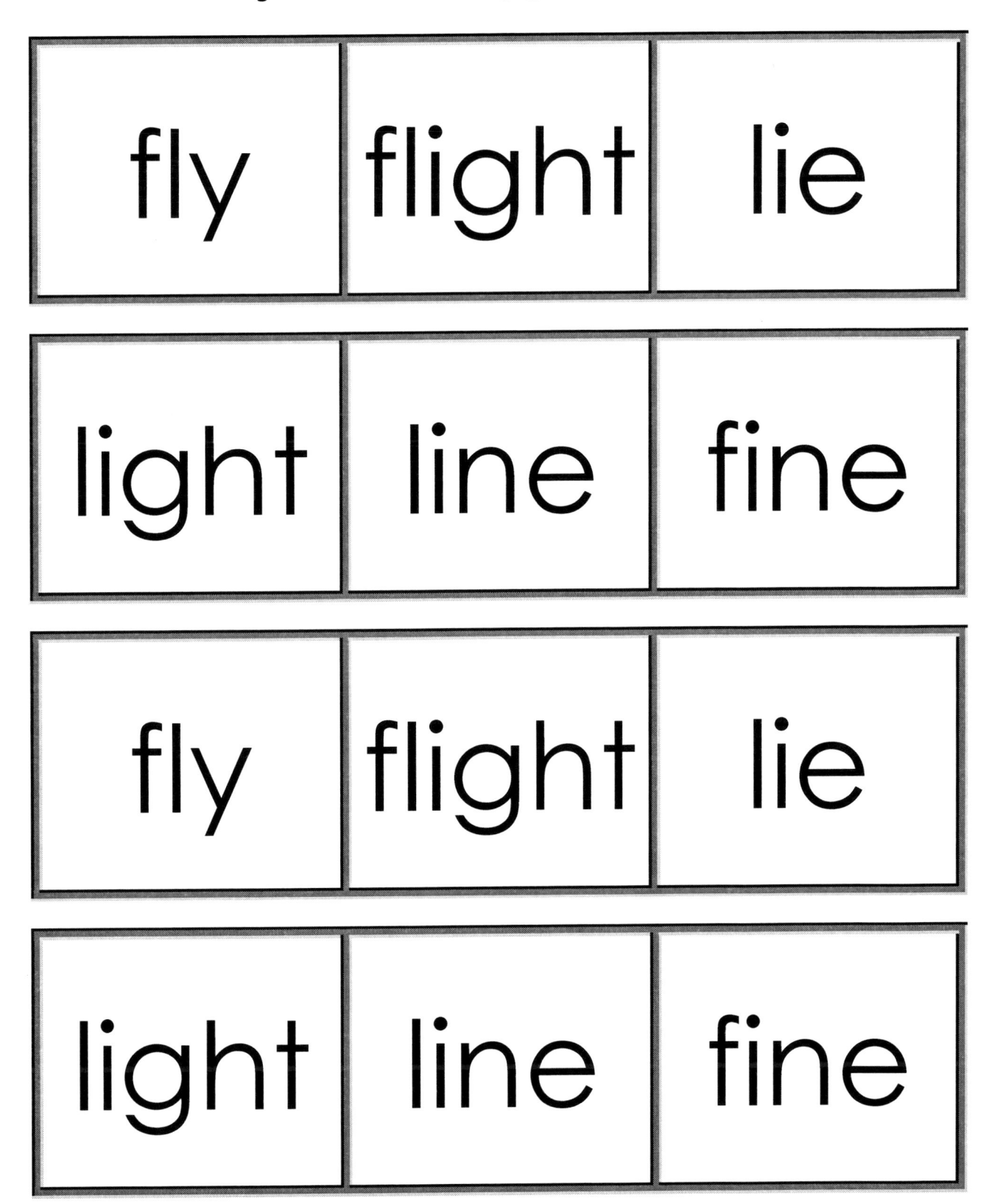

Review Week 8: Long Vowels Echo Game (page 2 of 3)

fly	flight	lie
light	line	fine
fly	flight	lie
light	line	fine

Copy onto cardstock. Laminate and cut into individual cards. There are two matching sets of cards per page. Clip each set of cards together. Follow directions on p. 10.

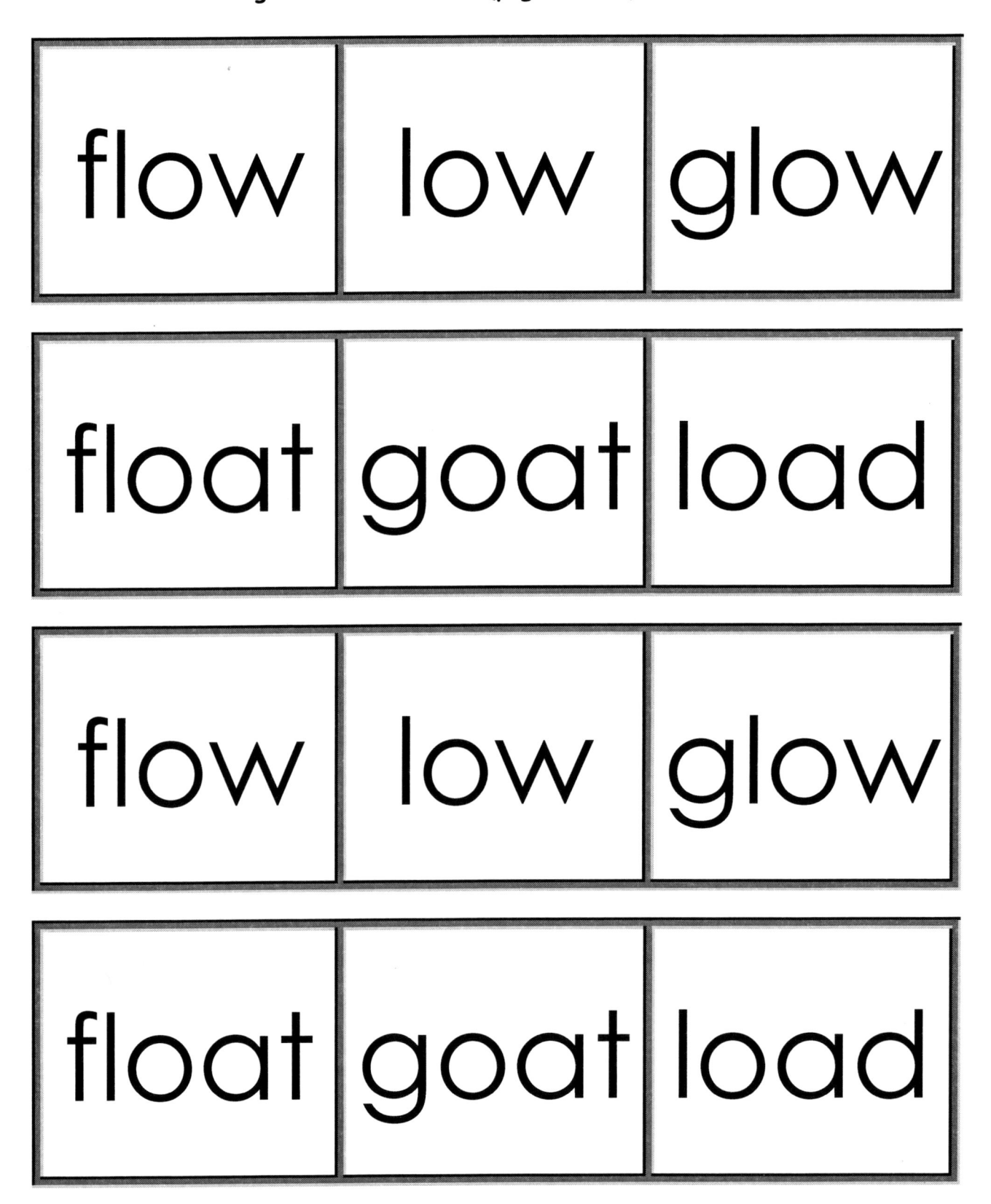

Review Week 8: Long Vowels Echo Game (page 3 of 3)

flow	low	glow
float	goat	load
flow	low	glow
float	goat	load

Copy onto cardstock. Laminate and cut into individual cards. There are two matching sets of cards per page. Clip each set of cards together. Follow directions on p. 10.

Review Week 8: Long Vowel Slinky Words

Slinky Words: tray, cheese, pie, snow, clay, wheel, fries, crow
Copy onto cardstock. Laminate and cut into individual cards. Follow directions on page 14.

©The Reading Teacher's Plan Book

Review Week 8: "Long Vowel Patterns" Word Hunt Writing Mats

Word Hunt Writing Mat

ay	ee	ie	ow

Word Hunt Writing Mat

ay	ee	ie	ow

Copy a Writing Mat for each student. Use with Word Windows (pgs. 383-384). Follow directions on p. 11.

Review Week 9: Long Vowel Patterns
Blending Cards

beach	flight	main
boat	grain	meat
bright	groan	night
clean	leaf	snail
coach	light	trail

Copy onto cardstock. Laminate and cut into individual cards. Follow directions on page 7 for Blending Practice.

Review Week 9: Long Vowel Patterns
Onset/Rime Cards and Mat

<u>m</u>	ain
<u>s</u>	eat
<u>r</u>	eal
<u>br</u>	ight
<u>l</u>	oad

Copy one Onset/Rime Cards and Mat for each student. The cards are on the left, and the mat is on the right. Cut along the dotted lines to make individual cards. Paper clip one set of cards to each mat. Follow directions on page 10.

Review Week 9: Long Vowel Patterns
Individual Sort Cards

ai	ea	igh
grain	beach	bright
main	clean	flight
snail	leaf	light
trail	oa	night
boat	coach	groan

Copy a set of Individual Sort Cards for each student. Cut into individual cards. Follow directions on p. 9.

©The Reading Teacher's Plan Book

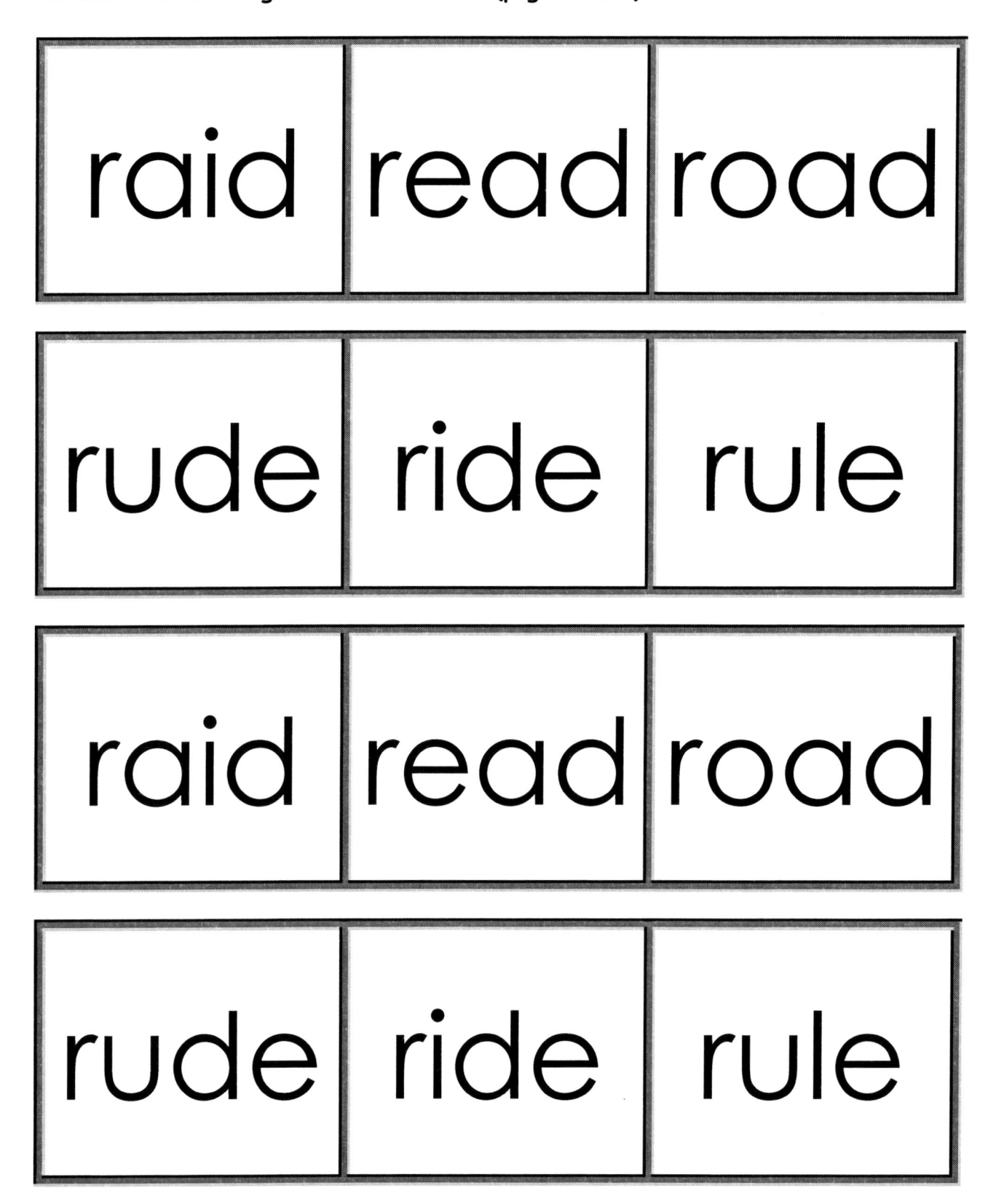

Review Week 9: Long Vowels Echo Game (page 1 of 3)

raid	read	road
rude	ride	rule
raid	read	road
rude	ride	rule

Copy onto cardstock. Laminate and cut into individual cards. There are two matching sets of cards per page. Clip each set of cards together. Follow directions on p. 10.

Review Week 9: Long Vowels Echo Game (page 2 of 3)

tray	tree	train
true	try	treat
tray	tree	train
true	try	treat

Copy onto cardstock. Laminate and cut into individual cards. There are two matching sets of cards per page. Clip each set of cards together. Follow directions on p. 10.

Review Week 9: Long Vowels Echo Game (page 3 of 3)

bait	beat	boat
bite	bead	bail
bait	beat	boat
bite	bead	bail

Copy onto cardstock. Laminate and cut into individual cards. There are two matching sets of cards per page. Clip each set of cards together. Follow directions on p. 10.

Review Week 9: Long Vowel Slinky Words

Slinky Words: paint, peach, knight, float, snail, dream, light, toast
Copy onto cardstock. Laminate and cut into individual cards. Follow directions on page 14.

©The Reading Teacher's Plan Book

Review Week 9: "Long Vowel Patterns" Word Hunt Writing Mats

Word Hunt Writing Mat

ai	ea	igh	oa

Word Hunt Writing Mat

ai	ea	igh	oa

Copy a Writing Mat for each student. Use with Word Windows (pgs. 383-384). Follow directions on p. 11.

Review Week 10: Long Vowel Patterns
Blending Cards

bay	peach	stay
crow	play	sway
cry	slow	throw
fly	speak	try
neat	squeak	why

Copy onto cardstock. Laminate and cut into individual cards. Follow directions on page 7 for Blending Practice.

Review Week 10: Long Vowel Patterns
Onset/Rime Cards and Mat

b	ay
m	eat
tr	ied
cr	ow
sh	y

Copy one Onset/Rime Cards and Mat for each student. The cards are on the left, and the mat is on the right. Cut along the dotted lines to make individual cards. Paper clip one set of cards to each mat. Follow directions on page 10.

Review Week 10: Long Vowel Patterns
Individual Sort Cards

ay	**ea**	**y**
bay	neat	cry
play	peach	fly
stay	speak	try
sway	**ow**	why
crow	slow	throw

Copy a set of Individual Sort Cards for each student. Cut into individual cards. Follow directions on p. 9.

Review Week 10: Long Vowels Echo Game (page 1 of 3)

meat	mean	main
moan	mow	may
meat	mean	main
moan	mow	may

Copy onto cardstock. Laminate and cut into individual cards. There are two matching sets of cards per page. Clip each set of cards together. Follow directions on p. 10.

Review Week 10: Long Vowels Echo Game (page 2 of 3)

fly	flight	try
tray	tight	ray
fly	flight	try
tray	tight	ray

Copy onto cardstock. Laminate and cut into individual cards. There are two matching sets of cards per page. Clip each set of cards together. Follow directions on p. 10.

Review Week 10: Long Vowels Echo Game (page 3 of 3)

snow	slow	low
slay	sly	slot
snow	slow	low
slay	sly	slot

Copy onto cardstock. Laminate and cut into individual cards. There are two matching sets of cards per page. Clip each set of cards together. Follow directions on p. 10.

Review Week 10: Long Vowel Slinky Words

***Slinky Words:** hay, beach, blow, fly, spray, treat, row, spy*
Copy onto cardstock. Laminate and cut into individual cards. Follow directions on page 14.

©The Reading Teacher's Plan Book

Review Week 10: "Long Vowel Patterns" Word Hunt Writing Mats

Word Hunt Writing Mat

ay	ea	y	ow

Word Hunt Writing Mat

ay	ea	y	ow

Copy a Writing Mat for each student. Use with Word Windows (pgs. 383-384). Follow directions on p. 11.

Review Week 11: "A Patterns"
Blending Cards

ball	flash	park
card	grand	place
chain	lawn	small
face	mail	start
flame	make	stray

Copy onto cardstock. Laminate and cut into individual cards. Follow directions on page 7 for Blending Practice.

Review Week 11: "A Patterns"
Making Words Letter Cards

a	i	b	f	l	l	r	s	t
a	i	b	f	l	l	r	s	t
a	i	b	f	l	l	r	s	t
a	i	b	f	l	l	r	s	t
a	i	b	f	l	l	r	s	t
a	i	b	f	l	l	r	s	t

Make these words: bat, bar, ball, bail, fail, fall, far, star, stall, tall, tail, rail, rat Copy onto cardstock. Use one row of letters per student. Cut into individual letter cards. Follow directions on p. 9.

Review Week 11: "A Patterns" Word Hunt Writing Mats

Word Hunt Writing Mat

short a	ar	all	ay

Word Hunt Writing Mat

short a	ar	all	ay

Copy a Writing Mat for each student. Use with Word Windows (pgs. 383-384). Follow directions on p. 11.

©The Reading Teacher's Plan Book

Review Week 12: "E Patterns"
Blending Cards

brew	fern	screw
cheese	germ	spell
chest	grew	spend
clerk	please	street
dream	queen	treat

Copy onto cardstock. Laminate and cut into individual cards. Follow directions on page 7 for Blending Practice.

Review Week 12: "E Patterns"
Making Words Letter Cards

a	e	c	h	k	n	p	r	t	w
a	e	c	h	k	n	p	r	t	w
a	e	c	h	k	n	p	r	t	w
a	e	c	h	k	n	p	r	t	w
a	e	c	h	k	n	p	r	t	w
a	e	c	h	k	n	p	r	t	w

Make these words: perk, peak, peck, neck, new, net, neat, heat, cheat, chew Copy onto cardstock. Use one row of letters per student. Cut into individual letter cards. Follow directions on p. 9.

©The Reading Teacher's Plan Book

Review Week 12: "E Patterns" Word Hunt Writing Mats

Word Hunt Writing Mat

short e	ea	ew	er

Word Hunt Writing Mat

short e	ea	ew	er

Copy a Writing Mat for each student. Use with Word Windows (pgs. 383-384). Follow directions on p. 11.

Review Week 13: "I Patterns"
Blending Cards

bring	knight	swirl
crisp	might	third
drink	rice	tries
file	spice	twine
flies	swing	twist

Copy onto cardstock. Laminate and cut into individual cards. Follow directions on page 7 for Blending Practice.

Review Week 13: "I Patterns"
Making Words Letter Cards

i	e	g	h	k	n	p	r	s	t
i	e	g	h	k	n	p	r	s	t
i	e	g	h	k	n	p	r	s	t
i	e	g	h	k	n	p	r	s	t
i	e	g	h	k	n	p	r	s	t
i	e	g	h	k	n	p	r	s	t

Make these words: stir, sir, sigh, sight, sit, pit, pie, tie, tin, pin, pine, pink, sink, sing, ring Copy onto cardstock. Use one row of letters per student. Cut into individual letter cards. Follow directions on p. 9.

Review Week 13: "I Patterns" Word Hunt Writing Mats

Word Hunt Writing Mat

short i	ing	i_e	igh

Word Hunt Writing Mat

short i	ing	i_e	igh

Copy a Writing Mat for each student. Use with Word Windows (pgs. 383-384). Follow directions on p. 11.

©The Reading Teacher's Plan Book

Review Week 14: "O Patterns"
Blending Cards

boy	fork	pond
broom	glow	shout
choice	groan	spoil
cook	ground	spoke
crown	how	sprout

Copy onto cardstock. Laminate and cut into individual cards. Follow directions on page 7 for Blending Practice.

Review Week 14: "O Patterns"
Making Words Letter Cards

a	o	b	g	n	r	t	w	y
a	o	b	g	n	r	t	w	y
a	o	b	g	n	r	t	w	y
a	o	b	g	n	r	t	w	y
a	o	b	g	n	r	t	w	y
a	o	b	g	n	r	t	w	y

Make these words: *grow, row, Roy, boy, bow, boat, goat, go, to, toy, tow, town, torn, worn* Copy onto cardstock. Use one row of letters per student. Cut into individual letter cards. Follow directions on p. 9.

Review Week 14: "O Patterns" Word Hunt Writing Mats

Word Hunt Writing Mat

short o	ow	or	ou

Word Hunt Writing Mat

short o	ow	or	ou

Copy a Writing Mat for each student. Use with Word Windows (pgs. 383-384). Follow directions on p. 11.

Review Week 15: "U Patterns"
Blending Cards

blue	curl	prune
bruise	flute	stung
clue	fruit	suit
crunch	glue	thump
cube	hurt	turn

Copy onto cardstock. Laminate and cut into individual cards. Follow directions on page 7 for Blending Practice.

Review Week 15: "U Patterns"
Making Words Letter Cards

e	u	b	c	l	n	r	t
e	u	b	c	l	n	r	t
e	u	b	c	l	n	r	t
e	u	b	c	l	n	r	t
e	u	b	c	l	n	r	t
e	u	b	c	l	n	r	t

Make these words: blue, clue, cue, cub, cube, tube, tub, but, bun, burn, turn Copy onto cardstock. Use one row of letters per student. Cut into individual letter cards. Follow directions on p. 9.

**Review Week 15:
Word Hunt Cube
"U Patterns"**

Copy onto cardstock. Laminate and cut along the outside edges. Fold along the lines and assemble with hot glue. Use with "U Patterns" Word Hunt Mats. Follow Word Hunt directions on page 11.

ur

u   **u-e**   **ue**

ur

u

Review Week 15: U Patterns

Review Week 15: "U Patterns" Word Hunt Mats

burn	glue	jump
stuck	shut	mule
hurt	cute	true

tube	duck	burp
blue	cue	June
lump	shrub	curb

must	tune	plum
Sue	slurp	clue
cube	truck	nurse

Copy a mat for each student. (Three mats are provided.) Provide an assortment of bingo chips. Use with "U Patterns" Word Hunt Cube. Follow directions on page 11.

Advanced Week 1: Syllabication – Double Consonants
Group Sort Cards (Page 1 of 2)

tt	**bb**	**nn**
attic	bubble	dinner
butter	rabbit	tunnel
fatten	ribbon	channel
kitten	rubber	funny

Copy onto cardstock. Laminate and cut into individual cards. Follow directions on page 8.

Advanced Week 1: Syllabication – Double Consonants
Group Sort Cards (Page 2 of 2)

letter	**mm**	**pp**
matter	common	puppy
pretty	summer	support
rotten	**dd**	wrapper
ladder	sudden	zipper

Copy onto cardstock. Laminate and cut into individual cards. Follow directions on page 8.

Advanced Week 1: Double Consonants
Syllable Match-Up (page 1 of 2)

lit	ter	bon	net
zip	per	tun	nel
lad	der	fun	ny

Copy onto cardstock. Laminate. Cut each strip into four cards and clip together. Keep sets separate. Follow directions for "Syllable Match-Up" on page 9.

©The Reading Teacher's Plan Book

Advanced Week 1: Double Consonants
Syllable Match-Up (page 2 of 2)

rab	bit	pup	py
but	ter	din	ner
bat	ter	wrap	per

Copy onto cardstock. Laminate. Cut each strip into four cards and clip together. Keep sets separate. Follow directions for "Syllable Match-Up" on page 9.

©The Reading Teacher's Plan Book

Advanced Week 2: Syllabication - Consonant + le
Group Sort Cards (Page 1 of 2)

-ble	-ple	-gle
bubble	apple	bugle
dribble	maple	giggle
marble	purple	jungle
noble	sample	angle

Copy onto cardstock. Laminate and cut into individual cards. Follow directions on page 8.

Advanced Week 2: Syllabication – Consonant + le
Group Sort Cards (Page 2 of 2)

-tle	pebble	gurgle
battle	table	wiggle
cattle	tumble	gentle
kettle	simple	mantle
little	staple	title

Copy onto cardstock. Laminate and cut into individual cards. Follow directions on page 8.

Advanced Week 2: Consonant + le
Syllable Match-Up (page 1 of 2)

jun	gle	bat	tle
bub	ble	daz	zle
pur	ple	un	cle

Copy onto cardstock. Laminate. Cut each strip into four cards and clip together. Keep sets separate. Follow directions for "Syllable Match-Up" on page 9.

©The Reading Teacher's Plan Book

Advanced Week 2: Consonant + le
Syllable Match-Up (page 2 of 2)

fid	dle	gig	gle
sam	ple	lit	tle
fiz	zle	sim	ple

Copy onto cardstock. Laminate. Cut each strip into four cards and clip together. Keep sets separate. Follow directions for "Syllable Match-Up" on page 9.

©The Reading Teacher's Plan Book

Advanced Week 2: Syllabication – Consonant + le
Individual Sort Cards

-ble	**-ple**	**-gle**
bubble	simple	wiggle
dribble	purple	giggle
marble	staple	jungle
table	apple	gurgle
pebble	maple	bugle

Copy a set of Individual Sort Cards for each student. Cut into individual cards. Follow directions on p. 9.

Advanced Week 3: Syllabication – Suffixes
Group Sort Cards (Page 1 of 2)

-ful	**-less**	**-ly**
careful	careless	bravely
cheerful	colorless	friendly
colorful	endless	happily
helpful	flawless	kindly

Copy onto cardstock. Laminate and cut into individual cards. Follow directions on page 8.

Advanced Week 3: Syllabication – Suffixes
Group Sort Cards (Page 2 of 2)

hopeful	helpless	loudly
joyful	homeless	nicely
thankful	senseless	quickly
useful	tasteless	smoothly
wonderful	useless	sweetly

Copy onto cardstock. Laminate and cut into individual cards. Follow directions on page 8.

**Advanced Week 3:
Word Hunt Cube
Suffixes**

Copy onto cardstock. Laminate and cut along the outside edges. Fold along the lines and assemble with hot glue. Use with "Suffixes" Word Hunt Mats. Follow Word Hunt directions on page 11.

less

ly   ful   less

less

ful

Advanced Week 3: Suffixes

338   ©The Reading Teacher's Plan Book

Advanced Week 3: "Suffixes" Word Hunt Mats

hopeful	helpless	smoothly
sweetly	thankful	careless
homeless	colorful	happily

colorless	grateful	useful
quickly	nicely	flawless
joyful	endless	friendly

loudly	senseless	cheerful
helpful	kindly	bravely
useless	tasteless	careful

Copy a mat for each student. (Three mats are provided.) Provide an assortment of bingo chips. Use with "Suffixes" Word Hunt Cube. Follow directions on page 11.

Advanced Week 3: Syllabication – Suffixes
Individual Sort Cards

-ful	-less	-ly
careful	careless	friendly
cheerful	endless	happily
helpful	helpless	nicely
hopeful	hopeless	quickly
useful	useless	smoothly

Copy a set of Individual Sort Cards for each student. Cut into individual cards. Follow directions on p. 9.

Advanced Week 4: Syllabication – Prefixes
Group Sort Cards (Page 1 of 2)

pre- (before)	**re-** (again)	**un-** (not)
precut	recall	unable
pregame	recount	unclean
preheat	repeat	uneven
prewash	replay	unfair

Copy onto cardstock. Laminate and cut into individual cards. Follow directions on page 8.

Advanced Week 4: Syllabication – Prefixes
Group Sort Cards (Page 2 of 2)

mis- (wrongly)	reread	unfriendly
miscount	retell	unkind
misfit	return	unlucky
mislead	rewind	unplug
misspell	rewrite	untie

Copy onto cardstock. Laminate and cut into individual cards. Follow directions on page 8.

Advanced Week 4:
Word Hunt Cube
Syllabication – Prefixes

Copy onto cardstock. Laminate and cut along the outside edges. Fold along the lines and assemble with hot glue. Use with "Prefixes" Word Hunt Mats. Follow Word Hunt directions on page 11.

re

mis | un | pre

re

un

Advanced Week 4: Prefixes

©The Reading Teacher's Plan Book

Advanced Week 4: "Prefixes" Word Hunt Mats

precut	unplug	repeat
recall	unlucky	unable
prewash	miscount	rewind

uneven	untie	recount
unkind	pregame	unlucky
misfit	replay	misspell

reread	return	mislead
unable	rewrite	unfair
unkind	prewash	preheat

Copy a mat for each student. (Three mats are provided.) Provide an assortment of bingo chips. Use with "Prefixes" Word Hunt Cube. Follow directions on page 11.

Advanced Week 4: Syllabication – Prefixes
Individual Sort Cards

pre-	re-	un-
precut	recount	unable
pregame	repeat	unclean
preheat	replay	unfair
preschool	retell	unkind
prewash	rewrite	unlucky

Copy a set of Individual Sort Cards for each student. Cut into individual cards. Follow directions on p. 9.

Advanced Week 5: Syllabication – Closed/Open Syllables
Group Sort Cards (Page 1 of 2)

1st syllable closed	1st syllable open	
batman	bonus	
cabin	crazy	
napkin	lady	
picnic	open	

Copy onto cardstock. Laminate and cut into individual cards. Follow directions on page 8.

Advanced Week 5: Syllabication – Closed/Open Syllables
Group Sort Cards (Page 2 of 2)

planet	predict	
robin	rodent	
sunset	secret	
tonsil	spider	
upset	table	

Copy onto cardstock. Laminate and cut into individual cards. Follow directions on page 8.

Advanced Week 5: Closed Syllables
Syllable Match-Up (page 1 of 2)

pic	nic	bas	ket
pump	kin	fin	ish
cab	in	plan	et

Copy onto cardstock. Laminate. Cut each strip into four cards and clip together. Keep sets separate. Follow directions for "Syllable Match-Up" on page 9.

©The Reading Teacher's Plan Book

Advanced Week 5: Closed Syllables
Syllable Match-Up (page 2 of 2)

sun	set	ton	sil
up	set	nap	kin
hat	box	rob	in

Copy onto cardstock. Laminate. Cut each strip into four cards and clip together. Keep sets separate. Follow directions for "Syllable Match-Up" on page 9.

©The Reading Teacher's Plan Book

Advanced Week 5: Syllabication – Closed/Open Syllables
Individual Sort Cards

1st syllable closed	1st syllable open	
cabin	bonus	
napkin	crazy	
picnic	predict	
robin	secret	
sunset	spider	

Copy a set of Individual Sort Cards for each student. Cut into individual cards. Follow directions on p. 9.

Advanced Week 6: Syllabication – Open/Closed Syllables
Group Sort Cards (Page 1 of 2)

1st syllable open	1st syllable closed	
baby	basket	
donut	comet	
female	fabric	
human	fossil	

Copy onto cardstock. Laminate and cut into individual cards. Follow directions on page 8.

Advanced Week 6: Syllabication – Open/Closed Syllables
Group Sort Cards (Page 2 of 2)

moment	habit	
music	husband	
program	kitten	
silent	pencil	
tiger	tractor	

Copy onto cardstock. Laminate and cut into individual cards. Follow directions on page 8.

Advanced Week 6: Open Syllables
Syllable Match-Up (page 1 of 2)

do	nut	fro	zen
mu	sic	pro	gram
si	lent	ti	ger

Copy onto cardstock. Laminate. Cut each strip into four cards and clip together. Keep sets separate. Follow directions for "Syllable Match-Up" on page 9.

©The Reading Teacher's Plan Book

Advanced Week 6: Open Syllables
Syllable Match-Up (page 2 of 2)

spi	der	se	cret
ro	dent	ta	ble
pre	dict	fo	cus

Copy onto cardstock. Laminate. Cut each strip into four cards and clip together. Keep sets separate. Follow directions for "Syllable Match-Up" on page 9.

©The Reading Teacher's Plan Book

Advanced Week 6: Syllabication – Open/Closed Syllables
Individual Sort Cards

1st syllable open	1st syllable closed	
baby	basket	
donut	comet	
music	fossil	
program	pencil	
silent	tractor	

Copy a set of Individual Sort Cards for each student. Cut into individual cards. Follow directions on p. 9.

Advanced Week 7: Syllabication - Silent E Pattern
Group Sort Cards (Page 1 of 2)

Silent E Pattern	No Silent E Pattern	
advice	absent	
boneless	basket	
donate	donut	
erase	grumble	

Copy onto cardstock. Laminate and cut into individual cards. Follow directions on page 8.

Advanced Week 7: Syllabication – Silent E Pattern
Group Sort Cards (Page 2 of 2)

excuse	hidden	
hopeless	lazy	
inside	magnet	
mistake	program	
refuse	silent	

Copy onto cardstock. Laminate and cut into individual cards. Follow directions on page 8.

Advanced Week 7: Silent E Pattern
Syllable Match-Up (page 1 of 2)

ad	vice	bone	less
do	nate	in	side
ex	plode	re	fuse

Copy onto cardstock. Laminate. Cut each strip into four cards and clip together. Keep sets separate. Follow directions for "Syllable Match-Up" on page 9.

©The Reading Teacher's Plan Book

Advanced Week 7: Silent E Pattern
Syllable Match-Up (page 2 of 2)

mis	take	hope	less
e	rase	ex	cuse
rep	tile	note	book

Copy onto cardstock. Laminate. Cut each strip into four cards and clip together. Keep sets separate. Follow directions for "Syllable Match-Up" on page 9.

©The Reading Teacher's Plan Book

Advanced Week 7: Syllabication – Silent E Pattern
Individual Sort Cards

Silent E Pattern	No Silent E Pattern	
boneless	basket	
explode	donut	
hopeless	grumble	
inside	hidden	
mistake	program	

Copy a set of Individual Sort Cards for each student. Cut into individual cards. Follow directions on p. 9.

Advanced Week 8: Syllabication – Vowel Team Patterns
Group Sort Cards (Page 1 of 2)

A patterns	E patterns	I patterns
jigsaw	agree	highlight
remain	mistreat	necktie
subway	repeat	replied
withdraw	unscrew	stoplight

Copy onto cardstock. Laminate and cut into individual cards. Follow directions on page 8.

Advanced Week 8: Syllabication – Vowel Team Patterns
Group Sort Cards (Page 2 of 2)

O patterns	U patterns	
classroom	clueless	fifteen
enjoy	suitcase	lookout
poison	untrue	snowplow
rowboat		trainer

Copy onto cardstock. Laminate and cut into individual cards. Follow directions on page 8.

Advanced Week 8: Vowel Team Pattern Syllables
Syllable Match-Up (page 1 of 2)

jig	saw	a	gree
high	light	class	room
sub	way	un	screw

Copy onto cardstock. Laminate. Cut each strip into four cards and clip together. Keep sets separate. Follow directions for "Syllable Match-Up" on page 9.

©The Reading Teacher's Plan Book

Advanced Week 8: Vowel Team Pattern Syllables
Syllable Match-Up (page 2 of 2)

neck	tie	row	boat
oat	meal	moon	light
rain	coat	with	draw

Copy onto cardstock. Laminate. Cut each strip into four cards and clip together. Keep sets separate. Follow directions for "Syllable Match-Up" on page 9.

©The Reading Teacher's Plan Book

**Advanced Week 8:
Word Hunt Cube
Syllabication – Vowel Team
Patterns**

Copy onto cardstock. Laminate and cut along the outside edges. Fold along the lines and assemble with hot glue. Use with "Vowel Team" Word Hunt Mats. Follow Word Hunt directions on page 11.

<u>A</u>
Patterns

<u>E</u>
Patterns

<u>I</u>
Patterns

<u>O</u>
Patterns

<u>E</u>
Patterns

<u>O</u>
Patterns

Advanced Week 8: Vowel Team Patterns

©The Reading Teacher's Plan Book

Advanced Week 8: "Vowel Team Patterns" Word Hunt Mats

jigsaw	agree	lookout
highlight	snowman	classroom
necktie	repeat	remain

display	replied	fifteen
mistreat	withdraw	cloudy
midnight	snowplow	enjoy

unscrew	repeat	necktie
rowboat	poison	sixteen
stoplight	trainer	subway

Copy a mat for each student. (Three mats are provided.) Provide an assortment of bingo chips. Use with "Vowel Team Patterns" Word Hunt Cube. Follow directions on page 11.

Advanced Week 8: Syllabication – Vowel Team Patterns
Individual Sort Cards

A Patterns	E Patterns	O Patterns
jigsaw	agree	enjoy
pigtail	fifteen	lookout
remain	mistreat	poison
subway	repeat	rowboat
withdraw	unscrew	snowplow

Copy a set of Individual Sort Cards for each student. Cut into individual cards. Follow directions on p. 9.

Advanced Week 9: Syllabication – Bossy R Patterns
Group Sort Cards (Page 1 of 2)

ar, are, air	er, eer, ear	ir, ire
careful	cheerful	birthday
dairy	gerbil	circus
garden	nearby	inspire
target	perfect	thirsty

Copy onto cardstock. Laminate and cut into individual cards. Follow directions on page 8.

Advanced Week 9: Syllabication – Bossy R Patterns
Group Sort Cards (Page 2 of 2)

or, ore, oar	ur	
aboard	curtain	
forty	disturb	
ignore	return	
normal	turnip	

Copy onto cardstock. Laminate and cut into individual cards. Follow directions on page 8.

Advanced Week 9: Bossy R Syllables
Syllable Match-Up (page 1 of 2)

care	ful	birth	day
per	fect	cir	cus
for	ty	thun	der

Copy onto cardstock. Laminate. Cut each strip into four cards and clip together. Keep sets separate. Follow directions for "Syllable Match-Up" on page 9.

Advanced Week 9: Bossy R Syllables
Syllable Match-Up (page 2 of 2)

bar	ber	tur	key
gar	den	a	board
cheer	ful	dis	turb

Copy onto cardstock. Laminate. Cut each strip into four cards and clip together. Keep sets separate. Follow directions for "Syllable Match-Up" on page 9.

©The Reading Teacher's Plan Book

Advanced Week 9: Syllabication – Bossy R Patterns
Individual Sort Cards

ar, are, air	er, eer, ear	or, ore, oar
careful	cheerful	aboard
carton	gerbil	explore
dairy	nearby	forty
garden	thunder	ignore
target	perfect	normal

Copy a set of Individual Sort Cards for each student. Cut into individual cards. Follow directions on p. 9.

Advanced Week 10: Syllabication – Syllable Patterns
Group Sort Cards (Page 1 of 2)

Look for an Ending or Suffix	Break into Compound Words	Look for a Prefix
drifted	armchair	mistreat
graceful	everywhere	preheat
painting	milkshake	recount
useless	seafood	unlucky

Copy onto cardstock. Laminate and cut into individual cards. Follow directions on page 8.

©The Reading Teacher's Plan Book

Advanced Week 10: Syllabication – Syllable Patterns
Group Sort Cards (Page 2 of 2)

Double Consonants	Look for chunks and patterns	
bubble	advice	
common	garden	
ladder	napkin	
puppy	purple	

Copy onto cardstock. Laminate and cut into individual cards. Follow directions on page 8.

Advanced Week 10: Word Hunt Cube "Breaking Words into Syllables"

Copy onto cardstock. Laminate and cut along the outside edges. Fold along the lines and assemble with hot glue. Use with "Breaking Words into Syllables" Word Hunt Mats. Follow Word Hunt directions on page 11.

- Look for Chunks and Patterns
- Look for a Prefix
- Consonant + le
- Look for an Ending
- Compound Words
- Double Consonants

Advanced Week 10: Breaking Words into Syllables

Advanced Week 10: "Breaking Words into Syllables" Word Hunt Mats

bubble	puzzle	careless
advice	armchair	unlucky
everywhere	drifted	purple

stable	washcloth	mistreat
milkshake	garden	puppy
friendly	swinging	common

drizzle	preheat	seafood
useless	ladder	graceful
napkin	cowboy	title

Copy a mat for each student. (Three mats are provided.) Provide an assortment of bingo chips. Use with "Breaking Words into Syllables" Word Hunt Cube. Follow directions on page 11.

Advanced Week 10: "Breaking Words into Syllables" Word Hunt Writing Mats

Word Hunt Writing Mat

Double Consonants	Compound Words	Endings or Suffixes

Word Hunt Writing Mat

Double Consonants	Compound Words	Endings or Suffixes

Copy a Writing Mat for each student. Use with Word Windows (pgs. 383-384). Follow directions on p. 11.

©The Reading Teacher's Plan Book

Advanced Week 10: Syllabication - Breaking Words into Syllables
Individual Sort Cards

Double Consonants	Compound Words	Endings or Suffixes
bubble	armchair	drifted
common	everywhere	friendly
drizzle	milkshake	graceful
ladder	seafood	painting
puppy	washcloth	useless

Copy a set of Individual Sort Cards for each student. Cut into individual cards. Follow directions on p. 9.

Sound/Spelling Boxes

Follow directions for Sound/Spelling Boxes on pages 13-14.

Name _____

Writing Sort

Follow directions for Writing Sorts on page 15.

©The Reading Teacher's Plan Book

Name _____

Writing Sort

Follow directions for Writing Sorts on page 15.

©The Reading Teacher's Plan Book

Name _____

Writing Sort

Follow directions for Writing Sorts on page 15.

©The Reading Teacher's Plan Book

Word Windows: Use with Writing Mats for Word Hunt activity.

Word Window

Word Window

Word Window

Follow directions for Word Hunt (Word Windows/Writing Mats) on page 11.

Word Windows: Use with Writing Mats for Word Hunt activity.

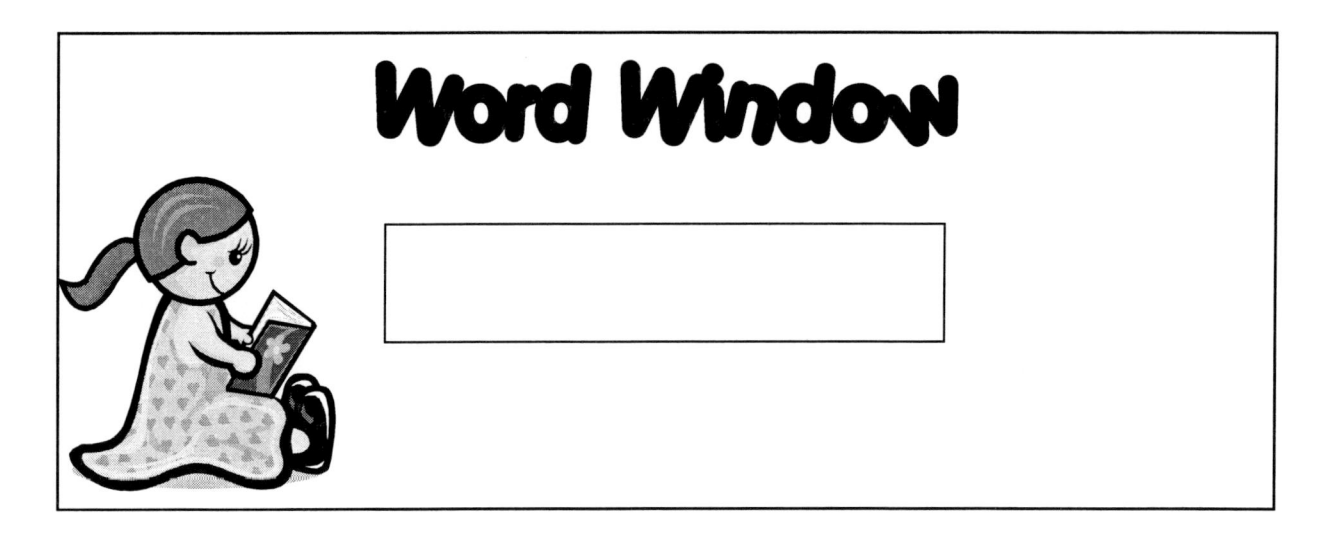

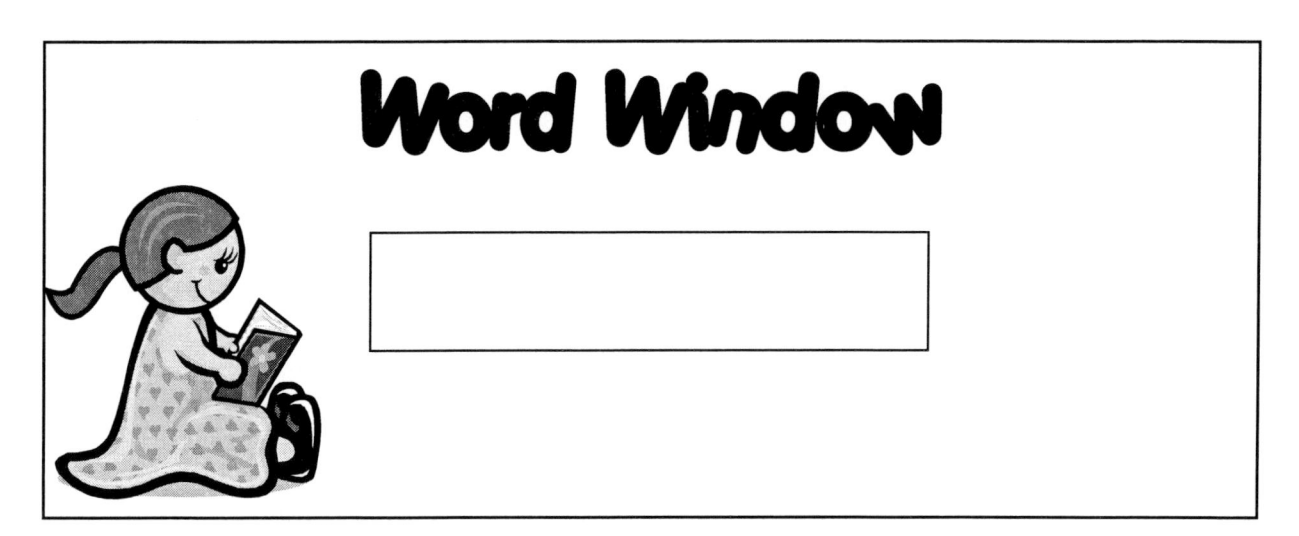

Word Window

Word Window

Word Window

Follow directions for Word Hunt (Word Windows/Writing Mats) on page 11.

384 ©The Reading Teacher's Plan Book

Name _____

Story Map

Characters	Setting
Story Problem	How the Problem Was Solved

Graphic Organizer

**Question/Answer Die
Use with Story Questions
Graphic Organizer**

Who?

Copy onto cardstock. Laminate and cut along the outside edges. Fold along the lines and assemble with hot glue. Use with "Story Questions" Graphic Organizer (page 387).

Where? What? When?

Why?

How?

©The Reading Teacher's Plan Book

Name _____

Story Questions

Who?	
What?	
Where?	
When?	
Why?	
How?	

Graphic Organizer – Use with Question/Answer Die (page 386).

Name _____

Words to Clarify

Word or Idea	Page	What It Means

Graphic Organizer

Name _____

Nonfiction News

Title of Book: _____

Interesting Fact	Interesting Fact
Interesting Fact	Interesting Fact

Graphic Organizer

Name _____

My Predictions

I predict . . .	I found out . . .
I predict . . .	I found out . . .

Graphic Organizer

©The Reading Teacher's Plan Book

Short Vowels

a	e	i	o	u

©The Reading Teacher's Plan Book

Long Vowels

a	e	i	o	u
a_e	e_e	i_e	o_e	u_e
ai	ee	ie	oa	
ay	ea	igh	ow	
	ie	_y	oe	
	e		o	
	_y			

The Spooky sound

oo
ew
ue
ui
u_e

The Whining sound

aw
au
all

©The Reading Teacher's Plan Book

The Bossy R Sounds

ar

er ir ur

The Hurt Sound

air are or ore

ow ou

©The Reading Teacher's Plan Book

The **Boxing** Sound

oo

The **Bouncy** Sound

oi
oy

©The Reading Teacher's Plan Book

The
Stick Out Your Tongue Sound

th

The **Quiet** Sound

sh

©The Reading Teacher's Plan Book

The Train Sound

Ch ch ch ch
Ch ch ch ch
Choo! Choo!

ch

©The Reading Teacher's Plan Book

Syllable Patterns

1. Some syllables are CLOSED.
They have 1 vowel in the middle. **cvc**
They make the **SHORT VOWEL** sound.

2. Some syllables are OPEN.
They end with 1 vowel.
cv or ccv
They make the **LONG VOWEL** sound.

3. Some syllables have a SILENT E pattern.
They end with a "silent e."
cvce
They make the **LONG VOWEL** sound.

4. Some syllables have a VOWEL TEAM.
They have 2 vowels together. **cvv or cvvc**
They make the **sound of the pattern.**

5. Some syllables have a BOSSY R pattern.
They have a **Bossy R** pattern.
They make a **BOSSY R** sound.

6. Some syllables have CONSONANT + LE.

ble, cle, dle, fle, gle, kle, ple, tle, zle

Breaking Words into Syllables

1. Look for an ENDING or SUFFIX.

-ed, -ing, -er, -est, -ful, -s, -es, -less, -ness, -y, -ly, -tion, -ible, -able, -ment, -ous, ...

2. Look for a PREFIX.

un-, re-, dis-, pre-, re-, ex-, com-, a-, be-, de-, ...

3. Look for a COMPOUND WORD.

mailbox   doghouse

4. Break the word BETWEEN DOUBLE CONSONANTS or 2 CONSONANTS.

mid/dle   cac/tus

5. Look for CHUNKS YOU KNOW.

Break the word into chunks.

6. Use what you know about SYLLABLE PATTERNS

to read each syllable.

©The Reading Teacher's Plan Book

Reading Strategy Chart

What Good Readers Do

Make Predictions

Summarize

Clarify words and ideas

Ask Questions